Understanding Intelligence in the Twenty-First Centu

G000160674

Intelligence has never been more important to world politics than it is now at the opening of the twenty-first century. The terrorist attacks on the United States on September 11, 2001, along with the politics and diplomacy of the second Gulf War, have brought intelligence issues to the forefront of both official, academic and popular discourse on security and international affairs. The emerging challenges posed by new forms of terrorism, together with the issues raised by the war on Iraq, have shown the value and limits of secret intelligence and generated fresh controversies for its proponents and for its critics. The need for better understanding of both the nature of the intelligence process and its importance to national and international security has never been more apparent. The aim of this collection is to enhance our understanding of this subject by drawing on a range of perspectives, from academic experts and journalists to former members of the British and American intelligence communities.

L.V. Scott is Professor of International Politics and Dean of Social Sciences at the University of Wales, Aberystwyth (UWA). **P.D. Jackson** is Senior Lecturer in International Politics at UWA. Professor Scott is Director of the Centre for Intelligence and International Security Studies (CIISS). Dr Jackson is Deputy Director of CIISS.

Also in the Intelligence Series

Understanding Intelligence in the Twenty-First Century

Journeys in Shadows

Edited by L.V. Scott and P.D. Jackson

Routledge
Taylor & Francis Group

LONDON AND NEW YORK

First published 2004
by Routledge
11 New Fetter Lane, London EC4P 4EE

Simultaneously published in the USA and Canada
by Routledge
29 West 35th Street, New York, NY 10001

Routledge is an imprint of the Taylor & Francis Group

Typeset in Times by
Integra Software Services Pvt. Ltd, Pondicherry, India
Printed and bound in Great Britain by TJ International Ltd, Padstow, Cornwall

British Library Cataloguing in Publication Data
A catalogue record for this book is available
from the British Library

Library of Congress Cataloging in Publication Data
A catalog record for this book has been requested

ISBN 0–714–65533–3 (hbk)
ISBN 0–714–68422–8 (pbk)

For our students, past and present

Contents

Foreword

Peter Hennessy

By the time you read this sentence, this book will itself have acquired the status of a historical artefact and one which teeters on the brim of being a primary source in its own right. For in intelligence terms, it is a piece of especially high-definition photo reconnaissance of the state of the craft in the fast-moving world between 9/11 and the 2003 war on Iraq. The Gregynog weekend in November 2002, during which many of these chapters were first presented, rippled with anticipation and anxiety about what was to come – anxiety because of real concerns, which we ventilated collectively, about the misuse of the intelligence process in Washington as part of making the politicians' case for a war of exemplary pre-emption in the Middle East that would topple Saddam Hussein.

As I write this foreword, the UK intelligence community is in a comparable dock. Sir Michael Quinlan, the former Whitehall permanent secretary who conducted an enquiry for the Prime Minister, John Major, in 1994 into the purposes of the British secret services, has captured succinctly the seriousness and centrality of the point at issue as his friend, Lord Butler of Brockwell, the former Cabinet Secretary, sets out at the request of Prime Minister Tony Blair to investigate those very UK intelligence processes and outputs in the run-up to the War on Iraq. The Whitehall Joint Intelligence Committee (JIC) system, Quinlan writes,

> is internationally admired as a major British strength, but its integrity and prestige are at risk if it is used not just for guidance before policy decisions but for public presentation after them. We must not slide towards the selectivity and advocacy which, in a different institutional environment, occasionally corrupts the use of intelligence in the United States.[1]

For older Whitehall hands, it is unbelievable that JIC assessments should see the light of day within weeks of drafting *and* that they should be used to buttress a government's arguments for going to war.

This very volume and its contents would cause comparably a sharp inhalation of breath on the part of some of the big figures of intelligence history past. It is, for example, only 20 years since Professor Sir Harry Hinsley took myself and Chris Andrew aside (separately) and warned us that if we went on writing as we did (me in the *Times*; Chris in journals and between hardcovers) we would risk prosecution under Section Two of the Official Secrets Act, 1911. Though when I pointed out that as his former pupils, Chris and I would expect Harry to turn up at the Old Bailey and speak on our behalf as character witnesses, he replied 'Of course, my boy'.

As for past prime ministers, the *existence* of the JIC, let alone the merest hint of its product, was a secret never to be breached. The day the Butler Inquiry was announced, a former Chairman of the JIC, Sir Rodric Braithwaite, and I sat in my study of Queen Mary in East London beneath a portrait of Clement Attlee discussing for the BBC World Service the remit of the Butler committee and the places it should probe deep in the JIC's processes and relationships with its customers. We turned our gaze on the old premier when we had finished and agreed he would have been horrified and utterly disapproving had he eavesdropped on our conversation.

Intelligence studies are entering their adolescence and, with genuine adolescents, the juices are flowing powerfully, sometimes confusingly and can lead to both obsessions and moodswings. The testosterone factor, in particular, is one which we all must avoid – that this is a subject for the hard and the tough, the 'now-it-can-be-told' brigade. Not for us the tedium of social policy, the dryness of economic history. Here is the missing ingredient that can pep up even diplomatic history. We must calm down. Our slice of history must be carefully contextualised and fitted into the whole. That said, there is one racy historical theme – perhaps the most elusive of all – which we must blend into our treatments of the mercurial realm of intelligence. I owe this thought to a seasoned member of the Canadian Intelligence Service, Gary Seroka. On the day the Hutton Report into the death of the weapons scientist, Dr David Kelly, was published in London in January 2004, I was, by long arrangement, to present a paper to the Canadian intelligence community in Ottawa. I wanted Gary to come. 'Are you cleared for all that?' I asked. 'Oh yes', he replied, 'I'm cleared all the way up to rumour and gossip!'[2] Point taken.

On returning to London, I chaired Queen Mary's annual Bagehot lecture given this time by Richard Ingrams and Paul Foot on the historical impact of the satirical and scuttlebutt-distributing magazine, *Private Eye*. Introducing them, I stressed that *theirs* was now the 'missing dimension' of history and that we professionals should do something about it. At the dinner afterwards I urged my Vice-Principal to advertise the world's first chair in the History of Rumour and Gossip. 'Why should I', Professor Philip Ogden replied, 'We already have you.'[3] Point taken.

We intelligence scholars are like travel writers. In a few short years we shall need a volume called *Still More Journeys in Shadows*. The study of intelligence will reach its early maturity in conditions of boom. *This* present volume will long stand as a benchmark in the process of take-off.

Notes

1 Michael Quinlan, 'Espionage on trial', *The Tablet*, 7 February 2004.
2 Conversation with Gary Seroka, 27 January 2004.
3 Conversation with Professor Philip Ogden, 3 February 2004.

Preface

Intelligence has never been more important in world politics than it is now at the opening of the twenty-first century. The terrorist attacks on the United States on September 11, 2001, along with the politics and diplomacy of the Second Gulf War, have brought intelligence issues to the forefront of both official and popular discourse on security and international affairs. The need for better understanding of both the nature of the intelligence process and its importance to national and international security has never been more apparent. The aim of this collection is to enhance our understanding of the subject by drawing on a range of perspectives, from academic experts to journalists to former members of the British and American intelligence communities.

The project *Journeys in Shadows* took shape in late 2000 with the aim of establishing a network of expertise on the study of intelligence and international politics. Initially, our central aim was to subject the emerging sub-discipline of intelligence studies to critical examination, considering the way the study has been studied, for what purposes and with what consequences. But both the context and contours of the project were overtaken and transformed by events. The impact of September 11 and the Second Gulf War left us no choice but to widen the conceptual parameters of our project to include reconsideration of the nature of intelligence and its role in national and international security. The emerging challenges posed by new forms of terrorism, together with the issues raised by the war on Iraq, have shown the value and limits of secret intelligence and generated fresh controversies for its proponents and for its critics. Studying intelligence has never been more relevant, nor more exhilarating.

This edited collection and the conference upon which it is based were funded jointly by the Arts and Humanities Research Board (AHRB) and the University of Wales, Aberystwyth, to whom we express our gratitude and indebtedness. The project involved a series of seminars and a symposium in the Department of International Politics at Aberystwyth in 2001/02, and a review conference at the University of Wales conference centre at Gregynog in Powys in November 2002. The collection of papers we publish here mostly comprises revised papers from the conference, together with additional contributions which develop themes and issues identified at the conference as particularly significant. One consequence is that some papers were completed before public crises developed over the use of intelligence in the war on Iraq, while others were able to reflect on emerging issues. Rather than delay publication in what is, in any case, a swiftly moving if extraordinary saga we decided against inviting contributors to further revisit their work.

One aim of the project was to explore different professional, methodological and national approaches to the study of intelligence and for that purpose we drew upon the views of academics, journalists and former practitioners to explore the way the subject is studied. The 'cast list' below illustrates the diverse professional and intellectual expertise we were able to draw upon, and to whom we express our gratitude. The following contributed papers and critiques in various fora: Richard Aldrich, Martin Alexander, Christopher Andrew, Ken Booth, Charles Cogan, Michael Cox, Toni Erskine, John Ferris, Peter Hennessy, Michael Herman, David Kahn, Pierre Lacoste, Andrew Linklater, Michael MccGwire, Eunan O'Halpin, Wolfgang Krieger, Colin McInnes, Michael Smith and Nigel West. Most of these attended the conference at Gregynog in November 2002 as did the following: Christopher Aaron, Marc Davies, Stephen Dorril, Peter Earnest, Olivier Forcade, Michael Goodman, Oleg Gordievsky, Frédéric Guelton, John Keiger, Florence Gauzy Krieger, Paul Maddrell, Joseph A. Maiolo, Wolfango Piccoli, Remy Porte, Guto Thomas, Stephen Twigge, Donald Watt, Andrew Webster and Neville Wylie.

Collections of essays vary in their cohesion and coherence. Our aim has been to provide an explicitly loose framework in which very different professional and methodological interpretations and agendas are facilitated. If the result tends toward the eclectic then we hope the reader will share our view that this is vindication of our editorial strategy rather than admission of editorial neglect.

Finally, we wish to record our thanks and appreciation to various people who assisted us in our endeavours: Richard Aldrich for his support and guidance; Lisa Hyde at Frank Cass for her patience and support; Jonathan Colman and Chester Cunningham for their help with research assistance. In addition, John Baylis, John Young, Martin Thomas and Zara Steiner all provided important support for the project during its initial phases. We would in particular like to thank our friend and colleague Gerry Hughes for his outstanding organisational skills, initiative and good humour, and for the vital role he played in our project.

Len Scott
Peter Jackson
Aberystwyth, October 2003

List of Abbreviations and Acronyms

ABM	Anti-Ballistic Missile
ATO	Air Tasking Orders
BBC	British Broadcasting Corporation
BND	*Bundesnachrichtendienst*, the West German intelligence service
C2W	Command and Control Warfare
C3I	Command, Control, Communications and Intelligence
C4ISR	Command, Control, Communications, Computers, Intelligence, Surveillance and Reconnaissance
CI	Counter-Intelligence
CIA	(US) Central Intelligence Agency
CFR	(US) Council of Foreign Relations
CPSU	Communist Party of the Soviet Union
DBK	Dominant Battlespace Knowledge
DCI	(US) Director of Central Intelligence
DDI	(US) Deputy Director for Intelligence (CIA)
DGSE	*Direction Generale de la Securite Exterieure*, the French intelligence service
DIA	(US) Defense Intelligence Agency
DNA	Deoxyribonucleic acid (biological carrier of genetic information)
DNI	Director of National Intelligence
DST	*Direction de la Surveillance du Territoire*, the French security service
EMI	Electro-Magnetic Interference
FBI	(US) Federal Bureau of Investigation
FCD	First Chief Directorate (of the KGB)
FISA	(US) Foreign Intelligence Surveillance Act
FOIA	(UK) Freedom of Information Act
FSB	Post-Soviet Russian security service
Gestapo	*Geheime Staatspolizei*, the Nazi secret state police
GC&CS	(UK) Government Code and Cypher School
GCHQ	(UK) Government Communications Headquarters

GPS	Global Positioning System
GRU	Soviet Military Intelligence
HIV/AIDS	disease of the human immune system
HUMINT	Human intelligence
IAO	(US) Information Awareness Office
ICSIS	Intelligence Community System for Information Security
IDC	(US) Information Dominance Center
IIHA	International Intelligence History Association
ILAR	Intelligence Liaison and Research Project
INO	Foreign Intelligence Department of Soviet Intelligence, 1920–41
IO	Information Operations
IR	International Relations
ISC	(UK) Intelligence and Security Committee
ISR	Information, Surveillance, Reconnaissance
IW	Information Warfare
JIC	(UK) Joint Intelligence Committee
KGB	Committee for State Security – Soviet intelligence and security service
MfS	(East Germany) Ministerium für Staatsicherheit; also known as the Stasi
MGFA	*Militärgeschichtliches Forschungsamt*
MI5	(UK) Security Service
NATO	North Atlantic Treaty Organisation
NCW	Netcentric Warfare
NIMA	(US) National Imagery and Mapping Agency
NKVD	People's Commissariat for Internal Affairs– Soviet Secret police
NRO	National Reconnaissance Organisation
NSA	(US) National Security Agency
NSC	(US) National Security Council
NATO	North Atlantic Treaty Organisation
NKVD	Soviet intelligence and security service – predecessor of KGB
ONA	Operational Net Assessment
OODA	Observe, Orient, Decide, Act
OSINT	Open Source Intelligence
OSS	(US) Office of Strategic Services
PFIAB	(US) President's Foreign Intelligence Advisory Board
PIRA	Provisional Irish Republican Army
PR	Political Intelligence department in KGB residencies
RAF	(UK) Royal Air Force
RDO	Rapid Decisive Operations
RMA	Revolution in Military Affairs
RUC	Royal Ulster Constabulary

SALT	Strategic Arms Limitation Talks
SIGINT	Signals intelligence
SIME	(UK) Security Intelligence Middle East
SIPRI	Stockholm International Peace Research Institute
SIPRnet	(US) Secret Internet Protocol Router Network
SIS	(UK) Secret Intelligence Service (MI6)
SOE	(UK) Special Operations Executive
SPECTRE	Special Executive for Counterintelligence, Terrorism, Revenge and Extortion
Stasi	East German intelligence and security service
SS	*Schutzstaffel* Nazi security service
SVR	Post-Soviet Russian intelligence service
UAV	Unmanned Aerial Vehicle
ULTRA	(UK) SIGINT in the Second World War
UNMOVIC	United Nations Monitoring, Verification and Inspection Commission
USAF	United States Air Force
UNSCOM	United Nations Special Commission
USSOCOM	United States Special Operations Command
USSR	Union of Soviet Socialist Republics
WMD	Weapons of Mass Destruction

List of Figures and Tables

Figures

Tables

List of Contributors

Christopher Andrew is Professor of Modern and Contemporary History at the University of Cambridge, Convenor of the Cambridge Intelligence Seminar, former Visiting Professor at Harvard, Toronto and the Australian National University, Official Historian of the Security Service (MI5), Honorary Air Commodore of No. 7006 (VR) Intelligence Squadron Royal Auxiliary Air Force, Chairman of the British Intelligence Study Group and Founding Co-Editor of *Intelligence and National Security*. His most recent book, with Vasili Mitrokhin, is *The Mitrokhin Archive*, Vol. 1: *The KGB in Europe and the West* (Penguin/Basic Books, 1999).

Jeremy Black is Professor of History at the University of Exeter. His books include *War: An Illustrated History* (Sutton Publishing, 2003); *World War Two: A Military History* (Routledge, 2003); *Modern British History* (Palgrave Macmillan, 2000); *Why Wars Happen* (Reaktion Books, 1998); *War and the World, 1450–2000* (Yale University Press, 1998); *Maps and History* (Yale University Press, 1997); *Maps and Politics* (Reaktion Books, 1997).

Dr Charles Cogan is a Senior Research Associate at the Kennedy School of Government, Harvard University. Earlier, he spent 37 years in the CIA, including as Chief Near East South Asia in the Directorate of Operations (1979–84) and as CIA Chief in Paris (1984–89).

Toni Erskine is Lecturer in International Politics at the University of Wales, Aberystwyth. Before taking up this post, she was British Academy Post-doctoral Fellow at Cambridge University. She researches in the areas of ethics and international relations and is author of *Embedded Cosmopolitanism: Duties to Strangers and 'Enemies' in a World of Dislocated Communities* (Oxford University Press, forthcoming).

John Ferris is a Professor of History at the University of Calgary. He has written widely on intelligence, strategy and military history. His most recent work, with Christon Archer, Holger Herwig and Tim Travers, is *A World History of Warfare* (University of Nebraska Press, 2002).

Robert Alan Goldberg is a Professor of American History at the University of Utah. His lastest book, *Enemies Within: The Culture of Conspiracy in Modern America*, was published by Yale University Press in 2001.

Michael Herman served as an intelligence officer at Government Communications Headquarters between 1952 and 1987. During this period he had spells at the Joint Services Staff College and in the Cabinet Office and the Defence Intelligence Staff. Between 1972 and 1975 he was Secretary of the Joint Intelligence Committee. Since retirement he has held research posts at Nuffield College Oxford and Keele University, and taught at King's College, London. He is an Honorary Fellow of the Department of International Politics at the University of Wales, Aberystwyth. He is author of *Intelligence Power in Peace and War* (Cambridge University Press, 1996) and *Intelligence Services in the Information Age: Theory and Practice* (Frank Cass, 2001).

Peter Jackson is Senior Lecturer in International Politics in the Department of International Politics at the University of Wales, Aberystwyth. He has published widely in the fields of intelligence and security studies, French strategy and diplomacy and the origins of the Second World War. His last book, *France and the Nazi Menace: Intelligence and Policy-making, 1933–1939*, was published by Oxford University Press in 2000. He is Deputy-Director of the Centre for Intelligence and International Security Studies at the University of Wales, Aberystwyth.

Wolfgang Krieger is Professor of Modern History/History of International Relations at Universität Marburg. He specialises in the history of international relations during the Cold War, particularly US–European relations, German and US foreign intelligence, and nuclear weapons. His most recent publication is an edited volume, *World History of Intelligence: Espionage and Covert Action from Antiquity to the Present* (C.H. Beck, 2003).

Gary T. Marx is Professor Emeritus at MIT. He is the author of many books and articles dealing with race relations, social movements and social control. With respect to intelligence his books include, *Undercover: Police Surveillance in America* (University of California Press, 1992) and *Windows Into the Soul: Surveillance and Society in an Age of High Technology* (University of Chicago Press, forthcoming).

Len Scott is Professor of International Politics at the University of Wales, Aberystwyth, where he is also Dean of Social Sciences. He specialises in intelligence and international history. Among his recent publications are *Macmillan, Kennedy and the Cuban Missile Crisis: Political, Military and Intelligence Aspects* (Palgrave, 1999) and *Planning Armageddon: Britain, the United States and the Command of Nuclear Forces, 1945–1964* (with Stephen Twigge) (Routledge, 2000). He is Director of the Centre for Intelligence and International Security Studies at the University of Wales, Aberystwyth.

Michael Smith is the Defence Correspondent of the *Daily Telegraph*. He served for ten years with the British Army's Intelligence Corps and is the author of a number of books on intelligence, including: *The Spying Game: The Secret History of British Intelligence* (Politicos, 2003), *Station X: The Codebreakers of Bletchley Park* (Channel 4 Books, 1999) and *Foley: The Spy Who Saved 10,000 Jews* (Hodder & Stoughton, 1999). He was also co-editor, with Ralph Erskine, of *Action This Day: Bletchley Park from the Breaking of the Enigma Code to the Birth of the Modern Computer* (Bantam, 2001).

Nigel West is an intelligence historian who has written several books on the subject and now teaches at the Centre for Counter-Intelligence and Security Studies in Washington, DC.

1 Journeys in Shadows

Len Scott and Peter Jackson

The first few years of the twenty-first century have witnessed a transformation in the role of secret intelligence in international politics. Intelligence and security issues are now more prominent than ever in Western political discourse as well as the wider public consciousness. Public expectations of intelligence have never been greater, and these demands include much greater disclosure of hitherto secret knowledge. Much of this can be attributed to the shock of the terrorist attacks of September 2001. These events drove home the vulnerability of Western societies and the importance of reliable intelligence on terrorist threats. But debates over the role of intelligence in the build-up to the Second Gulf War have played an equally important role in transforming the profile of the 'secret world' in Western society. As Christopher Andrew points out in his contribution to this collection 'In the space of only a year, the threats posed by Osama bin Laden and Saddam Hussein had succeeded in transforming British government policy on the public use of intelligence'.[1] The relationship between political leaders and their intelligence advisors came under unprecedented public scrutiny in both Britain and the United States. Both Prime Minister Tony Blair and President George W. Bush were widely charged with purposefully distorting intelligence information in order to justify their decision to make war on Iraq in April 2003. The need for a better understanding of both the nature of the intelligence process and its importance to national and international security policy has never been more apparent.

Understanding Intelligence in the Twenty-First Century draws upon the views of academics, journalists and former practitioners to consider the nature of intelligence and its evolving role in domestic and international politics. It also examines the development of intelligence as an area of academic study and assesses its emerging contribution to the study of international relations. An important aim is to explore the way the subject is studied, for what purpose and with what consequences.

It is nearly five decades since intelligence first emerged as a subject of serious academic study with the publication of Sherman Kent's *Strategic Intelligence for American Foreign Policy*.[2] It is some 20 years since two eminent British historians invoked Sir Alexander Cadogan's description of intelligence as the missing dimension of international affairs.[3] The development of intelligence studies as a sub-field of international relations has continued to gather momentum ever since. Initially the terrain of political scientists, the role of intelligence in domestic and international politics now attracts the attention of an ever larger number of historians. The subject is firmly established in centres of teaching and research in both Europe and North America. As a result, the study of international security has been increasingly influenced by a better understanding of the role of intelligence in policy making – although Christopher Andrew maintains that 'it is still denied its proper place in studies of the Cold War'.[4] And as Andrew argues persuasively in this collection, the specific and potentially crucial subject of signal intelligence remains almost wholly neglected in Cold War historiography.[5]

The rapid growth of intelligence as a focus of academic enquiry will surely continue. Recent progress in archival disclosure, accelerated by the end of the Cold War and by changing attitudes towards official secrecy and towards the work of the security and intelligence services, has further facilitated research, understanding and debate.[6] Newly released documents, along with a range of other sources, provide an opportunity to reconsider long-standing assumptions about the motives of policy makers and the institutional character of foreign and security policy making. The events of September 11 and the war on Iraq have focused attention on all aspects of the subject. In light of these developments, the time seems right to take stock of what has been accomplished in this relatively new area of scholarly enquiry, to reflect upon the various methodological approaches used by scholars as well as the epistemological assumptions that underpin research and writing about intelligence.

Scope and focus: What is intelligence? How do we study it?

Popular perceptions and general understanding of the nature of intelligence and its role in international relations leaves much to be desired. A starting point is the question: what is intelligence? The way intelligence is defined necessarily conditions approaches to research and writing about the subject. Sherman Kent's classic characterisations of intelligence cover the 'the three separate and distinct things that intelligence devotees usually mean when they use the word': knowledge, the type of organisation that produces that knowledge and the activities pursued by that organisation.[7] In most contemporary analyses, intelligence is understood as the process of gathering, analysing and making use of information. Yet beyond such basic definitions are divergent conceptions of exactly what intelligence is and what it is for. This is perhaps because, as James Der Derian has observed, intelligence is the 'least understood and most "undertheorized" area of international relations'.[8] David Kahn, one of the most eminent scholars in the field, similarly laments that '[n]one of the definitions [of intelligence] that I have seen work'.[9] A brief survey of various approaches to the study of intelligence illuminates the difficulties inherent in any search for an inclusive definition.

Many observers tend to understand intelligence primarily as a tool of foreign and defence policy making. Others focus on its role in domestic security. Still others concentrate on the role intelligence services have played as mechanisms of state oppression.[10] One interesting divergence of views pertains to the basic character of intelligence. Michael Herman (a former practitioner) treats it as a form of state power in its own right and this conceptualisation is at the heart of the analysis in his influential study *Intelligence Power in Peace and War*.[11] John Ferris (an historian) proffers a different view, judging that 'Intelligence is not a form of power but a means to guide its use, whether as a combat multiplier, or by helping one to understand one's environment and options, and thus how to apply force or leverage, and against whom.'[12] Whichever formulation one adopts and whatever the quality of intelligence on offer it is the judgement of political leaders and their grasp of the value and limitations of intelligence that is most crucial.[13]

So how do we define intelligence work? Should we make a distinction between 'secret' and 'open source' information? Does the internet change how we evaluate 'open source' information? What distinguishes the intelligence process from the information gathering activities of other government agencies? Michael Herman has offered a solution to this problem by identifying 'government intelligence' as 'the specialised organizations that have that name, and what they do and produce'.[14] This distinction can become problematic, however, when it comes to analysing the impact of intelligence on decision making. Assessments drafted by intelligence agencies are usually based on a combination of 'secret' and 'open' source information. And a substantial percentage of the information from open sources is quite often drawn from material acquired and processed by other government departments, the popular media and even work that has been contracted out to non-government agencies. Since all of these areas cannot reasonably be defined as intelligence activity, this suggests that the essence of intelligence lies at the level of analysis or assessment.[15] The problem is that assessments are only one element in the decision-making process, and the illumination that they provide may only complement information provided by other government agencies or other sources of information at the level of decision. It therefore remains difficult to make confident judgements about exactly what intelligence is and precisely how it influences decision making. Should scholars accept this level of imprecision as inevitable? Or, conversely, should we continue to strive to come up with a definition of intelligence that resolves this uncertainty?

A good illustration of the difficulties inherent in defining intelligence is the controversial question of secret intervention in other societies (most commonly referred to as 'covert action'). Scholars have frequently ignored covert action in their analyses of intelligence. As Elizabeth Anderson has argued: 'the specific subject of covert action as an element of intelligence has suffered a deficiency of serious study'. She further observes that

> while academics have developed different theoretical concepts to explain other instruments of international relations – for example, weapons, trade and diplomacy – the separation of covert action from 'traditional' foreign policy instruments means that these same concepts have not been applied to covert action.[16]

There is a clear need to locate 'covert action' within the study of international relations in general and within intelligence in particular. This may also pose an interesting challenge for theorists of intelligence because considering covert action as intelligence work means that intelligence might be better understood as a tool *for the execution* of policy as well as a tool *to inform* policy. Since September 11 the political context, both national and international, has changed. Amid widespread calls for intelligence reform in the United States there are those who argue for a radical new conceptualisation of the role of intelligence in national security policy. In this collection Charles Cogan, a former senior officer in the American Central Intelligence Agency (CIA), advocates, *inter alia*, a change in the orientation of US intelligence from gathering information to hunting the United States' adversaries. Such a transformation may require a new conceptual architecture for intelligence reflecting its new role in the exercise of US military power.

There is also substantial, if rarely articulated, divergence in approaches to studying intelligence. Scholars tend to approach the subject from three relatively distinct perspectives, in the pursuit of relatively distinct objectives. The first approach, favoured among international historians in particular, but also characteristic of theoretical approaches that seek to explain the relationship between organisational structure and policy making, conceives of the study of intelligence primarily as a means of acquiring new information in order to explain specific decisions made by policy makers in both peace and war. Close attention is paid by these scholars to the process of intelligence collection, to the origin and nature of individual sources of intelligence, and to the precise use that is made of intelligence as it travels up the chain of decision. A thorough understanding of the organisational structure of government machinery, and of the place of intelligence within this machinery, is crucial to this approach. This literature overlaps with journalistic endeavours that focus on particular cases of espionage and biographies of individual officials and agents.

A second approach strives to establish general models that can explain success and failure in the intelligence process. Characteristic of political science approaches to the discipline, it focuses almost exclusively on the levels of analysis and decision. Decisive importance is attributed by adherents of this approach to structural and cognitive obstacles to the effective use of intelligence in the policy process. The aim is to identify and analyse the personal, political and institutional biases that characterise intelligence organisations and affect their performance in the decision-making process. The emphasis is on the role of preconceptions and underlying assumptions in conditioning the way intelligence is analysed and used. The result has been a range of insights into the nature of perception and misperception, the difficulty in preventing surprise, and the politicisation of the intelligence process.[17] Both of the first two conceptual approaches focus primarily on intelligence as a tool of foreign and defence policy making.

A third approach focuses instead on the political function of intelligence as a means of state control. The past decade, in particular, has seen the appearance of a range of historical and political science literature on this subject. If the Gestapo has long been a subject of historical study, recently released archival material has enabled scholars to study the role of state security services in political and social life in the USSR and Eastern bloc states after 1945. This has provided a stimulus for a new wave of scholarship on state control since 1789. Historians are now working on a wide range of topics from the role of British and French intelligence services in maintaining imperial control overseas to the activities of security services such as MI5 or the FBI and their impact on political culture in Britain and the United States.[18] Many of the scholars engaged in this research would not consider themselves as contributing to 'intelligence studies'. Their focus is instead the use of intelligence sources to understand better the role of ideology and state power in political, social and cultural life. Yet there are strong arguments for embracing this scholarship under a broader definition of 'intelligence studies' and no reason to remain confined by disciplinary boundaries that are porous and arbitrary. One area of contemporary social science that has clear relevance to intelligence studies is the concept of surveillance. The potential of this area of enquiry is demonstrated in this volume by Gary Marx in his analysis of the new forms of surveillance in both official and private contexts. Marx explores an 'empirical, analytic and moral ecology' of surveillance and demonstrates how the evolution of information technology poses serious challenges to existing conceptions of individual liberty and security.[19]

The best writing about intelligence incorporates all three of the above approaches in different ways. But there are nearly always differences in emphasis even in the seminal works that have been crucial in pushing research forward. At the heart of these divergences, arguably, is disagreement concerning the extent to which political assumptions and political culture shape the intelligence process at all levels. Few would deny that the process of identifying threats is inextricably bound up with political choices and assumptions. The same can be true for the gathering, assessment and dissemination of information on these threats. Yet how we understand political processes and political culture is crucial. Scholars vary in the importance that they attribute to political culture and to ideology. Christopher Andrew, for example, argues in this collection that, 'For the conceptual framework of intelligence studies to advance further, it is essential to make a clearer distinction than is usually made at present between the roles of intelligence communities in authoritarian and democratic regimes.'[20] It is interesting to note, for example, that the first two lines of enquiry tend to pay less attention to the importance of ideological assumptions in the business of gathering, analysing and using intelligence than does the third.

One notable area where differing approaches converge is research into the role of Soviet and other Communist intelligence organisations, whose study has been facilitated by (some) declassification in former communist states. One especially fascinating area that has begun to be illuminated is nuclear threat perception. It now seems clear that in the early 1960s and in the 1980s Soviet authorities became genuinely concerned about the prospect of imminent US nuclear attack.[21] The role of Soviet intelligence in generating these perceptions was crucial and study of this issue offers fertile ground for exploring the role of cognitive, bureaucratic and ideological obstacles to the effective assessment of intelligence.

Moreover, such revelations have cast new light on the nature of the Cold War in general and the danger of inadvertent nuclear war in particular.

Another crucial set of questions concerns the methodological and epistemological assumptions underpinning the way the subject is studied. There has been insufficient consideration of these issues on either side of the Atlantic. Richard Aldrich has cautioned against interpreting the official records of the Public Record Office 'as an analogue of reality'.[22] He has argued persuasively that British archives are a highly manipulated source of evidence for historians. The British government's success in controlling knowledge of its wartime achievements in signals intelligence and strategic deception is a good example of official policy shaping the parameters of historical enquiry. There are almost certainly other such cases that are yet to come to light. One does not need to embrace a conspiratorial view of contemporary politics to appreciate the ramifications of this state practice for the generation of knowledge. These questions are especially important to consider in light of criticisms of studies of Soviet security and intelligence services that have been based on partial and controlled access to Soviet records.[23] When advancing such criticisms, we are obliged to consider whether recent archive-based histories of British or US intelligence are based on a more comprehensive and reliable sample of the documentary record.

And what of other sources, in particular oral testimony and interviews? Many journalists have written authoritative and well-researched accounts of intelligence-related issues, which rely on extensive contacts with officialdom.[24] Are these accounts more or less reliable than those based on the written archival record? Are they more or less prone to manipulation? And what of memoirs? And spy fiction? In his essay on 'Fiction, Faction and Intelligence' Nigel West demonstrates that behind the supposedly impenetrable veil of British official secrecy, many former intelligence officers have written accounts (factual, fictional and factional) of their experiences. While this material cannot take the place of greater transparency and oversight, it does provide an interesting perspective on how various former members of the secret services choose to represent the world of intelligence to the wider public. The extent to which British intelligence memoirs and spy fiction can function as propaganda for the secret services remains an open question. While this material must be used with care, it should not be ignored by scholars of British intelligence. There are areas, such as the role of women in espionage/intelligence and the perspective of gender where so far the study of the subject has often been dependent on such sources.[25]

Questions about the manipulation of intelligence have been underlined by September 11 and by allegations that the British government 'sexed up' intelligence to mislead the public about Iraqi Weapons of Mass Destruction (WMD). It was through the media that details of al-Qaeda operations and plans were made known to Western populations. For the student of intelligence – as for the practitioner – the provenance and credibility of the source remains central to understanding. Yet where the dissemination of knowledge accords with discernable agendas, how we deal with the problem of knowledge is crucial. Claims made about contacts between Mohammed Atta and Iraqi intelligence officers in Prague have now been shown to be false. Yet they were of potential importance in helping prepare the public and political ground for an attack on Iraq. The same is true of claims about Iraqi attempts to acquire uranium from Niger. Whether the claim about al-Qaeda represents misinformation or disinformation, it underlines the fact that we learn of some events because those in control of relevant information wish us to learn of them, and what we learn may inform broader political perceptions. Michael Smith's paper in this collection is a reminder of the tension between disclosing intelligence and risking sources, and how different leaders in different political cultures view their options and responsibilities differently.[26] These issues are of central importance to any attempt to establish the methodological foundations necessary for the effective study of intelligence.

Intelligence and the study of international relations

A further objective of this volume is to assess both the influence and importance of intelligence studies in broader debates concerning the history and theory of international relations. Intelligence has attracted limited interest from scholars of political philosophy and International Relations (IR) theory. Tsun Tzu is much quoted for the importance he attaches to military intelligence, but later thinkers on war were less interested and less impressed. Von Clausewitz held that knowledge of 'the enemy and his country' was 'the foundation of all our ideas and actions'.[27] Yet much of the knowledge or 'information' obtained in war is 'false' and 'by far the greatest part is of a doubtful character'. How the information was acquired and processed did not detain Clausewitz, who looked to officers with a 'certain power of discrimination' to guide their analysis.

Clausewitz's omissions are shared by many political and international theorists, including classical realists and contemporary neo-realists. Machiavelli, for example, demonstrates understanding of, and enthusiasm for, what the twentieth century would come to know as strategic deception: 'Though fraud in other activities be detestable, in the management of war it is laudable and glorious, and he who overcomes an enemy by fraud is as much to be praised as he who does so by force.' Yet elsewhere in the Discourses, when reflecting on conspiracy, he shows no understanding of the opportunities for espionage and counter-espionage in dealing with the conspiracies of coup plotters.[28] On the other hand, Toni Erskine makes clear in her essay in this collection that Thomas Hobbes, writing in the seventeenth century, understood the potential importance and value of espionage.[29]

Writing in 1994 Michael Fry and Miles Hochstein observed that, while intelligence studies had developed into an identifiable intellectual community, there was a noticeable 'failure to integrate intelligence studies, even in a primitive way, into the mainstream of research in international relations'.[30] In Britain the academic study of intelligence has developed overwhelmingly within international history, and thus reflects the methodological predisposition towards archive-based research characteristic of this sub-discipline. Common methodological cause between British and US historians has not prevented robust and fruitful exchanges and debates on the subject.[31] In North America, however, political scientists have played at least as prominent a role as historians in the study of intelligence in international relations. Their contributions have provided students of intelligence with a range of theoretical reflections on the nature of intelligence and its role in decision making. But interest in intelligence within the political science community has been confined mainly to those scholars working on theories of decision making. Intelligence is all but absent, conversely, in the work of most international relations theorists, and does not figure in key IR theory debates between realist, liberal institutionalist, constructivist and post-modernist approaches. It is interesting to note that, while there exists an implicit (and sometimes explicit) assumption that the study of intelligence falls within the realist camp, contemporary neo-realist writers have largely ignored intelligence in their reflections. The literature on US covert action for example, is ignored by leading neo-realist theorist, Stephen Krasner, in his analysis of the systematic violations of sovereignty in world politics. Although he advances trenchant arguments about the 'organised hypocrisy' of international discourse on sovereignty, he does not explore the potential role of intelligence as a source of both evidence and theoretical insight.[32]

The neglect of intelligence is apparent in other areas of international relations. Although one prominent item on the post-Cold War agenda was the role of intelligence in support of the United Nations and its agencies, the role of intelligence has not engaged the attention of those writing about humanitarian intervention, even though it is clear that intelligence has various roles to play, not least in providing evidence in war crimes tribunals. The role of intelligence services in promoting (or retarding) human rights is an area particularly worthy of exploration. Similarly, in debates about the democratic peace (whether democracies are less likely to engage in military operations against other democracies), attempts at regime change by clandestine means are an important dimension illuminated by the history of US covert operations in various democracies (Chile, Italy, Iran and so forth). How far the events of September 11 and the war on Iraq may help change academic attitudes and research agendas in these areas remains to be seen.

If international relations theory has shown limited interest in intelligence, to what extent have students of intelligence engaged with international relations theory? It seems clear that different theoretical perspectives are beginning to permeate the sub-field of intelligence. The journal *Intelligence and National Security* has carried important theoretical contributions which reward Fry and Hochstein's optimistic assertions that international relations and intelligence studies can fruitfully search for common ground. One notable example is Andrew Rathmell's essay on the potential importance of post-modern theorising to the practice of intelligence.[33] Rathmell argues that intelligence services must make radical changes in terms of both conceptual approach and organisational structure to adapt to the social, cultural and technological conditions of the twenty-first century. He posits that existing state-based intelligence agencies are products of modernity, but that the political and economic conditions of the modern era are disappearing. Capital intensive modes of mass production in highly urbanised nation-states are giving way, in the age of the world-wide web and digital technology, to 'knowledge intensive, dispersed globalized systems'. The end result is what Rathmell calls the 'fragmentation' of threat. What is needed, he argues, are different conceptual approaches to understanding the nature of security threats and radical changes in the way intelligence agencies collect and process knowledge on these threats. Obvious questions arise about how these new approaches might be implemented in practical terms. What is also necessary is greater awareness of the political role of the analyst in the construction of threats and threat assessments for makers of security policy of all kinds.[34]

The need to engage constructively with post-modernist thinking on security will surely increase, and this includes identifying areas where post-modernists themselves need to reflect further on existing approaches. The history of intelligence before the onset of the Cold War, for example, is often neglected. One resulting misconception is that open sources have only recently risen to prominence. The reality is that open sources have nearly always provided the majority of information for intelligence services during peacetime. It is also misleading to describe the emergence of 'globalised' threats as a 'post-modern' phenomenon. Imperial intelligence services faced such challenges throughout the nineteenth and twentieth centuries. Information technology has changed many aspects of intelligence work, but the intellectual challenges of dealing with security problems across immense spaces and over different cultures are by no means exclusively 'post-modern'. This is admirably demonstrated by the fascinating recent work of Martin Thomas.[35] It is also the case that the threat from non-state actors did not arrive with the end of the Cold War, as the history of the Anarchists and the Fenians well testifies.

An important argument made by Rathmell is that intelligence communities must become less hierarchical and more based on the concept of information 'networks' with a greater focus on 'open' sources of information. Here, the challenges identified by Rathmell and others have stimulated rather different diagnoses and prognoses. Writing before September 11, and from a very different ontological perspective, Bruce Berkowitz also argues the case for breaking down 'hierarchies and stovepipes' that restrict information flows within the intelligence community.[36] Berkowitz's article is notable for his analysis of the litany of what he terms US intelligence failures. The pressure to reform structure and culture in the US intelligence community is strengthened, and in some cases even driven, by advances in information technology. These trends and pressures are critically examined by John Ferris in his article in this collection. Where post-modernism rejects the notion of an absolute truth, the epistemological goal of those who proselytise the revolution in information warfare is perfect battlefield knowledge. Ferris casts doubt on their various assumptions and moreover reminds us that concerns with hierarchies and structures are crucial in communications security and counter-intelligence. He rightly observes that web-based nets within the US intelligence community are the 'richest treasure ever for espionage' and a grave potential vulnerability.[37]

Other theoretical innovations may well have something to offer. Recent constructivist theorising about the importance of identity and political culture in shaping both elite and public perceptions of international politics is a case in point. Its focus on identity as a central factor in the process of threat identification has obvious relevance to the study of security and intelligence. The same is true with the emphasis on cultural–institutional contexts of security policy. Intelligence services certainly have their own institutional cultures and a focus on the rules and norms which govern intelligence work in different national contexts has much to offer intelligence studies.[38] Reluctance to engage with this and other currents in international relations theory will not help efforts to expand the conceptual parameters of intelligence studies. In addition, a reluctance to engage with different strains of social theory may also comply with the intentions of those who seek to configure and inform public understanding of intelligence through the control of information. The way we choose to study the subject informs our analysis and our conclusions. As Aldrich warns, taking the archive as analogue of reality is a methodological and epistemological trap that can inadvertently legitimise activities that merit a much more critical approach.

Speaking 'truth unto power' or 'power unto truth'?

Much of the study of intelligence concerns the relationship between power and knowledge, or rather the relationship between certain kinds of power and certain kinds of knowledge. A sophisticated exponent of this view has been Michael Herman, writing on the basis of 25 years' experience at Government Communications Headquarters (GCHQ) and the Cabinet Office. Herman has received wide acclaim for his expositions of the process of intelligence and has been described as 'an historian and philosopher of intelligence'.[39] Although an advocate of broadening the scope of the subject, Herman's primary aim is to promote greater public understanding of intelligence. Yet, it is also undeniable that, in engaging with critical issues about the practice of the intelligence process, Herman seeks to legitimise that process. The same goals of education and legitimisation may also be ascribed to other intelligence mandarins who have written about intelligence after their retirement, notably Sir Percy Cradock, former Chairman of the Joint Intelligence Committee (JIC).[40] The work of both Herman and Cradock epitomises the prevalent self-image of the intelligence mandarin as providing objective, 'policy-free' analysis to decision makers. Sir Percy Cradock's characterisation of the JIC and its staff as 'having an eye always to the future and to British interests, and free from the political pressures likely to afflict their ministerial masters' reflects the self-image of the intelligence community as guardian of the national interest against transient and feckless politicians.

The role of the intelligence official in the British context is therefore represented as 'speaking truth unto power'. This self-image, so central to the identity of the public servant, has been the cornerstone of both the structure and the culture of British intelligence. It is represented as the fundamental safeguard against the politicisation of intelligence, which is often alleged to be a defining characteristic of autocratic and totalitarian regimes. Clearly this image of an independent and apolitical intelligence community has been called into serious question by the 'Iraq Dossier' affair.

In the summer of 2003 the British government and intelligence community became embroiled in one of the most serious political controversies in recent memory amid charges that intelligence on Iraqi weapons of mass destruction was politicised in order to bolster support for the government's bellicose posture towards the regime of Saddam Hussein. The publication of an intelligence dossier, written by the chair of the JIC, John Scarlett, included both Joint Intelligence Committee assessments and raw human intelligence obtained by the Secret Intelligence Service (SIS). The aim was to strengthen support both at home and abroad for war with Iraq. It was claimed in the dossier that 'The Iraqi military are able to deploy [chemical and biological] weapons within 45 minutes of a decision to do so.'[41] When introducing the dossier in the House of Commons, Prime Minister Tony Blair explained that it concluded

> that Iraq has chemical and biological weapons, that Saddam has continued to produce them, that he has existing and active military plans for the use of chemical and biological weapons, which could be activated within 45 minutes, including against his own Shia population, and that he is actively trying to acquire nuclear weapons capability.[42]

In this instance, intelligence was clearly employed to gain public support for government policy rather than as a guide for policy makers. Intelligence information was selected and presented in such a way as to emphasise the need to deal forcefully with the Iraqi regime. As Michael Handel observed nearly two decades ago, the closer the relationship between intelligence assessment and policy making, the greater the likelihood that the whole process will become politicised.[43] Indeed, a former Chairman of the JIC, Sir Rodric Braithwaite, has criticised his successors with the observation that JIC members went 'beyond assessment to become part of the process of making and advocating policy. That inevitably undermined their objectivity.'[44] Contemporary concern with use of intelligence should not obscure the fundamental reality that intelligence informs but rarely drives policy: Joint Intelligence Committees propose and Prime Ministers dispose. Another serious indictment of the Blair government policy concerns its commitment to counter-proliferation. If the Iraqi state possessed WMD, the destruction of that state means that ownership and control of these weapons are dispersed. These events could hasten the nightmare scenario of terrorist use of WMD against centres of population.

As Christopher Andrew points out in his contribution to this volume, the publication of Joint Intelligence Committee assessments is unprecedented. It is unlikely to remain so rare, however. Changes in the international system will likely make the public use of intelligence common practice. The decline of the Westphalian principle of non-intervention in the affairs of other states, along with the effects of September 11 and the 'war on terror', have led to the emergence of the doctrine of 'pre-emptive self defence' in the United States. This has introduced an important new dimension to the role of intelligence in international relations which students and practitioners have yet fully to comprehend. In this context it will be essential to establish the existence of a threat before public opinion in order to provide legitimacy for pre-emptive interventions. Despite the political problems created by the public use of intelligence to justify the invasion of Iraq, intelligence will remain central to debates about future pre-emptive action. Pressure on governments to disclose secret intelligence will lead to pressure on intelligence services to meet public needs. This was almost certainly the case in the months leading up to the Second Gulf War. It is a trend that will surely grow as long as the doctrine of pre-emptive intervention holds sway in Western foreign policy.

All this means that we need to evaluate critically this image of the intelligence official as apolitical interpreter of the real world for political decision makers. The dangers of not doing so are clear. The case of government deception over the role of British intelligence during the Second World War is just one example of the state's willingness to intervene in an effort to shape the conceptual horizons of intellectual enquiry. An uncritical acceptance of official or semi-official representations of the intelligence process as singularly free of ideological assumptions and political biases leaves the intelligence scholar open to the familiar charge that she or he is merely legitimising and perpetuating the ideology of the state. These issues are of central concern for all scholars interested in the relationship between power and knowledge. Again it seems clear that intelligence studies and international relations theory would both benefit from greater engagement with one another.

The idea of speaking truth unto power also has clear relevance to debates over the proper relationship between government and academia.[45] Among academics, notions and theories of truth and power are more explicitly contested. Claims of objectivity run counter to concern with developing multiple rather than unitary narratives of the past. This, of course, is the very antithesis of Whitehall's immaculate conception of a Joint Intelligence Committee. At the same time, official practice and academic study exercise an undeniable attraction to one another. But there are obstacles in the way of sustained engagement between the government and the academy. Intelligence is probably the field of academic enquiry over which the British government has been most anxious to exert control. Despite a recent trend toward more openness, particularly on the part of the British Security Service (MI5), access to archival material remains tightly regulated, though the National Archives (formerly the British Public Record Office) and the Lord Chancellor's Advisory Council on Public Records have endeavoured to engage British historians in the development of declassification policy. Yet it should be noted that, although the Freedom of Information Act (FOIA) will be fully enacted in January 2005, the intelligence agencies are specifically exempt from its provisions.[46]

In the United States the relationship between academics and government has always been much more porous. Since the formation of the first centralised US intelligence agency, the Office of Strategic Services, during the Second World War, academics have played a prominent role in the evolution of US intelligence policy. The study of intelligence is often informed by quasi-official links, and the CIA has been keen to promote the academic study of the subject. Both the National Security Agency and the CIA each employ their own team of full-time professionally trained historians. Each has also invited 'scholars in residence' to spend extended periods working within the agencies. Such links have at times generated debate about the proper limits and intellectual integrity of such endeavours.[47] But the overall benefits of these relationships are widely acknowledged.

In Britain it has long been difficult to discern any comparable relationship. A greater distance has generally been maintained between 'academics' and 'practitioners'. And, as Wolfgang Krieger demonstrates in this volume, the situation in Germany, as elsewhere in Europe, shows even less engagement.[48] There have been important exceptions to this general trend, most notably the scholars who were given privileged access to official records in order to write the official histories of the Second World War. Another notable exception is Christopher Andrew, whose collaborations with KGB defectors Oleg Gordievsky and Vasili Mitrokhin have illuminated KGB activities as well as British (and particularly SIS) successes in the espionage war. But it is only recently that a culture of greater openness has led to greater engagement between Britain's intelligence community and its universities. A good illustration of this trend was the willingness of Sir Stephen Lander, then Director-General of MI5, to attend academic meetings and conferences on the study of intelligence over the past few years. Further evidence of greater openness, at least on the part of the Security Service, is MI5's recent appointment of an academic historian, Christopher Andrew, to write its centenary history. Yet there are those who would argue that this kind of engagement is not without costs. For some academics the Ivory Tower should remain a sanctuary from the compromises of officialdom and provide a panorama (or a *camera obscura*) on the world outside. For others, academics are there to tell the world about the world. Yet, while many academics aspire to policy relevance, intelligence is one area where officialdom may remain sceptical about the value of engagement with the academy.

Dark sides of moons

Reflecting on the work of the JIC, Sir Percy Cradock has observed that 'it has a predilection for threats rather than opportunities, for the dark side of the moon'.[49] Certainly the issues of strategic surprise and of intelligence failure have loomed large in the evolution of the study of intelligence. This is unlikely to change significantly. Providing warning against surprise is central to both official and public perceptions of the fundamental role of intelligence services. The events of September 11, 2001 have clearly reinforced this trend. Desmond Ball has described September 11 as 'the worst intelligence failure by the US intelligence community since Pearl Harbor'.[50] Yet such judgements also raise questions about the meaning we give to the term intelligence failure as well as to how we explain and assign responsibility for what happened. Historians and political scientists will continue to study Pearl Harbor, the Tet offensive, the Yom Kippur War,

Argentina's seizure of the Falklands/Malvinas, Iraq's invasion of Kuwait, and, of course, the terrorist attacks on the World Trade Center and the Pentagon. But they will also need to revisit from time to time the conceptual foundations of their studies.

Recent developments in the study of security in international politics have attempted to broaden predominant conceptions of security to provide a more sophisticated understanding of the problem of instability in international society. The study of intelligence, with its focus on the identification and interpretation of threat, and on the architecture of threat perception, has much to offer and much to gain from greater engagement with new approaches to security. Contemporary intelligence agendas (both official and academic) range from economic security to environment to health to organised crime, as well as to more traditional areas of arms transfers, proliferation of WMD, and UN peace keeping and peace enforcing. Changes in world politics since the end of the Cold War have created greater awareness of the importance of these issues. The fact that the CIA has primary responsibility for the HIV/AIDS threat suggests that official thinking in Washington has responded to these trends in ways that have not always been acknowledged. Intelligence communities must play closer attention to the many dimensions of global insecurity, not least so that policy makers can better understand the need to alleviate social and economic conditions that are one source of disaffected recruits for extremist groups. In short, the practice of intelligence will change and adapt to new political problems facing world politics, as well as to more long-standing concerns with injustices that lie at the heart of much global instability. The same is true of the study of intelligence. The aim of this collection of essays is to stimulate reflection upon what new directions might be taken.

The role of threat perception in the policy process is bound to remain a central concern in the study of intelligence. The same is true of the relationship between 'producers' and 'consumers'. But it is important to remember that many intelligence services do more than just collect and process information. Many internal security agencies in democratic as well as non-democratic states possess powers of arrest and thus function as tools of state power. Indeed the Gestapo, the KGB and the Stasi are only the most notorious examples of the potential threat to individual freedom posed by domestic security and intelligence services. Yet another controversial and problematic area of intelligence activity is that of secret intervention in the affairs of other states (and non-state actors). As noted above, the case of 'covert action' provides an interesting perspective on the role of intelligence and intelligence services in the exercise of power. Over the past half-century, covert action has often undermined the legitimacy of Western intelligence services both domestically and internationally. A fundamental question is therefore: to what extent and in what ways should covert action be considered a function of intelligence and intelligence services. One answer is provided by Sherman Kent in his arguably tautological observation that intelligence is what intelligence services do. A variation on this might be to say that intelligence knowledge is power, and other exercises of power by intelligence services fall within the same ambit. A rather different view would be to suggest that secrecy, rather than power or knowledge, is the unifying theme of intelligence discourse. This is the line of argument pursued by Len Scott in this collection; a more radical perspective on secrecy is proffered by Robert A. Goldberg who argues that secrecy plays a crucial and perfidious role in sustaining conspiracy theories.[51]

The distinction between gathering intelligence and intervening in the internal affairs of other states, and thus the distinction between intelligence as a guide to policy rather than a tool of policy, can be misleading. This is particularly true in the realm of human intelligence, where the idea of an agent of influence, for example, challenges a simple distinction between gathering knowledge and taking action. It is interesting to compare the British and US literature on covert action. In the United States there has been long-standing awareness of the subject that has generated both public and scholarly debates. More recently, systematic declassification of files dealing with covert action has made a significant contribution to understanding the origins and dynamics of the Cold War. The declassification of CIA records has more clearly revealed the scope and scale of operations from Cuba to Chile to Indonesia to Guatemala. Indeed, in the view of some scholars, the history of covert action compels revision of the historical and political accounts of the Cold War, and fatally weakens the view that the US policy was simply concerned with containment.[52] These issues have not received the attention they deserve in the study of British intelligence so far. Although recently published studies by Richard Aldrich and Stephen Dorril have illuminated a great deal, British covert action in both Cold War and post-imperial contexts is an area that requires further study. Here the endeavours of senior intelligence mandarins to divert the focus to the sanitised and cerebral contexts of Whitehall analysis may reflect a conscious (or unconscious) attempt to divert attention away from the more dramatic and controversial question of covert action. It may be that such activities are marginal to the primary missions of the British intelligence services. Yet the fact is that this question remains shrouded in uncertainty.

Intelligence and ethics

One contribution of the (largely US) study of covert action has been to bring together ethics and intelligence studies. There is a significant literature which has been largely ignored by scholars working on the role of intelligence in policy making.[53] The ethical and legal dimensions of intelligence are rarely analysed, particularly in historical accounts – although in the United States ethical issues have frequently been explored within debates over intelligence accountability. The need for an explicit concern with moral issues has been identified by Michael Herman, who has begun to explore ethical dimensions of intelligence in a broader sense.[54] Herman has argued that intelligence requires 'a similar ethical foundation' to the use of armed force. An equally telling and compelling observation is his view that 'Ethics should be recognized as a factor in intelligence decisions, just as in anything else.'[55] Such a view compels attention not least given its provenance. This is not an entirely new concern. Abram Shulsky has also contended that an ethical case for conducting intelligence operations can be found in Tsun Tsu as early as the fifth century BC.[56]

In his famous essay on 'The Profession and Vocation of Politics', Max Weber observes that 'No ethics in the world can get round the fact that the achievement of "good" ends is in many cases tied to the necessity of employing morally suspect or at least morally dangerous means.'[57] This dilemma is a central concern for all those interested in the role of intelligence in politics. To what ends should the 'morally suspect' means of intelligence be put? For whose 'good ends' should these means be employed? To whom, or to what, should they be ultimately responsible? Can their responsibilities ever be to the universal or will they always be to the particular? The crux of the issue, according to Weber, is a crucial dilemma of politics: that the interests of particular communities or polities will not always be compatible with the wider interests of humanity. Weber rejects the universalist assumptions of the 'ethics of principled conviction' for their disregard of the consequences of political choice. He argues instead that the first responsibility of those involved in politics must be to their own community.[58] These questions are addressed by both Michael Herman and Toni Erskine in their contributions to this volume. Michael Herman reflects further on the ethical justifications for intelligence and explores the opportunities for doing so in the wake of September 11.[59] In her contribution, Toni Erskine locates emerging ethical reflections on intelligence gathering within the traditional frameworks of realist, consequentialist and deontological traditions.[60] Such an approach offers new vistas for potential research and has obvious relevance to efforts to combine intelligence and security concerns with an 'ethical foreign policy'.

Hitherto ethics has remained an under-explored area in intelligence studies. A former permanent secretary at the Ministry of Defence, Sir Michael Quinlan, who played a key role in British thinking about the morality of nuclear deterrence and was also responsible for an official overview of British intelligence in the post-Cold War era, has remarked upon the lack of a conceptual structure for studying the morality of espionage. Quinlan has lamented the absence of a doctrine for what he terms 'Just Espionage'.[61] On the other hand, Quinlan fascinatingly refers to ethical problems as a 'cost' of intelligence. The tension between these two positions suggests that intelligence may often be situated at the fault-line between the theory and practice of international politics. In any case, this is a fascinating and important aspect of intelligence that bears further reflection and research.

Ethics are not only relevant at the level of high-policy. The ethical ethos of an intelligence organisation is of great importance to understanding it as an institution. Studying that ethos remains a significant methodological hurdle. How intelligence services and intelligence officers view their responsibilities to their agents and to others, for example, is a potentially fascinating question. How far intelligence agencies will go to protect their sources is an ethical and operational matter that has surfaced for example in accounts and allegations concerning British security activities in Northern Ireland. The codes of conduct – both written and unwritten – of intelligence services provide one potential avenue for exploring the ethical constraints and dilemmas involved in human intelligence gathering as (to a lesser extent) do the ethical views of the individual agents. This is an aspect on which there has been little systematic study, though memoirs and other accounts of operations, including authoritative accounts by journalists, provide vignettes and insights.[62]

Debate about a range of ethical issues concerning the conduct of intelligence in war extends to legal questions about whether prisoners should be taken and how they should be treated. In the United States and elsewhere there has been serious public discussion about the use of torture in extracting information from terrorist suspects, reflecting the dramatic impact of events on public debate. US debates about the use of assassination as an instrument of statecraft have been rekindled.[63] Ethics seems destined to be ever more closely entwined with public debate and discourse concerning intelligence. Yet public perceptions of what intelligence is and what it does owe as much to fictional representations as to public debate in the 'real' world of international politics.

Popular culture and intelligence

At least since the aftermath of the Franco-Prussian war in 1871, popular culture has often played an important role in shaping both official and public attitudes towards intelligence. Michael Miller has demonstrated the way fears of foreign espionage and national insecurity gripped the French imagination during this period. The Dreyfus Affair, which had such grievous consequences for French intelligence, unfolded in an atmosphere of spy mania over the machinations of an imaginary army of German spies in France controlled by the notorious spymaster Wilhelm Stieber. The fact that there was no army of spies and Stieber was a police chief rather than a master of espionage did not matter. Through to the outbreak of war in 1914 spy mania was created and sustained by memories of France's defeat in 1871 and by a spy literature which played on national anxieties about France's vulnerability to foreign espionage.[64] The British public demonstrated a similar appetite for espionage stories and invasion scares, of which some of the most widely read were produced by William Le Queux. It was in the context of a wave of greatly exaggerated official and popular concern over the threat of foreign espionage that a British security service was established in 1909.[65]

Fictional representations of international politics as a struggle for survival between national intelligence services thus played an important role in the evolution of both French and British intelligence before the First World War. Between the two World Wars, spy adventures stories, and even spy films, became a permanent fixture of Western popular culture. This trend continued through the Cold War era. Graham Greene, John Le Carré, Ian Fleming and Tom Clancy are only the most prominent of several generations of novelists who used intelligence as both medium and metaphor when interpreting the era of superpower rivalry for the reading public. For most of the twentieth century, representations of intelligence in popular culture were far and away the most influential factors shaping public attitudes and perceptions. Yet, with a few notable exceptions, scholars have been reluctant to reflect upon the implications of this in their analyses of the relationship between intelligence and politics. Once again, there is potentially interesting work being done in the cognate field of cultural history which could enrich the study of intelligence. Cultural historians, especially those interested in Cold War popular and political culture, have begun to pay careful attention to the role of film and fiction in shaping both elite and popular attitudes towards international politics. The intersection between this work and the study of intelligence has not received the attention it deserves.

Jeremy Black provides an interesting perspective on the issue of popular culture in his exploration of the geopolitics of James Bond. Of particular interest is his analysis of the way Anglo-American relations are represented in the Bond genre.[66] Fictional representations of intelligence form the basis of much public understanding. As Nigel West observes, no less an authority than former SIS Chief, Sir Colin McColl, considered Bond 'the best recruiting sergeant the service ever had'[67] – perhaps the converse view of intelligence critic Philip Knightley who complained that the 'fictional glorification of spies enables the real ones to go on playing their sordid games'.[68] A more perplexing if intriguing relationship between reality and fiction is illustrated by the occasion recounted by Jeremy Black when the Soviet Politburo issued instructions to the KGB to acquire the gadgetry displayed in the latest Bond film.

Fiction provides a range of ethical representations of intelligence.[69] Jeremy Black observes that 'the world of Bond is not characterized by ambiguity... there is good (including good rogues...) and bad.'[70] Other representations convey a very different moral reality. One of Le Carré's characters, Connie Sachs, characterises Cold War espionage as 'half angels fighting half devils'.[71] This can be read as Le Carré's own perspective on intelligence and intelligence work. It stands in contrast to the self-image of Western intelligence officers proffered by a former senior member of the Secret Intelligence Service: 'honesty inside the service, however much deception might be practiced outside it, and never descend to the other side's methods'.[72] Fiction also illustrates specific ethical problems and dilemmas. How far an intelligence organisation is prepared to risk or sacrifice its own 'side' in pursuit of a 'higher' objective is a popular theme, well illustrated in Le Carré's *The Spy Who Came in From the Cold*.[73]

Other representations of intelligence go further in this regard. In the 1975 film *Three Days of the Condor*, for example, the CIA assassinates its own officers to protect its designs for global control of oil resources. The film illustrates various themes commonly found in conspiracy theories, not least that intelligence services are malign and all-pervasive. This manner of representing the ethics of intelligence services is very common in both literature and in film. A more recent example is the 2002 film version of Robert Ludlum's *The Bourne Identity* – which depicts the CIA as both omnipotent and utterly immoral.[74] The extent to which these types of cultural representations are influenced by public disclosure of intelligence activities would be an interesting avenue for further research.

Fictional conspiracy theories frequently accord with the genuine kind in giving meaning to events. As Robert Goldberg argues in his essay for this volume:

> Despite their weaknesses, conspiracy theories offer much to believers. If slippery in their logic and often careless of facts and assumptions, they order the random and make consistent the paradoxical. In the face of national crisis and human failure, conspiracy theorists rush to find purpose in tragedy and clarity in ambiguity. They also respond to the traumatized who cry for vengeance and demand the identities of those responsible. Conspiracy thinking thus becomes an antidote to powerlessness.[75]

Some of these observations resonate with James Der Derian's analysis of Hollywood's representation of conspiracy when he writes of:

> the conspiratorial aesthetic, which produces and is sustained by the tension between fear and desire. The world system might, on the face of it, be speeding out of control, yet we cling to metaphysical faith and find perverse pleasure in cinematic confirmation that somewhere under the table, in the highest corporate or government office, someone is pulling the strings or at the very least is willing with the best technology, fastest speed and longest reach to intervene secretly, if sinisterly, when necessary. It then makes sense to find in coeval events, synchronicities, even odd accidents, the intellectual evidence and psychological comfort of the hidden hand.[76]

Yet, merely because there are individual or collective psychological needs in a hidden hand does not mean that hidden hands do not exist. One reason why there are conspiracy theories is because there are conspiracies. Indeed the history of covert action is the history of conspiracy. While it would be simplistic to suggest that the former begat the latter, covert action is nevertheless the sturdy twin of conspiracy theory. The suggestion, for example, that the British state undertakes the murder of its citizens for political purposes is a familiar trope in popular representations of intelligence activity. The suggestion that Hilda Murrell, an elderly anti-nuclear protester, was killed by the security service in an operation against nuclear protesters gained surprising currency. MI5's website currently proclaims that 'We do not kill people or arrange their assassination.'[77] Yet it is now clear that there was collusion between British officials and loyalist paramilitaries in murders and other crimes in Northern Ireland.[78] As Sir John Stevens has commented: 'the unlawful involvement of agents in murder implies that the security forces sanction killings'.[79]

Fictional representation thrives on the plausibly implausible. Had the events of September 11 been crafted by a script writer, they may well have been dismissed as incredible and fanciful (even if they would have gained attention for transgressing Hollywood's devotion to happy endings). In the aforementioned *Three Days of the Condor* the CIA analyses books to check whether they depict actual CIA operations. After September 11 there are indications of new-found interest in how fiction writers conceptualise and represent threat. Conspiracy and conspiracy theory will remain inextricably linked with intelligence in popular perception and cultural representation. Disentangling the two remains an essential part of the enterprise. Michael Smith's defence of Prime Minister Churchill's use of intelligence on Nazi atrocities in the Soviet Union is a good illustration of how this can be done.[80] The issue of how far fiction corresponds to reality is linked to questions concerning the way we perceive and construct reality. Le Carré's novels are widely accepted as authentic depictions of the techniques and tradecraft of espionage – though his representation of the ethics of the service provoked anger from within.[81] More recently, the film *U-571* was criticised for depicting the seizure of the German naval Enigma by US rather than by British forces.[82] There is of course a long tradition of changing or manipulating historical 'events' for dramatic effect. But to what extent do such fictional representations actually shape popular attitudes? This is a question that awaits systematic exploration. How far fictional representations are *intended* to frame popular understandings has received rather more attention – particularly in the recent boom of studies of the cultural history of the Cold War.[83] The events of September 11 and the 'war on terror' have given these questions a new saliency and urgency. How Hollywood will now depict intelligence services and how it will represent the US government will be issues to watch carefully.

A final 'missing dimension': national and international intelligence co-operation

One other relatively neglected aspect in the study of intelligence is co-operation between different intelligence services at both the national and international levels. At the national level, efficient co-operation between secret services is crucial to the effective exploitation of intelligence. The importance of a rational system of inter-service co-ordination was highlighted, once again, by the events of September 11, 2001. Insufficient co-operation between various US security and intelligence services is consistently cited as a central factor in the failure to prevent the successful attacks on the World Trade Center and the Pentagon. The 858-page Congressional Report on these events published in July 2003 severely criticised both the CIA and the FBI for failing to develop an effective system for sharing intelligence on terrorist activity inside the United States with one another and with other departments concerned with national security.[84] Yet, despite the valuable start made by pioneers, this is a field that has not received systematic study by either political scientists or historians.[85] A comparative study, examining different national approaches to solving this problem, would be particularly valuable and policy relevant.

The question of intelligence co-operation at the international level has received more attention, particularly from historians. The origins, development and functioning of Anglo-American 'intelligence alliance' since 1940 have been the subject of relatively intense study from a range of perspectives.[86] Important research has also been done on such diverse subjects as intelligence sharing between the West and the Soviet Union during the Second World War, on intelligence collaboration within the Soviet bloc during the Cold War and between Soviet and Cuban intelligence, and between Western intelligence and former Nazi intelligence officers.[87] We also have a very useful collection of essays on the subject of 'Knowing One's Friends' that provides fascinating insights into the ambiguous role of intelligence between friendly states.[88]

Michael Herman and Richard Aldrich have both provided useful reflections on the nature of international intelligence co-operation.[89] This will assist the growing number of scholars now researching the potential role of intelligence in international organisations such as NATO, the European Union or the United Nations.[90] Important work has also been undertaken on the role of intelligence in international police work. The changing parameters of intelligence collaboration after September 11, and increased public awareness of this co-operation, suggest that this will be an area of great potential growth in the field. When a British arms dealer was arrested in August 2003 attempting to sell a surface-to-air missile to FBI agents posing as terrorists, news of the role of SIS and MI5 was immediately made public, illustrating changing attitudes towards disclosure as well as in practice.[91] One neglected aspect identified by Len Scott in this collection is the role of intelligence services in conducting clandestine diplomatic activities with adversaries, both states and non-states.[92]

All of this augurs well for opening new avenues for students of intelligence and security in contemporary international relations. Yet the research trends outlined above remain disparate. There are still few monographs or collections of essays devoted to the specific question of co-operation and collaboration between national intelligence services. Nor has sufficient research and reflection been given to the delicate relationship between intelligence and political relations between states. The successful prosecution of the present 'war on terror' depends largely on the ability of national intelligence services to collaborate with one another effectively in rooting out international terrorist cells. The relationship between politics and intelligence has never been more important. There is a clear need for more systematic study of this area.

Conclusion

The publication in 1946 of the lengthy and detailed Congressional Report on the Pearl Harbor attack provided the primary raw material for one of the founding texts in the intelligence studies canon.[93] Roberta Wohlstetter's marriage of communications theory with detailed historical research in *Pearl Harbor: Warning and Decision* demonstrated the rich potential of an interdisciplinary approach to the study of intelligence and policy making.[94] Whether or not the recently published Congressional Report on the surprise attacks of September 11 produces another seminal text, the events of the past three years are bound to have profound implications for the study of intelligence.

Michael Herman has argued that, 'Governments' and peoples' views of intelligence will be permanently affected by the events of September 11.'[95] While this is debatable, it is undeniable that intelligence occupies a more prominent place in the public sphere than ever before. Quite apart from the publication of secret intelligence on Iraq, debates about the practice of intelligence now take place on a scale and at a level that would have been inconceivable three years ago. Issues such as the relative importance of human intelligence as against 'technical assets', the importance of international intelligence collaboration and the cognitive obstacles to effective analysis and warning have all been debated. As Wesley Wark is surely right to argue: 'Learning to live with an open-ended "war on terrorism" will mean learning to live with intelligence.'[96] These developments will doubtless provide both challenges and opportunities to scholars interested in the study of intelligence.

Should the terror attacks in New York and Washington force us to rethink the subject we are studying? Will they change the nature and conduct of intelligence operations forever? If so, how will this affect the study of intelligence and its role in world politics? These are questions that bear further reflection in any exercise aimed at establishing a future agenda for intelligence studies. The evidence so far suggests that, while the role of intelligence in international politics has certainly evolved, and scholars will have to adjust to its evolution, the changes may not be as revolutionary as they at first appeared. As in other areas of world politics, the immovable object of change confronts the irresistible force of continuity.

It is true that there was no Pearl Harbor precedent for the debates about the ethical restraints on intelligence activity. Nor was there much public discussion of the need for trans-national intelligence co-operation. These differences reflect changes that have taken place in world politics since the Second World War. International norms have evolved and now place greater limitations on the exercise of power than those that existed during and after the Second World War. Globalisation, and in particular advances in information technology, have thrown up new challenges that require new solutions. But there are nonetheless remarkable parallels between debates over Pearl Harbor and the aftermath of September 11. In both instances, predictably, the overwhelming focus was on learning lessons and prescribing policies. Many of the themes are very similar: the inability to conduct effective espionage against a racially or culturally 'alien' adversary; the failure to organise and co-ordinate inter-service intelligence collection and analysis; the lack of resources for both gathering, translating and analysing intelligence and, finally, the failure of political leaders to understand the value and limitations of intelligence. The surprise attack on United States territory in December 1941 killed over 2,000 people and precipitated the United States' entry into war in Europe and Asia. Pearl Harbor portended a transformation in the US role in world politics, and indeed in world politics itself. The surprise attack on United States territory on September 11, 2001 killed a similar number of people (though these were not military personnel and included many hundreds of non-Americans). It too precipitated US wars – in Afghanistan and Iraq. How far it has transformed world politics will remain open to debate. The context in which intelligence is conducted and studied continues to change. *Journeys in Shadows* will hopefully provide some guidance and illumination along the dimly lit pathways that lie ahead.

Notes

We are grateful to Tim Dunne and Toni Erskine for comments on earlier drafts.

1 Christopher Andrew, 'Intelligence, International Relations and "Under-theorisation"', this volume, pp. 29–30.
2 Sherman Kent, *Strategic Intelligence for American World Policy* (Princeton, NJ: Princeton University Press, 1949).
3 Christopher Andrew and David Dilks (eds), *The Missing Dimension: Governments and Intelligence Communities in the Twentieth Century* (Urbana, IL: University of Illinois Press, 1984).
4 Christopher Andrew, 'Intelligence in the Cold War: Lessons and Learning', in Harold Shukman (ed.), *Agents for Change: Intelligence Services in the 21st Century* (London: St Ermin's Press, 2000), pp. 1–2.
5 Andrew, 'Intelligence, International Relations', pp. 29–41. For recent research on signals intelligence, see Matthew Aid and Cees Wiebes (eds), *Secrets of Signals Intelligence during the Cold War and Beyond*, Special Issue of *Intelligence and National Security*, 16, 1 (2001).
6 An important recent development in the evolution of more liberal classification and declassification policies in the United States is the implementation of Executive Order 12958 'Classified National Security Information' in April 1995, although the significance of this has been contested. The Blair government has been largely unsuccessful in its attempts to establish a similar regime in Britain. For an interesting perspective on US attitudes towards government secrecy see the report of the 'Commission on Protecting and Reducing Government Secrecy' established in Washington in 1995: *Secrecy: Report of the Commission on Protecting and Reducing Government Secrecy* (Washington, DC: Government Printing Office, 1997); and Daniel Moynihan, *Secrecy* (New Haven, CT: Yale University Press, 1998). On the British side see David Vincent, *The Culture of Secrecy* (Oxford: Oxford University Press, 1998).
7 Kent, *Strategic Intelligence*, p. ix.
8 James Der Derian, *Antidiplomacy: Spies, Terror, Speed and War* (Oxford: Blackwell, 1992); see also Michael Fry and Miles Hochstein, 'Epistemic Communities: Intelligence Studies and International Relations' in Wesley K. Wark (ed.), *Espionage: Past, Present, Future?* (London: Frank Cass, 1994), pp. 14–28 (also published as a Special Issue of *Intelligence and National Security*, 8, 3 (1993)).
9 David Kahn, 'An Historical Theory of Intelligence', *Intelligence and National Security*, 16, 3 (2002), p. 79. For a thoughtful comparative analysis of the concept of intelligence in different national contexts see Philip H.J. Davies, 'Ideas of Intelligence: Divergent National Concepts and Institutions', *Harvard International Review* (Autumn 2002), pp. 62–6. For an earlier valuable collection of essays dealing with these issues see Kenneth G. Robertson (ed.), *British and American Approaches to Intelligence* (Basingstoke: Macmillan, 1987).
10 Examples include Richard Thurlow, *The Secret State: British Internal Security in the Twentieth Century* (Oxford: Blackwell, 1994), Amy Knight, *Beria: Stalin's First Lieutenant* (Princeton, NJ: Princeton University Press, 1993), Robert Gellately, *The Gestapo and German Society: Enforcing Racial Policy 1933–1945* (Oxford: Oxford University Press, 1990).
11 Michael Herman, *Intelligence Power in Peace and War* (Cambridge: Cambridge University Press, 1996).
12 John Ferris, 'Intelligence' in R. Boyce and J. Maiolo (eds), *The Origins of World War Two: The Debate Continues* (Basingstoke: Palgrave, 2003), p. 308.
13 For an excellent analysis of US presidents and their use of intelligence see Christopher Andrew, *For the President's Eyes Only: Secret Intelligence and the American Presidency from Washington to Bush* (London: HarperCollins, 1995).

14 Michael Herman, 'Diplomacy and Intelligence', *Diplomacy & Statecraft*, 9, 2 (1998), pp. 1–2.
15 For discussion see Herman, *Intelligence Power* and Abram Shulsky, *Silent Warfare: Understanding the World of Intelligence* (London: Brassey's US, 1993).
16 Elizabeth Anderson, 'The Security Dilemma and Covert Action: The Truman Years', *International Journal of Intelligence and CounterIntelligence*, 11, 4 (1998/99), p. 404.
17 See, for example, Michael I. Handel, *The Diplomacy of Surprise* (Cambridge, MA: Center for International Affairs, Harvard University, 1980), idem, 'Intelligence and Military Operations' in idem (ed.), *Intelligence and Military Operations* (London: Frank Cass, 1990), pp. 1–95; Richard Betts, 'Analysis, War and Decision: Why Intelligence Failures are Inevitable', *World Politics*, 31, 1 (1978), pp. 961–88; and Robert Jervis, 'Intelligence and Foreign Policy', *International Security*, 2, 3 (1986/87), pp. 141–61.
18 See Martin Thomas, 'French Intelligence Gathering and the Syrian Mandate, 1920–1940', *Middle Eastern Studies*, 38, 2 (2002) and his forthcoming, *Intelligence and Empire: Security Services and Colonial Control in North Africa and the Middle East, 1919–1940* (Berkeley, CA: University of California Press, forthcoming). See also Richard J. Popplewell, *Intelligence and Imperial Defence: British Intelligence and the Defence of the Indian Empire, 1904–1924* (London: Frank Cass, 1995).
19 See Gary Marx, 'Some Concepts that may be Useful in Understanding the Myriad Forms and Contexts of Surveillance', this volume, pp. 78–98. For an authoritative overview of the concepts and context of surveillance in social and political theory see Christopher Dandeker, *Surveillance, Power and Modernity* (Oxford: Polity Press in association with Blackwell, 1990).
20 Andrew, 'Intelligence, International Relations', p. 34.
21 See in particular Aleksandr Fursenko and Timothy Naftali, *'One Hell of a Gamble': Khrushchev, Castro, Kennedy and the Cuban Missile Crisis 1958–1964* (London: John Murray, 1997); Christopher Andrew and Oleg Gordievsky, *KGB: The Inside Story* (London: Hodder & Stoughton, 1990); and Benjamin B. Fischer, *A Cold War Conundrum: The 1983 Soviet War Scare* (Washington, DC: Central Intelligence Agency, Center for the Study of Intelligence, 1997).
22 Richard Aldrich, *The Hidden Hand: Britain, America and Cold War Secret Intelligence* (London: John Murray, 2001), p. 6. On this important methodological issue see also idem, *Intelligence and the War against Japan* (Cambridge: Cambridge University Press, 2000), pp. 385–7, and P. Jackson, 'The Politics of Secret Service in War, Cold War and Imperial Retreat', *Twentieth Century British History*, 14, 4 (2003), pp. 423–31.
23 See Sheila Kerr, 'KGB Sources on the Cambridge Network of Soviet Agents: True or False', *Intelligence and National Security*, 11, 3 (1996), pp. 561–85, and 'Oleg Tsarev's Synthetic KGB Gems', *International Journal of Intelligence and Counter-Intelligence*, 14, 1 (2001), pp. 89–116; see Nigel West's rejoinder, 'No Dust on KGB Jewels', *International Journal of Intelligence and CounterIntelligence*, 14, 4 (2001–2002), pp. 589–92.
24 See for example, Mark Urban, *UK Eyes Alpha: The Inside Story of British Intelligence* (London: Faber & Faber, 1996) and Michael Smith, *New Cloak, Old Dagger: How Britain's Spies Came in From the Cold* (London: Victor Gollancz, 1996). The pre-eminent figure in combining recently released archival material with the fruits of personal disclosure and oral testimony is undoubtedly Peter Hennessy; see his *The Secret State: Whitehall and the Cold War* (London: Allen Lane Penguin Press, 2002).
25 For recent examples of writing on women, gender and intelligence see Sandra C. Taylor, 'Long-Haired Women, Short-Haired Spies: Gender, Espionage, and America's War on Vietnam', *Intelligence and National Security*, 13, 2 (1998), pp. 61–70 and Tammy M. Proctor, *Female Intelligence: Women and Espionage in the First World War* (New York and London: New York University Press, 2003); see also the journal, *Minerva:*

Women and War published by Taylor & Francis. We are grateful to Jenny Mathers for this information.

26 Michael Smith, 'Bletchley Park and the Holocaust', this volume, pp. 111–21.

27 Carl von Clausewitz, *On War* (ed. by Anatol Rapoport, New York: Pelican, 1968), p. 162. For analysis of Clausewitz on intelligence see John Ferris and Michael I. Handel, 'Clausewitz, Intelligence, Uncertainty and the Art of Command in Military Operations', *Intelligence and National Security*, 10, 1 (1995), pp. 1–58.

28 John Plamenatz (ed.), *Machiavelli, The Prince, Selections from the Discourses and other Writings* (London: Fontana/Collins, 1975), pp. 252–71.

29 Toni Erskine, '"As Rays of Light to the Human Soul"? Moral Agents and Intelligence Gathering', this volume, pp. 195–215.

30 Fry and Hochstein, 'Epistemic Communities', p. 14.

31 See in particular the reflections of John Lewis Gaddis, 'Intelligence, Espionage, and Cold War Origins', *Diplomatic History*, 13 (Spring 1989), pp. 191–212, and D. Cameron Watt, 'Intelligence and the Historian: A Comment on John Gaddis's "Intelligence, Espionage, and Cold War Origins"', ibid, 14 (Spring 1990), pp. 199–204.

32 Stephen D. Krasner, 'Rethinking the Sovereign State Model', in Michael Cox, Tim Dunne and Ken Booth (eds), *Empires, Systems and State: Great Transformations in International Politics* (Cambridge: Cambridge University Press, 2001). We are grateful to Tim Dunne for drawing our attention to this.

33 Andrew Rathmell, 'Towards Postmodern Intelligence', *Intelligence and National Security*, 17, 3 (2002), pp. 87–104. See also the work of James Der Derian who has written extensively on aspects of intelligence from a post-modern perspective. See, for example, his *Antidiplomacy*.

34 This is a central focus of the interesting and important work being done in France by scholars such as Didier Bigo and others, whose work is most often published in the journal *Cultures et Conflits*.

35 See Thomas, 'French Intelligence Gathering' and *Intelligence and Empire*.

36 Bruce Berkowitz, 'Better Ways to Fix US Intelligence', *Orbis* (Fall 2001), pp. 615–17.

37 John Ferris, 'Netcentric Warfare, C4ISR and Information Operations: Towards a Revolution in Military Intelligence?', this volume, p. 64.

38 For constructivist approaches to IR see, for example, the essays in Peter J. Katzenstein (ed.), *The Culture of National Security* (New York: Columbia University Press, 1996), and Alexander Wendt, *Social Theory of International Politics* (Cambridge: Cambridge University Press, 1999).

39 Hennessy, *Secret State*, p. xiii. See also Lawrence Freedman, 'Powerful Intelligence', *Intelligence and National Security*, 12, 2 (1997), pp. 198–202.

40 Percy Cradock, *Know Your Enemy: How the Joint Intelligence Committee Saw the World* (London: John Murray, 2002).

41 *Iraq's Weapons of Mass Destruction: The Assessment of the British Government* (London: The Stationery Office, 24 September 2002), p. 17.

42 *Hansard, HC deb*. Vol. 390, Col. 3, 24 September 2002.

43 Michael Handel, 'The Politics of Intelligence', in idem, *War, Strategy and Intelligence* (London: Frank Cass, 1987), pp. 187–228.

44 Richard Norton-Taylor, 'Intelligence Heads Under Fire', *The Guardian*, 6 December 2003.

45 See William Wallace, 'Truth and Power, Monks and Technocrats: Theory and Practice in International Relations', *Review of International Studies*, 22, 3 (1996), pp. 301–21 and replies: Ken Booth, 'A Reply to Wallace', *Review of International Studies*, 23, 3 (1997), pp. 371–7 and Steve Smith 'Power and Truth: a Reply to William Wallace', *Review of International Studies*, 23, 4 (1997), pp. 507–16.

46 We are grateful to Stephen Twigge for this information.

47 For scrutiny of the relationship between US academia and US intelligence see Robin Winks, *Cloak and Gown: Scholars in the Secret War* (New York: William Morrow, 1987).

48 Wolfgang Krieger, 'German Intelligence History: A Field in Search of Scholars', this volume, pp. 42–53.

49 Cradock, *Know Your Enemy*, p. 4.

50 Desmond Ball, 'Desperately Seeking Bin Laden: The Intelligence Dimension of the War Against Terrorism', in Ken Booth and Tim Booth (eds), *Worlds in Collision: Terror and the Future of Global Order* (Basingstoke: Palgrave Macmillan, 2002), p. 60.

51 Len Scott, 'Secret Intelligence, Covert Action and Clandestine Diplomacy', this volume, pp. 162–79; Robert A. Goldberg, '"Who Profited from the Crime?" Intelligence Failure, Conspiracy Theories and the Case of September 11', this volume, pp. 99–110.

52 Sara-Jane Corkem, 'History, Historians and the Naming of Foreign Policy: A Postmodern Reflection on American Strategic Thinking during the Truman Administration', *Intelligence and National Security*, 16, 3 (2001), pp. 146–63.

53 See for example, John Barry, 'Covert Action can be Just', *Orbis* (Summer 1993), pp. 375–90; Charles Beitz, 'Covert Intervention as a Moral Problem', *Ethics and International Affairs*, 3 (1989), pp. 45–60; William Colby, 'Public Policy, Secret Action', *Ethics and International Affairs*, 3 (1989) pp. 61–71; Gregory Treverton, 'Covert Action and Open Society', *Foreign Affairs*, 65, 5 (Summer 1987), pp. 995–1014; idem, *Covert Action: The Limits of Intervention in the Postwar World* (New York: Basic Books, 1987), idem, 'Imposing a Standard: Covert Action and American Democracy', *Ethics and International Affairs*, 3 (1989), pp. 27–43.

54 Michael Herman, 'Modern Intelligence Services: Have They a Place in Ethical Foreign Policies?', in Shukman, *Agents for Change*, pp. 287–311.

55 Cited in Herman, 'Modern Intelligence Services', ibid., pp. 305 and 308 respectively.

56 Shulsky, *Silent Warfare*, p. 187.

57 Max Weber, 'The Profession and Vocation of Politics', in *Political Writings* (Cambridge: Cambridge University Press, 1994), p. 360.

58 Ibid., pp. 357–69.

59 See Herman, 'Ethics and Intelligence after September 11', pp. 180–94.

60 Erskine, 'Rays of Light to the Soul'.

61 Michael Quinlan, 'The Future of Covert Intelligence', in Shukman, *Agents for Change*, pp. 67–8. Michael Herman also embraces the Just War notion of proportionality as a criterion for determining what is acceptable in covert collection. Herman, 'Modern Intelligence Services', p. 308.

62 See Mark Urban, *Big Boys' Rules: The SAS and the Secret Struggle against the IRA* (London: Faber & Faber, 1992), Peter Taylor, *The Provos: The IRA and Sinn Fein* (London: Bloomsbury, 1997), and idem, *Brits: The War Against the IRA* (London: Bloomsbury, 2001).

63 See Jeffrey Richelson, 'When Kindness Fails: Assassination as a National Security Option', *International Journal of Intelligence and CounterIntelligence*, 15, 2 (2002), pp. 243–74.

64 See Michael Miller, *Shanghai on the Metro: Spies, Intrigue and the French* (Berkeley, CA: University of California Press, 1994), pp. 21–36.

65 On this question see Christopher Andrew, *Secret Service: The Making of the British Intelligence Community* (London: Sceptre, 1991) pp. 67–137 and Nicholas P. Hiley, 'The Failure of British Espionage Against Germany, 1907–1914', *Historical Journal*, 26, 2 (1983), pp. 866–81.

66 J. Black, 'The Geopolitics of James Bond,' this volume, pp. 135–46.

67 N. West, 'Fiction, Faction and Intelligence,' this volume, pp. 122–34.

68 Wesley K. Wark (ed.), *Spy Fiction, Spy Films and Real Intelligence* (London: Frank Cass, 1991), p. 9.

69 For discussion see J.J. Macintosh, 'Ethics and Spy Fiction' in ibid., pp. 161–84.

70 Black, 'Geopolitics of James Bond', p. 144.

71 J. Patrick Dobel, 'The Honourable Spymaster: John Le Carré and the Character of Espionage', *Administration and Society*, 20, 2 (August 1988), p. 192. We are grateful to Hugh Burroughs for drawing our attention to this source.

72 Shukman, *Agents for Change*, discussion of the 'The Future of Covert Action', pp. 91–2.

73 Le Carré, *The Spy Who Came in From the Cold* (London: Victor Gollancz, 1963). For discussion of these themes see Jeffrey Richelson, 'The IPCRESS File: the Great Game in Film and Fiction, 1953–2002', *International Journal of Intelligence and Counter Intelligence*, 16, 3 (2003), pp. 462–98.

74 *Three Days of the Condor* (Paramount Pictures, 1975); *The Bourne Identity* (Universal Pictures, 2002).

75 Robert A. Goldberg, 'Who Profited from the Crime? Intelligence Failure, Conspiracy Theories and the Case of September 11', this volume, pp. 99–110.

76 James Der Derian, 'The CIA, Hollywood, and Sovereign Conspiracies,' *Queen's Quarterly*, 10, 2 (1993), p. 343.

77 www.mi5.gov.uk/myths_misunderstandings/myths_misunderstandings_6.htm.

78 Stevens Enquiry, *Overview and Recommendations*, 17 April 2003, para. 4.8, www.met.police.uk/index/index.htm.

79 Ibid., para. 4.8. The collusion identified by Commissioner Stevens was by the Army and the RUC, and not by MI5 (or SIS).

80 Smith, 'Bletchley Park and the Holocaust'.

81 See Tom Bower, *The Perfect English Spy: Sir Dick White and the Secret War, 1935–1990* (London: Heinemann, 1995), p. 275 for the views of Sir Dick White, former Chief of SIS and Director-General of MI5, on Le Carré.

82 See www.home.us.net/~encore/Enigma/moviereview.html. For explanatory discussion of the historical reality see www.history.navy.mil/faqs/faq97-.htm. We are grateful to Gerald Hughes for drawing our attention to these sources.

83 See, for example, Frances Stonor Saunders, *Who Paid the Piper? The CIA and the Cultural Cold War* (London: Granta Books, 1999), Scott Lucas, *Freedom's War: The US Crusade Against the Soviet Union, 1945–1956* (Manchester: Manchester University Press, 1999) and Giles Scott-Smith and Hans Krabbendam (eds), *The Cultural Cold War in Western Europe 1945–1960* Special Issue of *Intelligence and National Security*, 18, 2 (2003).

84 *Report of the Joint Inquiry into the Terrorist Attacks of September 11, 2001 – by the House Permanent Select Committee on Intelligence and the Senate Select Committee on Intelligence,* www.gpoaccess.gov/serialset/creports/911.html.

85 See, for example, the reflections in Bradford Westerfield, 'America and the World of Intelligence Liaison', *Intelligence and National Security*, 11, 2 (1996), pp. 523–60, Herman, *Intelligence Power*, pp. 100–112, 165–83, and *Intelligence Services in the Information Age: Theory and Practice* (London: Frank Cass, 2001).

86 See, among others, Jeffrey Richelson and Desmond Ball, *The Ties that Bind: Intelligence Cooperation between the UK–USA Countries* (Boston, MA: Allen & Unwin, 1985); Christopher Andrew, 'The Making of the Anglo-American SIGINT Alliance', in Hayden Peake and Samuel Halpern (eds), *In the Name of Intelligence: Essays in Honor of Walter Pforzheimer* (Washington, DC: NIBC Press, 1994); Aldrich, *Hidden Hand*; idem, 'British Intelligence and the Anglo-American "Special Relationship" during the Cold War', *Review of International Studies*, 24, 3 (1998), pp. 331–51; David Stafford and Rhodri Jeffreys-Jones (eds), 'American–British–Canadian Intelligence Relations 1939–2000', Special Issue of *Intelligence and National Security*, 15, 2 (2000); Stephen Twigge and Len Scott, *Planning Armageddon: Britain, the United States and the Command of Western Nuclear Forces* (Amsterdam: Routledge, 2000).

87 Bradley Smith, *Sharing Secrets with Stalin: How the Allies Traded Intelligence, 1941–1945* (Lawrence, KS: University Press of Kansas, 1996); Paul Maddrell, 'Operation Matchbox', forthcoming in Jennifer Siegel and Peter Jackson (eds), *Intelligence and*

Statecraft (Westport, CT: Greenwood Press, 2004); Fursenko and Naftali, *'One Hell of a Gamble'*.

88 Martin Alexander (ed.), *Knowing One's Friends* (London: Frank Cass, 1998).
89 Herman, *Intelligence Power*, pp. 200–219, Aldrich, 'British Intelligence and the Anglo-American "Special Relationship"'.
90 An excellent example of such an approach is the important recent monograph by Cees Wiebes, *Intelligence and the War in Bosnia, 1992–1995* (Munster: Lit Verlag, 2003).
91 'Briton arrested in "terror missile" sting', www.news.bbc.co.uk/1/hi/world/americas/3146025.stm, 13 August 2003.
92 Scott, 'Secret Intelligence'.
93 *Hearings Before the Joint Committee on the Investigation of the Pearl Harbor Attack, 79th Congress* 39 vols (Washington, DC: United States Government Printing Office, 1946).
94 Roberta Wohlstetter, *Pearl Harbor: Warning and Decision* (Palo Alto, CA: Stanford University Press, 1962).
95 Herman, *Intelligence Services*, p. 228.

2   Intelligence, International Relations and 'Under-theorisation'[1]

Christopher Andrew

In both East and West the public face of twenty-first century intelligence changed dramatically in the months preceding the Gregynog conference, which gave rise to the studies in this volume. One of the distinguishing characteristics of the Soviet intelligence system from Cheka to KGB was its militant atheism. In March 2002, however, the FSB, the born-again post-Soviet successor to the domestic arm of the KGB, at last found God. A restored Russian Orthodox Church in central Moscow was consecrated by Patriarch Aleksi II as the FSB's parish church in order to minister to the previously neglected spiritual needs of its staff. The FSB Director, Nikolai Patrushev, who was present at the consecration, celebrated the mystical marriage of the Orthodox Church and the state security apparatus by a solemn exchange of gifts, presenting the Patriarch with ceremonial golden keys to the church and receiving in exchange two religious icons – the possession of which would formerly have been a sufficiently grave offence to cost any KGB officer his job. Those who visit the FSB Church when next in Moscow may like to stop for lunch, dinner or a cocktail in the nearby Shield and Sword Café, which takes its name from the traditional symbols of the KGB (inherited from the Cheka), and appears to cater to a clientele drawn largely from the nearby FSB headquarters. A bust of Yuri Andropov, the only KGB chief to become Soviet leader, stands on a pedestal draped with blue velvet in the lobby, while the restaurant itself is dominated by a statue of Felix Dzerzhinsky, the founder of the Cheka.[2]

The change at the beginning of the twenty-first century in the public face of British intelligence, which still lacks a parish church of its own and declines to sponsor a restaurant, has been less spectacular but ultimately perhaps more significant than the recent changes in Russia. In September 2002 the Blair government issued a now-celebrated 55-page dossier on Iraqi weapons of mass destruction, the first published official document based on detailed Joint Intelligence Committee (JIC) assessments. Tony Blair says in his introduction, 'It is unprecedented for the Government to publish this kind of document.'[3] There was, however, one partial precedent. The government statement in October 2001 on al-Qaeda's responsibility for September 11, though much briefer and making no reference to the JIC, also derived from JIC assessments.[4] In the space of only a year, the threats posed by Osama bin Laden and Saddam Hussein had succeeded in transforming British government policy on the public use of intelligence.

Tony Blair has finally laid to rest the traditional taboo that British governments do not mention their intelligence services. The classic formulation of that taboo was Austen Chamberlain's stern injunction as Foreign Secretary to the House of Commons in 1924: 'It is of the essence of a Secret Service that it must be secret, and if you once begin disclosure it is perfectly obvious to me as to hon. Members opposite that there is no longer any Secret Service and that you must do without it.' The astonishing thing was that Hon. Members opposite, both Labour and Liberal, did accept the crude illogicality of Chamberlain's all or nothing argument. A bipartisan consensus to protect the intelligence community from any parliamentary discussion remained unchallenged for another 60 years. Sir Michael Howard complained in 1985 that, 'So far as official government policy is concerned, the British security and intelligence services, MI5 and MI6, do not exist. Enemy agents are found under gooseberry bushes and intelligence is brought by the storks.'[5]

Britain's longest-serving Labour Prime Minister, Harold Wilson, stoutly defended the storks and gooseberry bush tradition in his exposition of the constitutional wisdom, *The Governance of Britain*, published in 1976. Wilson's chapter on 'The Prime Minister and National Security' is probably the shortest ever written by a British politician. It quotes approvingly Harold Macmillan's dictum that it is 'dangerous and bad for our general national interest' to discuss security and intelligence matters at all, then concludes after less than a page: 'The Prime Minister is occasionally questioned on [security] matters...His answers may be regarded as uniformly uninformative. There is no further information that can usefully or properly be added before bringing this Chapter to an end.'[6]

It is difficult to credit now that it was not until 1992, long after most other major states, that the British government finally admitted for the first time that it actually has a foreign intelligence service. When it made that overdue acknowledgement not a single peacetime assessment by the JIC, even for the early years of the Cold War, had yet been released. Today, Tony Blair, David Blunkett and Jack Straw, like Robin Cook when he was Foreign Secretary, regularly pay public 'tribute to our Intelligence and Security Services for the often extraordinary work that they do'. And most JIC assessments are now subject, like most other government documents, to the 30-year rule (though there is still some catching up to do).[7]

The facts that the President of the United States spends the first hour of each working day with his intelligence chiefs and that the Prime Minister of the United Kingdom makes unprecedented public use of intelligence to put the case for his foreign policy attest to the fact that intelligence is more deeply and visibly embedded in the conduct of international relations today, over a whole range of issues from counter-terrorism to UN peacekeeping, than ever before in peacetime. The historical record suggests, however, that the points at which the intelligence cycle most frequently breaks down are in the assessment process and the policy interface rather than in collection. How and why that breakdown occurs require far more research – and research, first and foremost, in archives.

Len Scott's and Peter Jackson's bracing introduction to this volume rightly reminds us that in Britain, one of the dominant trends in intelligence studies has been a 'methodological predisposition towards archive-based research'. There is no alternative to this predisposition – unless it is argued improbably that so much reliable information is already available on intelligence collection, assessment, dissemination and use as to make further archival research of little value. Alan Bullock's classic biography of Ernest Bevin is only one of a series of major studies of British foreign and defence policy during the Cold War published over the last half-century which do not even mention the JIC. Much research still remains to be done on all stages of the intelligence cycle before it can be plausibly argued that the academic study of political history and international relations takes adequate account of the intelligence dimension.

In 1996 the former DDI, John Helgerson, produced a pioneering study of the CIA's early briefings of incoming presidents from Truman to Clinton, based both on unrestricted access to CIA files and on interviews with surviving presidents and their briefers. I wrote in a foreword to the unclassified version of Helgerson's study:

> Until similar volumes are available on the briefing of, among others, British prime ministers, German chancellors, French and Russian presidents, and leading Asian statesmen, the use made of intelligence by world leaders will continue to be a major gap in our understanding of both modern government and international relations.[8]

That major gap still remains. Basic questions about the attitude of most twentieth-century world leaders to intelligence have yet to be asked, let alone answered.

Why, for example, did Margaret Thatcher, develop such an interest in – perhaps even a passion for – intelligence? (Her memoirs briefly put on record her 'highest regard' for the former British agent inside the KGB, Oleg Gordievsky, and 'his judgement about events in the USSR' after his defection in 1985, but say nothing about the impact on her of the extraordinary intelligence he had supplied before his defection.)[9] Why, in contrast to Mrs Thatcher, did Helmut Kohl take such a jaundiced view of his intelligence services, whom he still accuses of giving him 'a lot of information that was quite simply false'?[10] Why was François Mitterrand more concerned than, apparently, any of his predecessors at the Élysée with tapping the telephones of so many rivals and opponents?[11] And why did his successor, Jacques Chirac, sack the heads of both the DST and the DGSE, after his election victory in 2002? *Le Monde* claimed that, 'The Élysée is accusing the secret services of having carried out investigations into M. Chirac under the Jospin government.'[12]

The attitude to intelligence of most Third World leaders remains at least equally mysterious. Why, for example, was Indira Gandhi convinced that the CIA was out to bring her down, perhaps even to assassinate her? In November 1973 she told Fidel Castro at a banquet in New Delhi, 'What they [the CIA] have done to Allende they want to do to me also. There are people here, connected with the same foreign forces that acted in Chile, who would like to eliminate me.'

The belief that Allende had been murdered in cold blood and that the Agency had marked her out for the same fate became something of an obsession. Dismissing accurate US claims that, in reality, Allende had turned his gun on himself during the storming of his palace, Mrs Gandhi declared, 'When I am murdered, they will say I arranged it myself.'[13] Tragically, Mrs Gandhi paid more attention to the imaginary menace of a CIA-supported assassination attempt than to the real threat from her own bodyguards.

As the paper by Peter Jackson and Len Scott reminds us, except for some work on the US–British Special Relationship, the important topic of relations between intelligence communities also remains an understudied aspect of international relations. This is at last being studied by the International Liaison and Research project (ILAR), an international research group founded in 2002, several of whose members attended the Gregynog conference. So I stand by my claim, quoted by Len Scott and Peter Jackson, that intelligence 'is still denied its proper place in studies of the Cold War' – and indeed of international relations in general. Part of the reason, of course, is the relative inaccessibility of the intelligence archive by comparison with other primary sources. The root of the problem, however, is cognitive dissonance – the difficulty of adapting traditional notions of international relations and political history to take account of the information now available about the role of intelligence agencies.

One striking example of this conceptual failure concerns SIGINT, a word still curiously absent from the great majority of histories of international relations. At the end of the Second World War, GCHQ wanted to keep the ULTRA secret indefinitely, but did not expect to be able to do so. The clues, it feared, were too obvious for historians to ignore: '[T]he comparing of the German and British documents is bound to arouse suspicion in [historians'] minds that we succeeded in reading the enemy ciphers.'[14] It now seems astonishing that for over a quarter of a century the great majority of historians suspected no such thing. With the gift of hindsight, some of the clues seem remarkably obvious. The fact that US cryptanalysts had broken the main Japanese diplomatic cipher in 1940 (known to the Americans as PURPLE) was extensively publicised during the Congressional enquiry into Pearl Harbor at the end of the war. It was also common knowledge that British cryptanalysts had broken German ciphers during the First World War; indeed one well-publicised German decrypt – the Zimmermann telegram – had hastened US entry into the war. But, until the revelation of ULTRA in 1973, almost no historian even discussed the possibility that German ciphers had been extensively broken during the Second World War as well as the First. The minority of academic historians who had served at Bletchley Park or had been 'indoctrinated' into ULTRA while writing official histories were thus in the remarkable position both of knowing that colleagues in their university departments who wrote about the Second World War misunderstood an important aspect of the war and of being forbidden by the Official Secrets Act to discuss this with them.

To a remarkable degree, the lack of interest in SIGINT by historians and specialists in international relations has survived even the revelation of the

ULTRA secret. Though no historian of the Second World War nowadays fails to make some mention of ULTRA, few stop to consider the influence of SIGINT on the rest of the twentieth century.[15] Even after the disclosure of ULTRA's role in British and US wartime operations, it took another 15 years before any historian raised the rather obvious question of whether there was a Russian ULTRA on the Eastern Front as well.[16] The great majority of histories of the Cold War do not refer to SIGINT at all. Though most studies of US Cold War foreign policy mention the CIA, there is rarely any reference to NSA – despite the public acknowledgement by George Bush (the elder) that SIGINT was a 'prime factor' in his foreign policy.[17] The small circle of those in the know in Washington used to joke that NSA stood for 'No Such Agency'. Most histories of the Cold War reflect a similar amnesia.

The virtual exclusion of SIGINT from the history of post-war international relations has distorted understanding of the Cold War in significant ways. That point is illustrated by the very first Cold War SIGINT to be declassified: the approximately 3,000 intercepted Soviet intelligence and other telegrams (later codenamed VENONA) for the period 1939–48, mostly decrypted by US and British codebreakers in the late 1940s and early 1950s. The decrypts have major implications for US political history as well as for Soviet–US relations.The outrageous exaggerations and inventions of Senator Joseph McCarthy's self-serving anti-communist witch-hunt in the early 1950s made liberal opinion sceptical for the remainder of the Cold War of the significance of the Soviet intelligence offensive. The evidence of Elizabeth Bentley and Whittaker Chambers, who had worked as couriers for Soviet intelligence, was widely and mistakenly ridiculed. VENONA provides compelling corroboration for both.

For many US liberals it became an article of faith that Alger Hiss and the Rosenbergs were the innocent victims of Cold War show trials. VENONA provides persuasive evidence that all were guilty (though that does not, of course, justify the death sentences passed on the Rosenbergs). Hiss (Agent ALES), who was a member of the US delegation at the Yalta Conference, was personally congratulated afterwards in Moscow by the Deputy Foreign Minister, Andrei Vyshinsky. Every major branch of the wartime Roosevelt administration was successfully penetrated by Soviet intelligence. Pat Moynihan, whose pressure was largely responsible for the declassification of VENONA, is right to claim that ignorance of what it revealed distorted the understanding by a generation of Americans of a decade of US history.[18]

VENONA was not officially declassified until 1996 but its existence was already known in the 1980s. Oleg Gordievsky and I referred in 1990 to the evidence it contained about Hiss, the Rosenbergs and others[19] – and we were not the first to do so. Until the late 1990s, however, most historians of US politics and policy during the early Cold War remained in denial. Instead of accepting or disputing the VENONA evidence, they preferred to ignore it. Since the declassification of VENONA, other fragmentary but important material on US, British, Canadian, Dutch, French, German, Russian and Scandinavian SIGINT during the Cold War has become available.[20] As I have argued elsewhere, 'Those who study the Cold

War [now] face a difficult but interesting challenge: either to seek to take account of the role of SIGINT – or to explain why they consider it unnecessary to do so.'[21]

Partly as a result of the continued gaps in our knowledge of intelligence history, intelligence remains, as Len Scott and Peter Jackson rightly remind us (quoting Der Derian), 'the most under-theorised area of international relations'. But though intelligence theory is thin on the ground, the work of at least a handful of scholars, notably in Britain that of Michael Herman,[22] gives grounds for guarded optimism.

For the conceptual framework of intelligence studies to advance further, it is essential to make a clearer distinction than is usually made at present between the roles of intelligence communities in authoritarian and democratic regimes. At the end of the Cold War, with former intelligence officers in East and West reminiscing nostalgically at international conferences about their past duels with each other, the impression was often given that their roles had been roughly similar. That false analogy also pervades the tendentiously sanitised multi-volume history of Russian intelligence in the Soviet era currently being published by the SVR.[23]

Despite the fact that NATO and the Warsaw Pact targeted each other and employed sometimes similar operational techniques, there was a fundamental asymmetry between intelligence operations in East and West. Similarities in intelligence vocabulary disguised basic differences of function. The same was true of many other professions. Economists in Moscow and London during the Cold War had, of course, certain functions in common, such as the massive production of statistics. But the striking contrast between the workings of the command and market economies meant that there were also fundamental differences in their roles. The similarly striking contrast between the two political systems meant that there were equally fundamental differences in the role of intelligence officers in East and West.

Modern intelligence systems have changed the nature of authoritarian regimes and with it the workings of the international system. The one-party state, the most malign political innovation of the twentieth century, depended on the creation of new intelligence agencies with an unprecedented ability to monitor and suppress dissent in all its forms. Though it is, of course, impossible to reduce the history of Stalin's Russia, Hitler's Holocaust, Saddam Hussein's Iraq or Kim Jong-Il's North Korea simply to the history of their intelligence and security services, all were heavily dependent on those services. The centrality of their intelligence communities to the functioning of one-party states and their systems of social control is frequently underestimated even in otherwise excellent political histories. The magnificent study by Orlando Figes on the Bolshevik Revolution and its aftermath, for example, tells us that the Cheka became 'a state within a state', in other words that it was central to the structure of the Soviet regime, but the perfunctory analysis of its role is the most inadequate part of a 900-page book.[24]

Intelligence communities in authoritarian regimes, especially one-party states, have at least two basic functions which distinguish them from their counterparts in parliamentary democracies. These two functions, first fully developed in the inter-war Soviet Union, have since been largely replicated in most other one-party states:

1   The intelligence community is central to the structure of the one-party state and to the systems of repression and social control which seek to suppress all challenges to its authority.
2   It also acts as a mechanism for reinforcing the regime's misconceptions of the outside world.

The suppression of challenges to the authority of one-party states is a job which their intelligence communities have learned to perform depressingly well. As a result of their successes, ranging from prison camps to election-rigging, the world's most unpleasant regimes have also become some of the longest-lasting. In October 2002, the Iraqi security system outdid even the KGB by securing a 100 per cent vote for Saddam Hussein – a dramatic 0.1 per cent swing since his previous electoral triumph.

It tends to be forgotten that the determination of one-party states to destroy all opposition has a major influence on their foreign as well as domestic intelligence operations. There were moments both before and after the Great Patriotic War when pursuit of 'enemies of the people' abroad by Stalin's intelligence agencies was an even greater priority than discovering the secrets of Western governments. In November 1937 Stalin told the Comintern leader, Georgi Dimitrov, that: 'The Trotsk[y]ists [in the Comintern] should be persecuted, shot, destroyed. These are worldwide provocateurs, the most vicious agents of fascism.' For Stalin the killing of the leading Trotskyists was a major foreign policy objective which could be accomplished only by the NKVD. At the beginning of 1940 he appears to have been more preoccupied by Trotsky than by Hitler. The final act of Stalin's foreign policy before he died in 1953 was a plan (abandoned after his death) to assassinate Josip Tito, who had succeeded Trotsky as the leading heretic of the Soviet Bloc.[25] Operations to liquidate dissidents abroad have also been a major priority of authoritarian regimes as various as those of Kim Il-Sung, Colonel Qaddafi, Todor Zhivkov and Saddam Hussein.

Though attempts to assassinate Soviet 'enemies of the people' who had taken refuge in the West almost ceased after the early 1960s, the KGB's war against the dissidents was, similarly, a central part of its foreign as well as domestic operations. Though it is predictably excised from the SVR official history of Russian foreign intelligence, some of the most important of these operations were jointly devised by senior officers of the First Chief (foreign intelligence) and Fifth (ideological subversion) Directorates. Early in 1977, for example, a total of 32 jointly devised 'active measures' operations designed to demoralise and discredit Andrei Sakharov and his wife, Elena Bonner, and discredit them abroad were either already in progress or about to commence both within the Soviet Union and abroad.[26]

In KGB jargon, the United States was known as the 'Main Adversary' (*glavny protivnik*) – just as the main adversary of the CIA was the Soviet Union. Unlike

US intelligence, however, the KGB had not one but two 'Main Adversaries'. The second was what the KGB called 'ideological subversion' – anything which threatened to undermine the authority of the communist one-party states in and beyond the Soviet Bloc. The simplest test ('Andrew's Test') by which to judge the importance attached to any intelligence report in any of the world's capitals is to ask this question: 'If it arrives in the middle of the night would you wake the Prime Minister, the President, or some other senior member of the government?' From the moment that test is applied, it quickly becomes clear that there were fundamental differences, as well as important similarities, between intelligence priorities in East and West during the Cold War. On 27 October 1978 the KGB resident in Oslo, Leonid Makarov, rang Mikhail Suslov, the senior Politburo member chiefly responsible for ideological purity, in the middle of the night. Why? Not to tell him that some great international crisis was about to break. Simply to inform him that the Russian dissident Yuri Orlov had not won the Nobel Peace Prize. So far from being reproved for waking Suslov in the early hours, the Oslo residency was warmly congratulated for the supposed 'operational effectiveness' of its 'active measures' (influence operations). By influencing both the Norwegian Labour Party and the Nobel Peace Prize Committee, the residency was wrongly believed to have ensured that the prize went to Sadat and Begin (who, in reality, had always been the clear favourites), rather than to Yuri Orlov (who had never had a realistic chance of beating them). The fact that Sadat and Begin, both of whom were *bêtes noirs* of the Centre (KGB HQ), were regarded as lesser evils than the little-known Orlov is, in itself highly revealing of KGB priorities.[27]

Seeking to discredit every well-known dissident who managed to get to the West was a major KGB priority – irrespective of whether the dissident's profession had, in Western terms, anything to do with politics at all. Though plans to maim Rudolf Nureyev, Natalia Makarova and other Soviet ballet dancers after their flight to the West seem never to have been implemented, great efforts were made to destroy their reputations. When Mstislav Rostropovich became director of the National Symphony Orchestra in Washington, the Centre seized on a solitary bad review in the *Washington Post*, and sent it to residencies with instructions to arrange for more of the same. At the world chess championships in the Philippines in 1978, when the dissident Viktor Korchnoi committed the unforgivable sin of challenging the orthodox Anatoli Karpov, the KGB sent 18 operations officers to try to ensure that he lost.[28]

The KGB campaign against 'ideological subversion' also extended to heretical tendencies within Western communist parties. At the height of Euro-Communism in the mid-1970s, the KGB was engaged in an active measures campaign to discredit the main Euro-Communist leaders: Enrico Berlinguer, who was accused of shady land deals in Sardinia; Georges Marchais, who was accurately accused of working voluntarily to build Messerschmitt planes during the Second World War; and Santiago Carillo, whose position as Spanish party leader the Centre sought to undermine.[29]

The most dangerous dissidents, in the Centre's view, were in the Soviet Bloc. One of the best indications of the importance which the First Chief Directorate attached to operations against them were the numbers of its elite corps of illegals which it used to penetrate their ranks. In only two months after the beginning of the 1968 Prague Spring, 15 KGB illegals posing as Westerners sympathetic to the attempt to create 'socialism with a human face' were posted to Prague.[30] No example has yet come to light of so many illegals being posted in such a short period of time for any operation in the West.

The second distinctive characteristic of the foreign intelligence agencies of authoritarian regimes is the way that they act as mechanisms for reinforcing the regimes' misconceptions of the outside world. A British intelligence chief once defined his main role as 'telling the Prime Minister what the Prime Minister does not want to know'. Though Western intelligence agencies sometimes fall short of this exalted calling, the problem of the politicisation of intelligence assessment in authoritarian regimes is different in kind as well as in scale. In all one-party states, intelligence analysis is necessarily distorted by the insistent demands of political correctness. Few, if any, analysts are willing to challenge the views of the political leadership. Ibrahim al-Marashi, who has made a detailed study of thousands of the Iraqi intelligence documents captured during the Gulf War in 1992, has found a level of sycophancy towards the political leadership reminiscent of the Soviet era.[31]

In Stalinist Russia the distortions produced by political correctness were made worse by a recurrent tendency to conspiracy theory (another common characteristic of authoritarian regimes), of which Stalin himself was the chief exponent. The tendency to substitute conspiracy theory for evidence-based analysis when assessing the intentions of the encircling imperialist powers in the 1930s was made worse by Stalin's increasing determination to act as his own intelligence analyst. Stalin, indeed, actively discouraged intelligence analysis by others, which he condemned as 'dangerous guesswork'. 'Don't tell me what you think', he is reported to have said, 'give me the facts and the source!' As a result, INO (the inter-war foreign intelligence department) had no analytical department. Soviet intelligence reports throughout, and even beyond, the Stalin era characteristically consisted of compilations of relevant information on particular topics tailored to fit the views of the political leadership, with little argument or analysis.[32]

At least until the Gorbachev era, the Soviet Union, like other authoritarian regimes, was far worse at intelligence analysis than at intelligence collection. Though the Soviet leadership never really understood the West until the closing years of the Cold War, it would have been outraged to have its misunderstandings challenged by intelligence reports. While KGB assessments of the world situation in 1984 emphasised the supposedly insoluble international contradictions which beset Western capitalism, they tactfully refrained from mentioning the far more serious problems of the Soviet economy. A review by the head of the First Chief Directorate, Vladimir Kryuchkov (later KGB Chairman), in February 1984, only 13 months before Mikhail Gorbachev became General Secretary, concluded that the West's 'deepening economic and social crisis' was so serious that it was leading imperialists to consider war as a possible way out of their insoluble problems. As one Line PR (political intelligence department in KGB residencies) officer later admitted, 'In order to please our superiors we sent in biased information, acting on the principle "Blame everything on the Americans, and everything will be OK".' In both the early 1960s and the early 1980s, the KGB reported to the Kremlin – with horrendous inaccuracy – that the United States was planning a nuclear first strike against the Soviet Union.[33]

For most of the Cold War, Western analysts failed to grasp the degree to which political correctness and conspiracy theory degraded Soviet intelligence assessment. Looking back on the Cold War, Sir Percy Cradock, former Chairman of the British Joint Intelligence Committee and Margaret Thatcher's Foreign Policy Advisor, is surely right to identify 'the main source of weakness' in the Soviet intelligence system as 'the attempt to force an excellent supply of information from the multi-faceted West into an oversimplified framework of hostility and conspiracy theory'.[34]

Among the most convincing evidence for the genuineness of Gorbachev's 'new thinking' during his early months in office was his denunciation of the political correctness of KGB political intelligence. In December 1985 Viktor Mikhailovich Chebrikov, KGB Chairman since 1982, summoned a meeting of the KGB leadership to discuss a devastating memorandum sent him by Gorbachev on 'the impermissibility of factual distortions in [KGB] messages and reports sent to the Central Committee of the CPSU and other ruling bodies' – a damning indictment of its previous obsequious political correctness. The KGB leadership sycophantically agreed on the need to avoid sycophantic reporting and instructed all KGB residencies to fulfil 'the Leninist requirement that we need only the whole truth'.[35]

The KGB First Chief Directorate (FCD) appears to have responded to Gorbachev's demand for more objective intelligence on the United States. According to Leonid Shebarshin, who became head of the FCD in 1988, 'the FCD no longer had to present its reports in a falsely positive light', though some of its officers doubtless found it difficult to throw off the habits of a lifetime. The intelligence from Aldrich Ames and Robert Hanssen, both of whom volunteered their services to the KGB in 1985, thus came at precisely the moment when the FCD was best equipped to make use of it. In assessing its significance, it is important to remember Eisenhower's dictum that negative intelligence on what the other side does not have or is not doing is sometimes as important as positive intelligence. According to Shebarshin, his main initial brief from Gorbachev was 'to ensure the West did not cheat' on arms control. The numerous highly classified documents provided by Ames and Hanssen, some of which corroborated each other, must surely have helped to reassure the Centre, and through the Centre Gorbachev, that US policy on arms control did not conceal a hidden agenda.[36] Whatever the limitations of glasnost and perestroika in other areas of Gorbachev's policy, they appear to have produced at least a partial transformation of the quality of Soviet foreign intelligence assessment.[37]

The 'under-theorisation' of intelligence studies is not simply a problem for academic research. It also degrades much public discussion of the role of intelligence. Since September 11, 2001 the media and even some learned journals have been full of claims of 'intelligence failure'. But the majority of those who use that phrase seem to have no coherent idea of what it means. Clearly, lack of a 100 per cent success rate does not constitute failure. Were that the case, most financial journalists (very few of whom foresaw the early twenty-first century slump in world stock-markets) and most political correspondents (almost none of whom predicted the defeat of the French Socialist Prime Minister, Lionel Jospin, by Jean-Marie Le Pen in the first round of the 2002 presidential elections) would be out of job. Confusion over the criteria for intelligence failure and success also pervades the final report of the US Congressional Joint Inquiry into the September 11 Terrorist Attacks.[38] Despite repeated use of the term 'failure', the report does not claim that the attacks on that day could have been averted. The approach of the British Intelligence and Security Committee (ISC) to these attacks is more sophisticated. While the Joint Inquiry was concerned to identify 'failure', the ISC preferred the term 'hindsight'.[39] The ISC fairly concludes 'with hindsight, that the scale of the threat and the vulnerability of Western states to terrorists with this degree of sophistication and a total disregard for their own lives was not understood'.[40]

The role and performance of the British intelligence community, a taboo subject for most of the twentieth century, has now entered the mainstream of twenty-first century political and media discussion. The disappointingly low level of much of that discussion derives chiefly from the lack of understanding of what intelligence communities can be reasonably expected to achieve. The best-informed public assessments of the performance of the British intelligence community over the last decade, the reports of the ISC, have, however, generally been too un-sensational to attract the degree of media attention they deserve.[41]

Notes

1 This is a revised version of a paper given to the Gregynog conference in November 2002, prior to the author's appointment as part-time official historian of the Security Service. The views expressed in this paper are those of the author alone.

2 Unpublished paper by Julie Elkner (King's College, Cambridge) on 'Recent Research in Russia' to the Cambridge Intelligence Seminar on 1 November 2002. Images of the FSB Church are available at www.fsb.ru/smi/liders/shults4.html; and www.politika-magazine.ru/%B955/_hram_sofii.html.

3 *Iraq's Weapons of Mass Destruction: The Assessment of the British Government* (London: The Stationery Office, 24 September 2002).

4 *Responsibility for the Terrorist Atrocities in the United States, 11 September 2001*, 4 October 2001; and *Responsibility for the Terrorist Atrocities in the United States, 11 September 2001 – An Updated Account*, 14 October 2001.

5 Christopher Andrew, 'The British View of Security and Intelligence', in A. Stuart Farson, David Stafford and Wesley K. Wark (eds), *Security and Intelligence in a Changing World: New Perspectives for the 1990s* (London and Portland, OR: Frank Cass, 1991).

6 Sir Harold Wilson (later Lord Wilson of Rievaulx), *The Governance of Britain* (London: Weidenfeld & Nicolson, 1976).

7 In recent years members of the Cambridge Intelligence Seminar have produced a number of important studies based on JIC records. The first was the ground-breaking 1999 Cambridge University Ph.D. thesis by Alex Craig, 'The Joint Intelligence Committee and British Intelligence Assessment, 1945–1956'. Other Seminar members are using the

JIC records to compare UK and US intelligence assessment; see, for example, Matthew Perl, 'Comparing US and UK Intelligence Assessment in the Early Cold War: NSC-68, April 1950', *Intelligence and National Security*, 18, 1 (2003).

8 John L. Helgerson, *Getting to Know The President: CIA Briefings of Presidential Candidates, 1952–1992* (Washington, DC: CIA Center for the Study of Intelligence, 1996).

9 Margaret Thatcher, *The Downing Street Years* (London: Harper Collins, 1993), p. 470.

10 *Ten Years After. Reflections on the Decade since the Velvet Revolution: An International Conference Held at Prague Castle, November 17–18, 1999* (Prague: EastWest Institute, 2000), p. 17.

11 Jean-Marie Pontaut and Jérôme Dupuis, *Les oreilles du Président – suivi de la liste des 2000 personnes "écoutées" par François Mitterrand* (Paris: Fayard, 1996).

12 'L'Elysée accuse les services secrets d'avoir enquêté sur M. Chirac sous le gouvernement de M. Jospin', *Le Monde*, 23 June 2002.

13 Katherine Frank, *Indira: The Life of Indira Nehru Gandhi* (London: HarperCollins, 2001), pp. 368, 374–5.

14 COS (45), confidential annexe, 31 July 1945, PRO (Public Record Office) CAB 76/ 36; Special Order by Sir Edward Travis (Director GCHQ), 7 May 1945, PRO FO371/ 39171: both cited by Richard J. Aldrich, *The Hidden Hand: Britain, America and Cold War Secret Intelligence* (London: John Murray, 2001), pp. 1–3.

15 The significance of SIGINT was made clear by David Kahn's pioneering *Codebreakers,* published in 1967. Though a bestseller, however, its contents appeared to stun, rather than to inspire, most historians of international relations.

16 Geoff Jukes, 'The Soviets and "Ultra"', *Intelligence and National Security*, 3 (1988). Though Jukes's conclusions are debatable, his article remains a ground-breaking study. Cf. Christopher Andrew and Vasili Mitrokhin, *The Mitrokhin Archive*, Vol. 1: *The KGB in Europe and the West* (London/New York: Penguin/Basic Books, 1999), pp. 125–7, 135–6.

17 Christopher Andrew, *For The President's Eyes Only: Secret Intelligence and the American Presidency from Washington to Bush* (London: HarperCollins, 1995), p. 5 and ch. 13. This volume attempts, *inter alia*, an assessment, on the fragmentary evidence available, of varying presidential attitudes towards SIGINT.

18 Daniel Patrick Moynihan, *Secrecy: The American Experience* (New Haven, CT: Yale University Press, 1998). Christopher Andrew, 'The VENONA Secret', in K.G. Robertson (ed.), *War, Resistance and Intelligence: Essays in Honour of M.R.D. Foot* (Barnsley: Pen & Sword, 1999).

19 Christopher Andrew and Oleg Gordievsky, *KGB: The Inside Story of its Foreign Operations from Lenin to Gorbachev* (London: Hodder & Stoughton, 1990), pp. 308–9, 313–14, 314, 325–9, 369–71.

20 See, for example, the pioneering study edited by Matthew M. Aid and Cees Wiebes, *Secrets of Signals Intelligence during the Cold War and Beyond* (London: Frank Cass, 2001) (also published as a Special Issue of *Intelligence and National Security*, 16, 1 (2001)). On Soviet SIGINT during the Cold War, see Andrew and Mitrokhin, *The Mitrokhin Archive*, Vol. 1; and David Kahn, 'Soviet Comint in the Cold War', *Cryptologia*, 22 (1998).

21 Christopher Andrew, 'Intelligence and International Relations in the Early Cold War', *Review of International Studies*, 24 (1998).

22 Michael Herman, *Intelligence Power in Peace and War* (Cambridge: Cambridge University Press, 1996); idem, *Intelligence Services in the Information Age: Theory and Practice* (London: Frank Cass, 2001).

23 Yevgeni Primakov *et al., Ocherki Istorii Rossiyskoy Vneshney Razvedki* (Moscow: Mezhdunarodyye Otnosheniya, 1995–); four volumes so far published.

24 Orlando Figes, *A People's Tragedy: The Russian Revolution 1891–1924* (London: Jonathan Cape, 1996).

25 Christopher Andrew and Julie Elkner, 'Stalin and Foreign Intelligence', in Harold Shukman (ed.), *Redefining Stalinism* (London: Frank Cass, 2003), pp. 84–9.

26 Andrew and Mitrokhin, *The Mitrokhin Archive*, Vol. 1, pp. 423–7.

27 Ibid., pp. 429–30. The names of the Peace Prize winners were not classified information and therefore did not require secure transmission. Makarov's telephone call was presumably in response to Suslov's insistence on being told as soon as the news was available.

28 Ibid., pp. 480–1, 727–8.

29 Ibid., ch. 18.

30 Ibid., ch. 15.

31 Ibrahim al-Marashi, 'Saddam Hussein's Intelligence Archive': paper to the Cambridge Intelligence Seminar on 15 October 2002.

32 Andrew and Elkner, 'Stalin and Foreign Intelligence', p. 75.

33 Christopher Andrew and Oleg Gordievsky, *Instructions From The Centre: Top Secret Files on KGB Foreign Operations, 1975–1985* (London: Hodder & Stoughton, 1990), chs 1, 4. Andrew and Mitrokhin, *The Mitrokhin Archive*, Vol. 1, pp. 235–8, 722.

34 Sir Percy Cradock, *Know Your Enemy: How the Joint Intelligence Committee Saw the World* (London: John Murray, 2002), ch. 17.

35 Raymond L. Garthoff, 'The KGB Reports to Gorbachev', *Intelligence and National Security*, 11 (1996), pp. 226–7.

36 Interview with Shebarshin, *Daily Telegraph*, 1 December 1992. On the material supplied to the KGB by Ames and Hanssen, see, *inter alia*, Pete Earley, *Confessions of a Spy: The Real Story of Aldrich Ames* (London: Hodder & Stoughton, 1997); David A. Vise, *The Bureau and the Mole: The Unmasking of Robert Hanssen, the Most Dangerous Double Agent in FBI History* (London: Atlantic Books, 2002).

37 As the Soviet Union began to crumble in 1990–91, however, Kryuchkov and others in the Centre began to revert to the old conspiracy theories about Western, especially US, plots to hasten its disintegration. Andrew and Gordievsky, *Instructions From The Centre*, ch. 10.

38 US Congress Joint Inquiry into the September 11 Terrorist Attacks. *Final Report of the Joint Inquiry into the September 11th Terrorist Attacks*, 10 December 2002. The full text of the report, published with some omissions in the summer of 2003, was released too late to be included in this article.

39 See, on this subject, the pioneering study by a member of the Cambridge Intelligence Seminar, Laura Winthrop, 'The Evolution of a Public Role for Secret Intelligence: The United States and Great Britain in the War on Terror' (Cambridge University M.Phil. thesis, 2003).

40 *Intelligence and Security Committee Annual Report 2001–2002*, Cmd. 5542, June 2002.

41 The best study so far of the origins and performance of the ISC is Angus Wood, 'The Construction of Parliamentary Accountability for the British Intelligence Community' (Cambridge University M.Phil. thesis, 2003).

3 German Intelligence History

A field in search of scholars

Wolfgang Krieger

While Anglo-Saxon scholars are producing books on intelligence history at an ever-increasing rate, the interest in this particular branch of historical studies has been scant in Germany. Throughout the United States intelligence history is taught and researched at university level. It has expanded dramatically over the past two decades and become something of an academic fashion. It has begun to develop in various places around Europe, except in Germany where historians have largely ignored this new field. This is unusual because they have been quite keen to follow academic fashions, particularly those in the United States.

Why has even the intelligence history of the Nazi era left so little trace in the voluminous German writings on Nazi history? Why has so little work been done on Cold War intelligence history, given Germany's geopolitical place in that epic struggle and considering that Berlin was a unique nerve centre of intelligence activities?

To be sure, as in *Asterix*, there are pockets of dissent, that is, small circles of German intelligence historians whose activities will be described in this paper. But the overall picture is undoubtedly one of neglect.

What may have led to this neglect? Surely not German popular culture. Germany is a large market for spy fiction and movies. James Bond is a household name. Tom Clancy and his brethren in spirit have been best-selling authors in Germany just as they have in their Anglo-Saxon homelands. We are therefore bound to look for the answer in German intellectual life and academic culture after 1945, because what is fashionable in historiography is largely defined by the surrounding intellectual atmosphere.

Arguably there are three factors at work. The first is access to sources, the second has to do with the peculiarities of post-1945 intellectual life in Germany, and the third concerns German bureaucratic culture.

A question of sources?

A lack of archival sources is often invoked as being the chief obstacle to research in German intelligence history. No doubt, compared to other subject areas of twentieth-century German history the surviving files from intelligence organisations amount to no more than a sad trickle. Many records relating to German military intelligence for the World Wars were either lost or, in 1918 and again in 1944/45, destroyed in the face of utter defeat. Perhaps the most severe losses occurred at the end of the First World War. As to the Cold War era, we may assume intelligence records were well kept but they are unavailable to researchers.[1] The *Bundesnachrichtendienst* (BND), the single German (until 1990 only West German) intelligence service responsible for foreign and for a good portion of military intelligence, has yet to declassify a single page from its files.

However, this lack of Cold War intelligence sources is nothing unusual. Except for the CIA and a few others, intelligence organisations the world over refuse to declassify their files. Nor should this obstruction on their part be a reason for refusing to ask research questions and ignoring other source materials. After all, historians, including German historians, routinely work on questions where sources are hard to find.[2] What is more, any student of contemporary history knows that government files are far from being the only sources of value to the researcher. Much information is in the public domain, even for German intelligence history. While autobiographies and published diaries of intelligence officials are a rare species in Germany, there are masses of press accounts, parliamentary documents and criminal court records which deserve careful study. The BND's relations with the press ought to be a subject of considerable interest, particularly under Reinhard Gehlen, its founder and president until 1968. The same goes for the varieties of control functions exercised by the Bundestag (German Federal Parliament).[3]

Throughout the Cold War the BND received a good deal of attention from the German press, though much of it was harmful to its reputation. A long list of spying scandals was revealed over the years. Those scandals can profitably be studied as manifestations of political culture. To the intelligence historian many of them offer a window into the inner workings of the BND. While not all of the evidence used in court against those spies or double-agents is in the public domain what is available deserves close scrutiny. At the very least those trials provide useful starting points for historians, among other things because they are based on the access given to judges and public prosecutors who have a lot more power to investigate a particular case than the historian is likely to have.

Such reports from court proceedings along with parliamentary papers, particularly records from parliamentary investigations, have long been used by journalists. In at least two cases journalists were given access to a wide range of secret intelligence files, obviously in an effort to encourage them to write books sympathetic to the BND.[4] (Nothing comparable ever happened to academic historians.) It is therefore quite obvious that the BND since its founding days in 1956 received, and even encouraged, plenty of journalistic attention. Consequently, no-one can argue that it was hidden from public debate or that nothing could be known about it.

The situation with respect to sources is of course completely different for East German intelligence history. The German *Ministerium für Staatssicherheit* (MfS) or Stasi as it is popularly known, left about 180 kilometres of files. Additional material can be found in the papers of the communist party Politburo and other agencies which were part of the intelligence loop. Since the fall of the East German regime in 1989 many of those files have become available. However, here we also have large gaps in the source materials because leading Stasi officials managed to destroy records, particularly those relating to foreign operations, or to hand them over to their Soviet partners in the KGB.

This archival bonanza might well have put intelligence history on the map in Germany. But it did not promote the study of intelligence in a broader sense. Most German historians see the Stasi as a special issue within East German history. Indeed, some have complained that too much emphasis on the Stasi would produce a distorted picture of the true nature of East German history.[5]

A question of academic culture?

This brings us to the second point in our search for reasons why intelligence studies have been neglected in Germany. We need to consider some peculiarities of German intellectual life after 1945.

Here we must look at a much broader issue, namely the study of power politics, of war and peace. For the study of external and military intelligence organisations usually takes place in the much wider framework of international security issues. It is here that German academic discourse after 1945 has most sharply differed from what developed in the Anglo-Saxon world. In German universities, international security studies remained a very small sub-discipline, and where they came into existence they were often pursued without the kind of 'hands on' approach which characterises Anglo-Saxon policy studies. Neo-Marxists and followers of the peace movements essentially saw them as an absurdity produced by capitalism, particularly in the United States, by the Cold War, or by a mixture of the two. Armed forces were associated with militarism, with capitalist and Stalinist paranoia. Wars in the Third World were explained away as consequences of 'imperialism'. Their deeper social and cultural roots were of little interest.

As a result such 'great debates', which took place among the Anglo-Saxon intelligentsia, between the competing scholarly camps labelled 'realism', 'idealism' and (later on) 'liberal institutionalism' had a much reduced echo in Germany. While institutionalism was readily taken up, the realist camp was excluded or marginalised within German history and political science departments. Few of the now classical works of the realist school(s) were translated into German. Nuclear strategy and the politics of nuclear weapons was the domain of small circles at most, as was the study of Soviet communism, particularly of its repressive apparatus, its military and its foreign policy.[6] Military history was (and still is) absent from nearly all German universities. C. Wright Mills would have been pleased to find so few 'NATO intellectuals' in West Germany, particularly after the student revolt of 1968.

Within the bounds of this short essay it is not possible to explore the deep structures of post-1945 intellectual life in Germany. In a sense, it is understandable that the Germans associated war so extensively with death, destruction and humiliation while the Anglo-Saxon perspective increasingly became one of seeing war as a heroic activity which leads to glory, liberation and free enterprise.

The 'lesson of Normandy' (1944) was that war, if properly conducted, can lead to liberty, prosperity and respect for international law. Western policy makers came to regard this as a fundamental 'law' of international relations which – along with the lessons of '1914' and of 'Munich' (1938) – never had the same echo in Germany. When federal President Richard von Weizsäcker, in a famous speech in May 1985, suggested that Germans had been 'liberated' by the military victory of the allied powers in 1945, few of them were emotionally willing to follow his logic.[7]

Why should Germany's fate in the Second World War be a reason for avoiding policy-oriented international security studies? A rather small number of scholars protested and participated in those (mostly Anglo-Saxon) debates on the nature of power politics. After all, the roots of 'realist' thinking had a distinctly German flavour. Some of the most prominent figures were either German émigrés in the United States (think of Hans Morgenthau, C.J. Friedrich or Henry Kissinger) or were their immediate disciples (such as Zbigniew Brzezinski, a disciple of C.J. Friedrich) or had studied in Germany (like the French sociologist Raymond Aron and the politically influential Hungarian physicist Edward Teller) or were at least keen students of Carl von Clausewitz (as Britain's Michael Howard or again Raymond Aron).[8] In other words, a German tradition of 'realism', far removed from Nazi thinking and policy making, was clearly available but largely forgotten in its country of origin.

After 1945, Clausewitz (and other theoreticians of war as a human activity) received little attention in Germany – apart from that usually misquoted and misunderstood phrase that 'war was the continuation of politics by other means'.[9] The new questions of war and peace in the nuclear, bipolar and post-colonial era played a very much less prominent role in German academic life than they did in the Anglo-Saxon world or in France and Israel (and presumably some other countries whose publications receive less attention in the 'global' academic discourses). With little exaggeration it can be said that international security studies as a vibrant branch of political science were largely shaped by those debates, at least during the first two post-war decades, and that Germany largely missed out.

The connection between marginalising both 'realism' and intelligence studies is all too obvious. Those who refuse to deal with the agonising issues of nuclear weapons politics, the 'delicate balance of terror', with world politics as essentially 'anarchical', those who refuse to believe that Soviet policy was essentially expansionist and aggressive – though cautiously executed for the most part – will most likely refuse to believe that intelligence services are essentially necessary and proper instruments of foreign policy making, even though their day-to-day practice may be unethical and certain aspects of their missions inherently impossible to achieve. This is not to say that intelligence services only make sense from a 'realist' point of view. Far from it. The purity of international relations theory is of little use to the historian anyhow and, one should add, to the policy analyst and policy maker in the real world. But the logical connection between international security studies and intelligence studies is too obvious to need further explaining.

The Nazi era left behind a deep intellectual confusion. Anti-communism, the main driving force behind Western Cold War policies and institutions, was compromised in Germany because it had been used by the Nazis to mobilise popular support, initially for their domestic policies, later for the conduct of the war at large. Many of those intellectuals who embraced post-war anti-communism did so to cover up their failure to foresee the consequences of Nazi rule or, much worse, their involvement in Nazi politics and atrocities. Though Konrad Adenauer and most of his political associates, who strongly supported anti-communist Western (that is, NATO) defence policies, were personally unblemished by the Nazi legacy, many of their eager followers were using anti-communism in an effort to reinvent themselves. Then, in the 1960s, when a younger generation took up the battle cry for 'coming to terms with the Nazi past', a battle largely fought in order to win their place at the top of the political table, Western intellectual discourse came under a strong neo-Marxist influence. While NATO-ism, as preached by German ex-Nazis, failed to appeal to many young intellectuals, neo-Marxism appeared to them as an international movement of high moral standing. It seemed to represent eternal peace and nuclear disarmament. Under the spell of the new thinking, history departments became increasingly preoccupied with various forms of social and cultural studies.

This was of course true not only in Germany but in most other Western countries, including the United States.[10] But it took a somewhat different turn in Germany, which no longer had a defining role in world politics, or even in the affairs of the Western camp. Rather than discussing what intellectual guidance they might have for their own political leaders, the new German intellectuals saw their mission in publicly criticising everybody else, particularly the United States for their policies around the globe. As the 2003 Iraq war showed, this mood has remained predominant far beyond the end of the Cold War.

To be sure, this is a rather short-hand, perhaps overly polemical reading of post-1945 intellectual life in Germany. A more balanced picture would require us to look at the efforts of those who disagreed with majority sentiments and intellectual positions. But the simple fact remains that Germany, even today, has few university centres where international security policy is taught intensely, 'hands-on' and successfully. Nowhere is there a university institute or a degree programme which could match Aberystwyth or King's College, London, in Britain or Harvard, Stanford and Georgetown in the United States – to name just a few. And there can be little doubt that the paucity of intelligence studies is a direct consequence thereof.

A growing interest in intelligence history?

This brings us back to *Asterix's* pockets of resistance. As elsewhere in the Western countries, political history somehow survived in the university departments and saw a modest expansion, due no doubt to the political world revolutions of 1989 and the fast-growing intensity of international competition or 'globalisation' which followed. At the same time, almost simultaneously, the CIA's 'openness' policy, the sudden availability of the Stasi archives and various encouraging moves in Moscow and elsewhere to release at least a few intelligence records created unexpected opportunities for research. In response a small number of German historians formed a study group for intelligence history. Over the years it came to hold annual conferences, it produced a newsletter, a website (www.intelligence-history.org) and several edited volumes. In 2001, it started the *Journal of Intelligence History*, edited by Michael Wala, and two years later a series of monographs.[11]

How does this initiative fit into the German academic community as described above? Not easily, to be sure. Significantly, that initiative came from three tenured professors, who were scholars of Anglo-American or British history, and a retired naval historian who had been among the first Germans to engage in the scholarly debates around ENIGMA and the history of Second World War codebreaking.[12] Thus the Anglo-Saxon inspiration was obvious and the professional risk involved in taking up this unpopular academic cause was nil. Those post-doctoral and doctoral students who joined them knew quite well that they were running a high professional risk in picking intelligence history as their specialty. (Some have since abandoned it.) They will eventually have to re-label themselves because no specific university appointments for intelligence history are available so far.

Not surprisingly, their fate is shared by a highly able cohort of young military historians who also have to re-label themselves as early modern or nineteenth- and twentieth-century specialists if they are to find a university post because only one chair in Germany is explicitly dedicated to military history.[13] While history departments may eventually warm up to military and intelligence history, the same cannot be said of political science departments where defence studies are very much of marginal concern. So far no German professor of political science, teaching at a German university, has labelled himself or herself as a specialist in intelligence studies. Indeed, no-one is doing any work in the field.[14] This is true even of the small band of those who work on defence and international security policy. In other words, the growing importance of intelligence in international security policy since 1989/91, has so far had little impact on Germany's political science departments.[15]

Even the blossoming of Stasi history has done little to change those structures. This is not surprising since the initiative for this fast-developing new field did not come from German academia but from the East German dissident movement. In the autumn of 1989, when immense amounts of Stasi files fell into their hands, it was far from clear that those records would be preserved and made available to researchers. Many in East and West Germany, Chancellor Helmut Kohl among them, wished to destroy them and to protect victims and perpetrators alike from extended public recriminations. But the East German victims of Stasi terror refused to accept such proposals. They insisted that special legislation was passed for establishing a new German federal authority which would manage those records and make them available to the public wherever possible.

This new institution, which came to be know as 'Gauck authority', named for its first director, not only took charge physically of the Stasi files but also set up an in-house historical research unit which has since produced an admirable number of scholarly studies, most of them of very high quality and filled with mind-boggling revelations. Next to those official historians a growing number of others have begun to publish studies on a variety of subjects. To be sure, the gaps in the records make it difficult to research some of the most interesting questions. The names of foreign agents must be reconstructed from index cards of which copies had fallen into the hands of the CIA and which have so far only been partially returned to Germany. Stasi relations with the Soviets are hard to explore because records were either destroyed or handed back to Moscow. Yet those new studies provide startling new insights into Cold War politics in the Soviet bloc. Germany could finally make a significant contribution to intelligence history.

Without going into the substance of what we have learnt and are likely to learn from those records, it may be worthwhile to point out that nearly all of those authors in and around the Gauck office are younger historians, some from eastern Germany, who have no previous experience in intelligence history. Few of them seem to have found the time to look beyond their immense stacks of Stasi records. Few appear to have explored intelligence history as a field with its own very peculiar challenges. Few also seem to have benefited from the hands-on experiences of either Western or Eastern intelligence practitioners.[16] This seems logical from the Eastern side, particularly with respect to the leadership which has used its forced retirement mostly to engage in exercises of denial.[17] But research is clearly impaired by the fact that no opportunities exist for checking the Stasi files against BND reports and studies. We have a few records on the counter-intelligence failures which were uncovered inside the BND after 1989 but little else on the Stasi–BND intelligence war. While the complete history of German and allied intelligence activities in and around Germany will take many more years to explore no-one can doubt that an impressive start has been made by those who have worked 'at the coal face' of Stasi history over the last decade.

Regrettably this research has had little impact so far beyond the narrow field of the history of communist East Germany. This is particularly true for the mainstream historical work done on Cold War western Germany even though, for obvious reasons, the Bonn republic had been the Stasi's number one target. We know that the Stasi had its agents placed throughout the government departments in Bonn, across the organisational structures of political parties, trade unions, churches, universities, research institutes and so on. They exerted much influence in the anti-nuclear and peace movements, in the media, and in the publishing industry. Numerous careers in West German public life were either built or destroyed through Stasi activity. And still, many in today's Germany prefer to ignore or to downplay those aspects. In other words, intelligence history has a hard time being taken seriously even where its scholarly results are beyond reasonable doubt. It remains to be seen if any of those young (and not so young) historians who have unearthed so much from the Stasi files will make it to senior posts in German universities.

Peculiar limits to professional mobility?

If intelligence history in Germany has been held back by a lack of sources and by specific characteristics of post-1945 intellectual life (and academic politics), a third point needs to be explored which sets Germany apart from the Anglo-Saxon countries. In Germany there is much less mobility between institutions and professions than in the United States or in Britain. To put it in US terminology, the 'revolving door' is much less common. A professional person working in a government department will rarely become a university professor and vice versa. A BND official in the higher-up ranks, where a university degree is required, will usually stay with the BND until his or her retirement. Early retirement and follow-up careers in journalism or think-tanking are rare exceptions, unless the person had a military career and can therefore retire in his mid- to late fifties. A number of retired Bundeswehr officers with extended tours in the BND have written books and articles, particularly in Soviet and Arabic studies and on arms-control topics. But they usually refrain from discussing any specifically intelligence-related angles of their topics.

With reference to intelligence studies this means that there is practically no-one in a university department who previously worked inside the BND. The same is true of the press. This type of mobility has simply not impacted on either historical or policy-oriented studies. The few memoirs published by senior BND officials take great pains to present the BND as a 'normal' government agency. Occasionally they refer to certain internal bureaucratic conflicts, usually those which were already discussed in the press, but offer virtually no insight into how the BND really operates.[18] There have been no Victor Marchettis or Robert Baers.

While the lack of mobility in and out of the BND is a special case even in the German higher civil service this is not to say that every Anglo-Saxon colleague writing on the subject is or was an intelligence official or was on the staff of the Congressional intelligence oversight committees. But it is quite obvious that a good number of them were and that many of those who were not have in the course of their research benefited from privileged access to written sources or to key intelligence officials. By contrast, the few cases in which the BND provided documentary support for book projects the authors were journalists rather than university scholars.[19] Consequently, their experiences did not come to benefit any graduate students or academic research projects.

With respect to professional mobility there is a significant difference between security and intelligence studies. German international security studies have strongly benefited from more than a handful of diplomats who left the German foreign service to work in think tanks or to teach part time at universities. Their ranks are reinforced by people who served as non-career officers, usually for 12 years including their military service. But, to repeat the point made above, those people rarely work in intelligence studies.

Apart from those long-retired professors who had once served in Wehrmacht intelligence, no historian or political scientist who has a tenured post at a German university has had any personal experience in intelligence, with the possible exception of military intelligence if he served as a non-career *Bundewehr* officer.[20] One only needs to study the CVs of our Anglo-Saxon colleagues to see the difference with Germany. Without the help of 'old hands' or of some kind of institutional access to where intelligence work is done or used the study of intelligence remains truly academic in the pejorative sense of the word.[21]

In pointing to the missing 'revolving door' between German government bureaucracy and academia one need not necessarily conclude that the extremely politicised US higher civil service should be the model to follow. There are many good reasons for preferring the European model of a thoroughly professionalised higher civil service which is much less exposed to the whims of political clans or parties.

Conclusion

There is an even larger question behind our search for a way to promote German intelligence history. Why did Germany never produce an intelligence culture before 1945, when it clearly pursued an expansionist foreign policy, when it wanted to be a global actor and might have found it useful to develop an intelligence tradition?

While historians usually do not deal with events which did not happen or traditions which did not develop, the reader may wish to reflect on a few rather basic observations.

It is perhaps useful to remember that intelligence traditions are often closely linked with the upkeep of an empire in which the imperial centre needs to control other nations or tribes or ethnic groups by means other than massive police and/ or military forces. Apart from its ancillary role in warfare, intelligence is a means of controlling subjected territories and peoples on the cheap. But Germany's small pre-1918 empire had little impact on the German polity and left few traces. Even Adolf Hitler, the German leader with the most ambitious imperialist agenda, had little interest in intelligence. His aim was not to manipulate foreign peoples but to kill them or to resettle them by force in order to gain space for German agricultural colonies in eastern Europe.

To be sure, during the two World Wars numerous German intellectuals became engaged in intelligence work. Many who later became leading figures in area studies such as in Russian or Balkan or Chinese or Arabic studies were employed by German intelligence, particularly military intelligence. The same was of course true of engineers, medical doctors, mathematicians and physicists – to name but a few branches of learning which were obviously needed in military intelligence. But few of them wrote about their experiences or even mentioned them privately after the war.

There is perhaps only one topic of mainstream German history in which intelligence officials played a prominent role which was recognised in the more popular history books. A number of intelligence officers were involved in the conspiracy against Hitler. Of those, Admiral Wilhelm Canaris, the military intelligence chief, was the most prominent figure to be killed by the Nazis in the aftermath of the failed coup d'état of 20 July 1944.[22] Significantly, however, a number of those who survived were quite reluctant to reveal their heroic stories. Take the example of Hans von Herwarth, a junior diplomat posted in Moscow who secretly informed the British and the Americans about the Nazi–Soviet negotiations which produced the pact of 23 August 1939. His story only became publicly known after two US diplomats, George Kennan and Charles Bohlen, published their memoirs. And even then it took a US scholar to get von Herwarth to write down his story.[23] Several Germans, business managers and technical specialists, who supplied intelligence material to the Allies in an effort to help them win the war against Hitler, were never publicly identified during their lifetime.[24] They preferred to be quiet heroes.

Perhaps this lack of heroic spies, or rather of heroic spies who make sure that their stories are widely publicised, is another factor which has hampered intelligence studies in Germany. Imagine Lawrence of Arabia or George Smiley without their literary promoters! The British gentleman spy, who is even unique in the Anglo-Saxon world, most definitely has no equivalent in Germany.

Notes

1 This guess is based on an official enquiry into the record keeping of the *Bundesnach-richtendienst* (BND), which was launched in connection with the Guillaume spying scandal of 1974.

2 Post-1945 German historiography has paid little attention to earlier periods of intelligence history for which sources are generally open to everyone. The recently published collection of essays, *Geheimdienste in der Weltgeschichte* (Munich: Beck 2003), edited by this author, hopes to encourage fresh studies in all historical periods.

3 Admittedly, German parliamentary papers are neither as voluminous nor as studded with hard facts – compared to US Congressional materials – but they still contain a good deal of information which has hardly been tapped. Stefanie Waske is preparing a dissertation on the subject. Meanwhile, cf. Shlomo Shpiro, *Guarding the Guard: Parliamentary Control of the Intelligence Services in Germany and Britain* (Sankt Augustin: Konrad-Adenauer-Stiftung, 1997).

4 Hermann Zolling and Heinz Höhne, *Pullach Intern: General Gehlen und die Geschichte des Bundesnachrichtendienstes* (Hamburg: Bertelsmann, 1971); Udo Ulfkotte, *Verschluss-Sache BND* (Munich: Heyne, 1997).

5 For an excellent new overview of GDR history, see Klaus Schroeder, *Der SED-Staat: Partei, Staat und Gesellschaft, 1949–1990* (Munich: Econ-Ullstein-List-Verlag, 1998). For details of the Stasi archive itself see their excellent website www.bstu.de.

6 Soviet studies was a highly unpopular field in Germany after the mid-1960s – in part because some of its leaders were compromised by their Nazi past. But even a man like Richard Löwenthal, a left-wing Jewish émigré who returned to Berlin to become a close associate of Willy Brandt's, was little appreciated for his insights into the nature of Soviet communism.

7 See my essay on the post-1945 German view of the 1944 Normandy invasion, 'Der 6. Juni 1944 im politischen Denken in Deutschland und bei den Alliierten', in Günter Bischof and Wolfgang Krieger (eds), *Die Invasion in der Normandie 1944* (Innsbruck: Studien Verlag, 2001). For a more recent illustration see the immense public response to a recent book on the allied bombing war, which was followed by a number of German television documentaries. In effect Germany came to be seen chiefly as a victim of 'inhuman Allied warfare' while the broader historical context was lost from

sight (Jörg Friedrich, *Der Brand: Deutschland im Bombenkrieg, 1940–45* (Munich: Büchergilde Gutenberg, 2002)).

8 Incidentally, the Clausewitz renaissance of the 1970s and 1980s largely bypassed Germany.

9 Sometime in the late 1970s, when this author was a lecturer at the German Armed Forces University, he was asked by a group of visiting American dignitaries how much time his officer students devoted to the study of Clausewitz. Diplomatically, perhaps cowardly, a truthful answer was avoided.

10 The key difference is perhaps that defence departments and certain non-profit organisations in the United States, Britain, France, Australia and Canada made sure that security policy or defence studies remained alive at least in some universities and think tanks while German governments did little in this direction – apart from handing out scholarships to those younger scholars who went abroad to study and work in Anglo-Saxon institutes of security studies. Later various 'peace research institutes' were sponsored by left-wing German provincial governments, though none reached the intellectual level of the Stockholm International Peace Research Institute (SIPRI).

11 For publications which evolved from the International Intelligence History Association (IIHA), founded by German scholars in 1993, see Wolfgang Krieger and Jürgen Weber (eds), *Spionage für den Frieden? Nachrichtendienste in Deutschland während des Kalten Krieges* (Munich: Olzog, 1997); Reinhard R. Doerries (ed.), *Diplomaten und Agenten: Nachrichtendienste in der Geschichte der deutsch-amerikanischen Beziehungen* (Heidelberg: Steiner Verlag, 2001); Heike Bungert, Jan G. Heitmann and Michael Wala (eds), *Secret Intelligence in the Twentieth Century* (London: Frank Cass, 2003). The first volume in the IIHA series is Cees Wiebes, *Intelligence and the War in Bosnia 1992–1995* (Münster: Lit, 2003).

12 The founders were Jürgen Rohwer, Reinhard R. Doerries, Jürgen Heideking and Wolfgang Krieger. Today about half of the membership comes from outside Germany.

13 The initiative for the reform of military history in Germany came from the German defence department's Office of Military History (*Militärgeschichtliches Forschungsamt* or MGFA) at Potsdam which, however, takes virtually no interest in intelligence history. The only chair in military history is held by Bernhard Kroener at Potsdam University.

14 My Marburg colleague Thomas Noetzel is the only exception I am aware of. His dissertation was on betrayal and decadence, a study of the Cambridge spies.

15 For example, in the magisterial 4-volume study of Germany's 'new foreign policy' after 1990, with contributions from virtually the entire 'establishment' of German political scientists, the brief essay on intelligence was contributed by Hans-Georg Wieck, a retired diplomat and former president of the BND (Karl Kaiser *et al.* (eds), *Deutschlands neue Außenpolitik*, 4 vols (Munich: Oldenbourg, 1997/98)). Wieck is also the author of a thoughtful study on 'intelligence and democracy' (*Demokratie und Geheimdienste* (Munich: Oldenbourg, 1995)). Together with Wolbert Smidt, a retired senior BND official, he founded a public forum on intelligence in Berlin in July 2003.

16 Only lower level ex-Stasi officials were hired to help locate files and to restore certain papers which were shredded but not entirely destroyed in the hasty clean-up of 1989/90.

17 Reinhard Grimmer *et al.* (eds), *Die Sicherheit: zur Abwehrarbeit des MfS*, 2 vols (Berlin: Ed. Ost, 2002) is a collection of essays to which virtually the entire leadership of the final years of the Stasi contributed. Other examples along those lines are: Klaus Eichner, *Headquarters German: die USA-Geheimdienste in Deutschland* (Berlin: Ed. Ost, 2001), and Werner Grossmann, *Bonn im Blick: die DDR-Aufklärung aus der Sicht ihres letzten Chefs* (Berlin: Das Neue Berlin, 2001). Grossmann succeeded Erich Mielke as head of the Stasi in 1989.

18 Waldemar Markwardt, *Erlebter BND: Kritisches Plädoyer eines Insiders* (Berlin: Tykuo Berlin, 1996); Reinhard Gehlen, *Der Dienst: Erinnerungen 1942–1971* (Mainz: Droemer-Knaur, 1971); English edition: *The Service* (New York: Collins, 1972).

19 Gert Buchheit, *Der deutsche Geheimdienst: Geschichte der militärischen Abwehr* (Munich: List, 1966); Jürgen Thorwald, *Die Illusion: Rotarmisten in Hitlers Heeren* (Zürich: Droemer-Knaur, 1974); see also the books by Zolling/Höhne and Ulfkotte (note 4 above).

20 Very different career patterns apply to those who were old enough to have served in the *Wehrmacht* before or during the Second World War and then went into academic careers thereafter (for memoirs and other intelligence-related writings, see Max Gunzenhäuser, *Geschichte des Geheimen Nachrichtendienstes: Literaturbericht und Bibliographie* (Frankfurt am Main: Bernard&Graefe, 1968)). There must be more than a few people who became prominent figures in area studies (such as Chinese, or Japanese or Latin American studies) or in linguistics, psychology and in law after having served as intelligence officers during the war. No systematic studies have been undertaken on what post-war German academic leaders in the humanities and the social sciences did during the war and to what extent there might be links of expertise between the two. Most recently, a vivid debate broke out over biographies of some of the most prominent historians who had undertaken various 'ethnic studies' during the Nazi era, possibly providing some of the conceptual and organisational foundations for the Nazi policies of ethnic cleansing in central and eastern Europe, including the Holocaust committed against the Jews and the gypsies. Those studies were only marginally related to intelligence organisations.

21 Only the annual conferences of the International Intelligence History Association provide opportunities to mix with intelligence officials, including those retired from the BND, and to solicit their critique of a scholarly presentation on intelligence history.

22 Heinz Höhne, *Canaris* (New York: Doubleday, 1979).

23 Much later, von Herwarth became West Germany's first ambassador to London. Hans von Herwarth with S. Frederick Starr, *Against Two Evils* (New York: Collins, 1971) is well worth reading.

24 Reginald V. Jones, *Most Secret War: British Scientific Intelligence 1939–1945* (London: Coronet Books, 1979); *Reflections on Intelligence* (London: Heinemann, 1989) by the same author.

4 Netcentric Warfare, C4ISR and Information Operations

Towards a revolution in military intelligence?

John Ferris

No military forces ever have placed such faith in intelligence as do US military forces today. The idea of a 'revolution in military affairs' (RMA) assumes that information and the 'information age' will transform the knowledge available to armed forces, and thus the nature of war. This faith is central to US doctrine and policy. Joint Visions 2010 and 2020, which guide strategic policy, predict forces with 'dominant battlespace awareness', and a 'frictional imbalance' and 'decision superiority' over any enemy. The aim is unprecedented flexibility of command: the ability to combine freedom for units with power for the top, and to pursue 'parallel, not sequential planning and real-time, not prearranged, decision making'.[1] Officials have created new concepts about intelligence and command. They hope to pursue power by using new forms of information technology in order to fuse into systems matters which once were split into 'stovepipes'. These concepts include netcentric warfare (NCW), the idea that armed forces will adopt flat structures, working in nets on the internet, with soldiers at the sharp end able to turn data processing systems at home into staffs through 'reachback', real time, immediate and thorough inter-communication; C4ISR (command, control, communications, computers, intelligence, surveillance and reconnaissance; loosely speaking, how armed forces gather, interpret and act on information); the 'infosphere', the body of information surrounding any event; and 'IO' (Information Operations), the actions of secret agencies. The aim is to realise the RMA, by creating a revolution in military intelligence. This paper will consider how far those ideas can be achieved, and how attempts to do so will affect the nature of power, intelligence and war in the twenty-first century. Progressives and revolutionaries debate the details of these issues (conservatives need not apply). The Marine Corps' draft doctrine on IO denies that technology can solve all problems and defends its 'timeless fighting principles'. Army doctrine too gives C4ISR a Clausewitzian cast, judging that it can 'reduce the friction caused by the fog of war' and help impose one's will on the enemy. But it also concludes that 'achieving accurate situational understanding depends at least as much on human judgment as on machine-processed information – particularly when assessing enemy intent and combat power... [U]ncertainty and risk are inherent in all military operations.'[2] But these judgements represent the cautious end of the spectrum of US military thinking about the future of warfare. Revolutionaries, conversely, assume C4ISR will function in a system precisely as a person sees the world, turns data to knowledge and acts on it. Enthusiasts believe armed forces can comprehend an enemy and a battle perfectly, and act without friction. David Alperts, a leading Pentagon figure in NCW, holds that

> we will effectively move from a situation in which we are preoccupied with reducing the fog of war to the extent possible and with designing approaches needed to accommodate any residual fog that exists to a situation in which we are preoccupied with optimizing a response to a particular situation... we will move from a situation in which decision making takes place under 'uncertainty' or in the presence of incomplete and erroneously [sic] information, to a situation in which decisions are made with near 'perfect' information.[3]

All sides in this debate assume intelligence will have great power. They take its triumphs for its norms. Thus, in 1995, the USAF chief, General Fogleman, discussing ULTRA and FORTITUDE, said, 'Throughout history, soldiers, sailors, Marines and airmen have learned one valuable lesson. If you can analyze, act and assess faster than your opponent, you will win!' Unless, of course, the enemy is stronger or smarter or luckier.[4]

The military exponents of Information Warfare (IW) assign unprecedented weight to intelligence in war. In 1995 George Stein wrote 'Information warfare, in its essence, is about *ideas and epistemology* – big words meaning that information warfare is about the way humans think and, more important they way humans make decisions... It is about influencing human beings and the decisions they make.' Colonel Szafranski spoke of '*targeting epistemology*'.[5] Faith in intelligence and IO underlies Command and Control Warfare, the main form of operations the United States plans to fight a version of blitzkrieg which seeks 'to deny information to, influence, degrade, or destroy' the enemy's 'information dependent process', so to shatter its ability to perceive and command.[6] Revolutionaries advocate a higher mode of war, Rapid Decisive Operations (RDO), which will open with the pursuit of a 'Superior Information Position (Fight First for Information Superiority)' and become 'knowledge-centric':

> The creation and sharing of superior knowledge are critical to RDO... Decision makers, enabled by study, judgment, and experience, convert information into knowledge and situational understanding, which is the key to *decision superiority* [original emphasis] – the ability to make better decisions faster than the adversary... IO are the information equivalent of manoeuvre and fire... In planning for effects-based operations, *knowledge* is paramount.[7]

The revolutionaries conceptualise war as game and strategy as shooting. They assume that to be seen is to be shot, to be shot is to be killed, and to be fast is to win. As USAF planner and theorist Colonel John Warden wrote, 'a very simple rule for how to go about producing the effect: do it very fast...the essence of success in future war will certainly be to make everything happen you want to happen in a very short period of time – instantly if possible'.[8] These tendencies are reinforced by the routine use of the 'OODA cycle' (Observe, Orient, Decide, Act), devised by strategic theorist Colonel John Boyd to describe all conflict on all levels of war, with the aim usually defined as moving through the cycle faster than one's opponent. Wiser heads urge that this gain in time be used to think more rather than simply act faster. Boyd's model, derived from his reflections on his experience as a fighter pilot in the Korean War, is a good means to conceptualise one-on-one combat. It is less useful for war. In a boxing match, speed may equal victory; in strategy, cries of 'faster! harder!' produce premature ejaculation. Focus on the OODA cycle, 'sensors to shooters', 'one shot one kill' weapons and the idea that armed forces can act almost without friction on near perfect knowledge, has led to a fetishisation of speed and the tacticisation of strategy.

These ideas frame much thinking about intelligence. The assumption is that intelligence will be an engine fit for a fine-tuned, high-performance, machine – reliable, understood, useful, usable and on-call. One can learn exactly what one wants to know when one needs to do so, and verify its accuracy with certainty and speed. The truth and only the truth can be known. It is further assumed that intelligence will show what should be done and what will happen if one does. According to this line of thought, action taken on knowledge will have precisely the effect one intends, nothing more or less.

Intelligence experts in the military–academic complex have attacked these ideas. Williamson Murray notes that a key to Rapid Decisive Operations, the idea that 'Operational Net Assessment' will turn knowledge to power by constantly updating and fusing all data on everything related to a war, ignores every known problem in intelligence. At a strategic level, says Murray, net assessment rarely did more than bean counting. It usually fell victim to worst- or best-case assessments and mirror-imaging. Achieving Operational Net Assessment would require 'a revolution in the culture of intelligence'. Such a revolution would entail a 'move away from the search for the predictive to an emphasis on a broader, intuitive understanding of potential opponents' – from a focus on collection and technology to an emphasis on the importance of foreign languages, culture and history. Michael Handel argued that intelligence, once undervalued, has become oversold. 'If it sounds too good to be true', he briefed officers, 'maybe it is'.[9] In their doctrine, too, all US services treat the relationship between intelligence and operations carefully and well.[10]

The Pentagon expects normal intelligence to be as good as it ever has been, more central to planning and operations, and to be transformed along with every other element of power. In January 2003, the Chairman of the Joint Chiefs of Staff, General Myers, noted that, we have always tended to have this situation where intelligence people are in one stove pipe and the operators in another and we are real happy if they talk together. When today's world requires that they be totally integrated…you can't have an intel pod, throw it over a transom to an operator and say, here's what we know. This has got to be continuous, 24/7 sort of relationship and synergistic to the point where operations help with intel and vice versa.[11]

Some months later, commenting on Operation Iraqi Freedom, the Pentagon's Director of Force Transformation, Admiral Cebrowski, noted that,

the intelligence analysis problem, where we have all of these intelligence sources, and they all produced their products and reports and fed databases, all of which are stove-piped. The analysis functions are similarly stove-piped. Essentially, we have an intelligence community that is organized by wavelength…But it needn't be that way. It could be more like this, where your intelligence is organized around the demand functions of warning, force protection, and warfighting intelligence, where you have data mediation layers that are able to pull together all source information, plot it geo-spatially, and generate the kinds of displays in which a senior leader's question can in fact be answered at very, very high speed.[12]

Cebowski advocated 'a new demand centred intelligence system'. He argued that since 1970 intelligence had become unbalanced. The quantity of information had risen exponentially, and the power of analysis only in a linear fashion, while specialists alone collected, processed (and hoarded) material from each source. This caused both overload and strangulation. Too much information was available, too little used and even less co-ordinated, because it was divided into watertight pots defined not by function but source. Never was all the data on any topic brought together. Agencies collected what they did because that was what they did; the customer was forgotten. So to solve these problems, material from all sources should go to an 'Information Dominance Center' (IDC) for analysis characterised by 'Continuous merge…Megadata, All Source, Open Source and Geospatial Data, Dynamic Collection, Visualisation'. This idea, like that of Operational Net Assessment, assumes analysts can constantly gather, analyse, synthesise, fuse and update intelligence from all sources on all aspects of an enemy in real time and make it useful to decision makers. This rolling product would be returned to agencies and to an office of an Under Secretary of Defense Intelligence, with three analytical–operational functions, 'Warning, CI/Force Protection and War-fighting intelligence'.[13]

At first glance, such a body might solve the problems caused by unco-ordinated single source agencies, but not that of information overload in analysis, unless one assumes that to centralise and automate and computerise information must transform its nature. This is precisely the assumption upon which much new thinking about 'operational net assessment' and 'knowledge-centric warfare' is based. As its name indicates, the IDC is intended to unleash the power of information: to bring intelligence into the information revolution, and vice versa.

Here, as often in the debates over the RMA and intelligence, vague language and jargon obscure a clash between ideas and agencies. Advocates of the RMA view the intelligence services which survived the Cold War as legacy forces, industrial age dinosaurs, muscle-bound and clumsy, too focused on technique, security, secrecy and the source of their collection as against the material it provides; too divided in acquiring their evidence and presenting their analyses; too reluctant to disseminate their data; providing too much useless information; too little able to answer key questions fast and accurately. In the Cold War, American intelligence focused on supporting millions of soldiers in a world-wide competition against a peer, with the trump suit being the collection of data on strategic issues through technical means. In the information age, the focuses are terrorists or expeditionary forces. To meet these needs, the revolutionaries want intelligence services to become nimble, to simplify their techniques and reduce their emphasis on them, to alter their priorities and their focus on one source; to cease being monopolists of knowledge and oracles of assessment; to distribute their material widely and freely, to fuse it constantly in a rolling fashion, to co-operate in assessment with each other and the military in ad hoc teams, and to emphasise broad strategic or political issues less and military operational ones more, to provide less but better information. Advocates of the RMA see the attack on the Twin Towers as illustrating the flaws in US intelligence, but their criticisms are more fundamental. They want a revolution in military intelligence.

These ideas have political consequences which are intended even if they are unspoken. If an IDC is created, one analytical bureau, a military one, reflecting its aims and means, will handle all information from all sources, and dominate analysis in the intelligence community. If Operational Net Assessment is practiced, power in analysis will move from Washington to theatre commands. All this will revive demarcation disputes between collectors and customers over priorities and between the military and the Central Intelligence Agency (CIA) in analysis. Again, the problems in US intelligence can be solved by many means, not merely those proposed by advocates of the RMA. Intelligence services can adapt to the times; they do so all of the time. Without transforming or detracting from other work, refined 'push' and 'pull' techniques should let them flexibly and immediately meet the needs of each of the five divisions in an expedition, a good thing in itself. However, such reforms (even more those in the revolutionary programme) raise the danger that intelligence will be militarised and tacticised. Junior commanders always want to control intelligence, more than ever in an era of C4ISR and expeditionary forces; yet such steps threaten to erode the advantages of critical mass or centralisation.

Another problem is that the rise of precision weapons and the idea of intelligence, surveillance and reconnaissance (ISR) further blurs the boundary between target acquisition and intelligence. Somehow, in moving from C3I to C4ISR, 'computers' have eaten qualities once assigned to 'command' while 'intelligence' has diminished, as an idea connoting 'to think' slips into one meaning 'to sense'. After Afghanistan, one intelligence officer noted 'As weapons [systems] become more "intel centric" the importance of ISR increases proportionately...Think of Intel as a modern gun director', while Myers said bombs 'can be used like bullets from a rifle, aimed precisely and individually'.[14] When considering C4ISR, it is tempting to focus on the aspects most easily changed, machines, and to assume improvements to them must in turn raise the performance of the human aspects of command and decision. It is similarly tempting to believe solutions to one set of problems (target acquisition) will solve another (net assessment). In fact, one can improve every technological aspect of C4ISR without aiding any of the human ones, possibly even harming their performance. The same action can help target acquisition and harm net assessment. These pressures bolster the tendency in US intelligence to focus on technology.

Some revolutionaries hold that only nonhuman means can allow a C4I and NCW system to work. Contributors to the *Air Force 2025* project, which framed the USAF's policy on these matters, predicted a C4ISR system with the self-awareness of a man, or a god. According to these theorists, the future of battlefield command will be characterised by 'a series of intelligent micro-processor "brains"...all-knowing, all-sensing' and 'an intelligence architecture with human-like characteristics...[which will]...simultaneously sense and evaluate the earth in much the same way you remain aware of your day-to-day surroundings'. One concludes that 'Future generations may come to regard tactical warfare as properly the business of machines and not appropriate for people at all.'[15] Against this pressure is the cry for 'HUMINT'. But this takes many forms. Many people call for a change in the culture of intelligence; others stress the need for human intelligence. Meanwhile, soldiers define 'HUMINT' vaguely, taking it to mean everything from cultural awareness or linguistic knowledge, to a focus on humans as sources of information and for subversion, to paying some attention to humans, or to anything but technology. Beneath the debate on intelligence is an inchoate struggle between emphasis on humans and reliance on machines.

Many of these ideas about intelligence are naive or misguided. Thus, C4ISR has solved only some problems of command and changed none of its conditions. As ever, the issue is how much information a system contains, how fast and flexibly it circulates, and how well it is used. In communications, intelligence and decision making, more or faster is not necessarily better; the value of multiplication depends on what is being multiplied; changes in quantity cause changes in quality, sometimes for the worse. Outside of fairy tales, rarely is intelligence self-evident and easy to use. The advocates of a revolution in military intelligence cannot achieve exactly what they intend. Still, their actions will have consequences. They may cause a revolution, even if it is not the one they plan. The RMA is the greatest matter affecting intelligence today, and its success depends on how far intelligence really can be transformed.

Ideas on these issues have affected US intelligence services, most notably those most closely linked to the military. Since 1995 these services have focused increasingly on serving C4ISR, especially by improving their databases, links with customers and reachback. The Defense Intelligence Agency (DIA) aims to provide 'Fused, Tailored Intelligence Essential to Battlefield Dominance' and 'Dominant Battlespace Intelligence for the Warfighter'. Similarly, among the five 'Core Competencies' in the National Security Agency's (NSA) 'National Cryptologic Strategy for the 21st Century' is the ability to 'ensure dominant battlespace knowledge through [the] integration of cryptology with joint operations'. The precise objective is to 'anticipate warfighter intelligence needs – on time, anywhere, at the lowest possible classification'.

3   Integration of cryptologic support to enable policy makers to promote stability and thwart aggression. NSA seeks to...

(b)   Work with policy customers to improve interoperability and ensure that intelligence can be tailored to meet customer needs.

(c)   Expand 'pull' dissemination capabilities to enable customers to initiate real time requests to improve crisis support.

(d)   Work with the I[ntelligence] C[ommunity] to create interactive databases that will enable searches for information gathered by members of the IC.

In Afghanistan during 2002 (and no doubt, Iraq in 2003), NSA personnel, 'integrated with the combatant commander staffs...ensured field commanders and others had access to NSA operations and crisis action centres; developed a collection system that supports military forces abroad' and co-ordinated reachback. On 17 October 2002, the NSA's Director, Michael Hayden, said, 'As we speak, NSA has over 700 people not *producing* SIGINT but sitting in our customer's spaces *explaining* and *sharing* SIGINT'. The National Imagery and Mapping Agency (NIMA), too, deployed 'the Target Management System Network', giving its 'customers direct access to targeting support and navigation data from the NIMA precise point database'.[16] By January 2003, NIMA and NSA exchanged personnel and combined imagery, geospatial and signals intelligence at the point of first production, before it was sent to consumers.[17] After Operation Iraqi Freedom, the director of the CIA praised 'the seamlessness, fusion, speed and quality of what is being provided on the battlefield' and held this proved his organisation must transform like other intelligence services.[18] These agencies all aim to distribute normal intelligence better than the best performance ever hitherto achieved. Though they are reforming rather than transforming, this pressure may reinforce the military's role in intelligence and the latter's tendency to focus on technology, technique and tactics, despite the rhetoric about the need to develop human sources and cultural awareness.

Meanwhile, the intelligence community began to enter the information age. By 2001 the US government had several web-based but enclosed intelligence intranets, linked to the military's 'SIPRnet' (Secret Internet Protocol Router Network), a self-contained internet gated from the conventional one. Intelligence and government agencies were joined to 'Intelink Intranet', which had further subsections. The latter included 'Intelink Commonwealth' (between US, Australian, British and Canadian agencies); 'Intelink-SCI' for the 'top-secret, compartmented intelligence level'; 'Intelink-S', an 'SIPRnet at the secret level' for military commands; and connections between the main intelligence agencies and their consumers, like the CIA's 'Intelink PolicyNet' and the DIA's 'Joint Intelligence Virtual Architecture', a web-based interactive system which joined 5,300 analysts world-wide for normal work and reachback. These nets were supported by steadily improving collection, search and analysis functions which, the head of the Joint Military Intelligence College noted, must allow 'mining of data not only of what the analyst knows is important but also of – while unthought-of by the analyst – what might be of importance'.[19] By 2003, the agencies were beginning to deploy an 'Intelligence Community System for Information Security system' (ICSIS), with secure gateways for the transfer of messages between networks of different security classifications.[20] The inability of the CIA, the NSA and the Federal Bureau of Investigation to co-ordinate their databases before the attack on the Twin Towers shows the limits to this work, but one should not over-generalise from that failure. Even on 10 September 2001, intelligence databases on traditional military and diplomatic matters probably were linked fairly well. No doubt they have been made to work rather better since.

These steps were in pursuit of greater visions. The 'Strategic Investment Plan for Intelligence Community Analysis' noted that by 2007,

> the agencies aimed to achieve a virtual work environment enabled by collaborative and analytic tools, and interoperable databases ... the breaking down of barriers and the sharing of databases of critical and common concern ... [a system] that connects databases across the IC and a security framework to allow analysts to share knowledge and expertise and link them to collectors, consumers, allies, and outside experts ... Efforts and electronic tracking and production systems to capture and make available intelligence 'products' that can be recovered and reused by customers and other analysts (knowledge warehouses).

The aim was to create the 'secure and classified sub-set' of the infosphere, 'the intelsphere, which is the virtual knowledge repository of authoritative intelligence information, relevant reference material, and resources used to store, maintain, access and protect this information'. The strategic investment plan noted that the DIA had taken the lead 'in developing the concepts underpinning knowledge management in order to provide full battlespace visualization to warfighters and military planners', but all military intelligence providers 'are automating their request, tasking, and response systems – at both the front and back ends – to serve a scattered and diverse constituency', and creating

> an integrated electronic production environment. The large organizations, for example, are making strides, albeit somewhat uneven, in tracking customer requests and in recording and capturing production flow, an effort that will become increasingly critical if we are to develop common 'knowledge warehouses' that are easily accessible to our customers and to each other.

To this system must be allied search techniques which would sidestep information overload, and 'reveal connections, facilitate analytic insights and deductions and streamline search by prioritizing information, automatically populating databases, and integrating data'. The ultimate aims of the strategic investment plan were threefold. First, to integrate national intelligence analysis from multiple sources with the timely reporting of tactical sensors, platforms and other battlefield information. Second, to provide customer, user and producer interfaces so that organisations at all levels (national–allied/coalition–theatre–tactical) have access to digital data that each can retrieve and manipulate. Third, to use advanced models, architectures, automated metrics/management tools and authoritative production templates within a collaborative environment to dynamically assign, prioritise, track and measure the operations/intelligence infosphere content.

By 2010, the intelligence community hopes to have 'a dynamic knowledge base...fully accessible from anywhere at any time by authorized users... Knowledge base linkage to collectors with information needs/gaps automatically identified'.[21] In a similar vein, the Army's Deputy Chief of Staff for Intelligence held that in the 'knowledgecentric' army,

> analytic operations will be executed collaboratively in a distributive environment with extensive use of virtual-teaming capabilities. Analysts at every level and in multiple locations will come together in virtual analytic teams to satisfy unit of action and employment intelligence requirements. Each analyst will have access to the entire body of knowledge on the subject at hand and will draw on interactive, integrated, interoperable databases to rapidly enable understanding. Communities of analytic interest will create and collapse around individual issues. The commander forward will be supported by the entire power of the formerly echeloned, hierarchical, analytic team. [22]

No doubt, some of this is mere rhetoric, a political response to pressure, while much that matters remains unsaid. Collectors and analysts fear the uncontrolled distribution of their best material, or that such a transformation in practices might degrade their work. According to Bruce Berkowitz (an academic with an intelligence background, seconded to the CIA during 2001–02) at that time its Directorates of Intelligence (DI) and Operations (DO), had incompatible databases. Each DI analyst had one computer linked to their own, poor, database, another to the internet, neither to other official systems. 'The CIA view is that there are risks to connecting CIA systems even to classified systems elsewhere.' Merely to send intranet e-mail to intelligence officers outside the agency was difficult. Few CIA computers were linked to the SIPRnet – though models which could receive but not send messages were quickly being introduced. The CIA disliked Intelink because it could not control dissemination of the documents which it provided to this database. It did 'post almost all of its products on CIASource, a website maintained on the Agency's network that is linked to Intelink' to which few outsiders had access. As a result, no-one outside the agency had much electronic access to CIA material. In order to study any topic, DI analysts had to search separate databases including the DI system, Intelink, and the internet. They often simply ignored the latter two. 'When it comes to it', Berkowitz notes,

> the CIA's approach is not 'risk management' but 'risk exclusion'. All this had cultural causes and consequences. Access by outsiders to CIA data threatened its hierarchical system of assessment and quality control, while by making technology a bogey-man rather than an ally, the CIA is reinforcing the well-known tendency toward introversion among most DI analysts.[23]

This critique was accurate for the time, but changes seem to have occurred since. The CIA now claims to be creating secure but flexible inter-agency databases and intranets, including the ICSIS (which had languished since 1998) and a browser-based system allowing document sharing and e-mail.[24]

In 1999, NSA Director Hayden had two teams investigate the NSA. Both condemned its culture and especially its rejection of the internet. The internal team noted 'we focus more on our own "tradecraft" than on our customers, partners, and stakeholders'. It advocated the NSA's 'transformation...from an industrial age monopoly to an information age organization that has entered the competitive market place', embracing 'the Internet as a force-multiplier...a means of creating numerous virtual centers of excellence with colleagues around the world'. The external team held that the NSA must be recentred around the internet, and overcome its 'culture that discourages sending bad news up the chain of command... a society where people were afraid to express their own thoughts'. It also called for changes in institutional culture. It observed that the 'NSA generally talks like engineers' and that '[it] will talk about the technical parameters of constructing a watch, describing gears and springs, when the customer simply wants to understand that we have just developed a better way to tell time. Even more important, NSA needs to learn to communicate what the ability to tell time might mean to a customer.'[25] Advocates of the information revolution view both the CIA and NSA as anal and ossified, unable to grasp the need to provide fast, flexible, fused material. Such criticisms have force. Yet, as Hayden noted, the NSA 'is a very conservative, risk-averse organization' because these characteristics, along with 'consistency and thoroughness and care', fit the Cold War.[26] They also suit any intelligence agency which dislikes error or insecurity.

But the rhetoric of transformation obscures the key issue – who gets what from whom? It is easy enough to produce good intelligence or co-ordinate analysts, or push material effectively in a crisis, or send fused information fast from Washington to a theatre command, or from there to an aircraft or unit commander. These are standard problems with school solutions: reachback, tailoring, fusion and pull techniques are old hat, they do not require transformation. To give thousands of people access to the databases of secret intelligence services, and to use them as they wish, however, is unprecedented. It gives intelligence services cause to fear for their security and tradecraft and the integrity of their data. There are concerns to be balanced. The question is, how?

Since 1995, the intelligence agencies have learned how better to push their product to the military, which have honed their means to pull it. Reachback is a reality, and will, in turn, reshape reality. Already, it has magnified the power of intelligence. Colonels can tap data from the centre to solve problems in the field and guide immediate strikes; junior analysts at home can warn sergeants at the sharp end of danger or promise just ahead. Yet in all fairy tales, curses accompany blessings. Search engines augment analysis but they cannot replace analysts. If intelnets work as advertised, collectors can more easily distribute their product and analysts find the material they want. Correlations can be made, expected or unexpected, and actions will be aided. Everyone will receive far more data than ever before – perhaps too much. So, to justify their existence, intelink agencies will stock 'knowledge factories' such as the projected IDC with reports in mass, many trivial, some competitive, all well-advertised. Analysts will be swamped in sites, losing their way down hot-linked detours. Analysis will be constipated by the quantity of information and by conflicts of interpretation and of interest. Need and politics will keep security restrictions in being, often blocking users precisely from the material they need or hiding all the best evidence.

This situation calls for education in intelligence and its pathologies, and the creation of a new culture for assessment and use. If this is achieved, analysts and engines will just be able to prevent the increased mass of detail from adding more friction to general decision making, while making great gains in two areas: when one knows what one wants to know, the answers will come with unprecedented power and speed; and the chances for discovery by serendipity will rise. If this aim fails, more will mean worse.

Again, by making intelligence more central than ever before, the United States has made C4ISR the centre of gravity for its power as well as its greatest vulnerability. All of this has also increased the importance and the difficulty of security. SIPRnet is the richest treasure ever for espionage, and intelink agencies are its crown jewels, which will shine the brighter the better intelligence is fused and distributed. In principle, the 'intelsphere' is walled from enemies but accessible to friends, who communicate with freedom. But if this firewall collapses, that web-based communication will become the equivalent of plain language traffic over wireless. If an enemy penetrates the 'intelsphere', it will have more chances than ever before to gather intelligence on you or to pirate intelligence and to use it as its own. It will also gain unprecedented ability to corrupt one's own data. The danger of penetration, indeed even the suspicion that databases are insecure, is the Achilles heel of the 'intelsphere'. If soldiers cannot trust the security of the 'intelsphere', how will they act on it? One successful corruption of information, producing one failure in the field, might cripple the machine or the trust on which it relies. A virus may be little more damaging than the fear of one.

Thus, as ever, security will trump flexibility. Databases are most easily defended when they are accessible only to regulated computers. SIPRnet, however, is easily accessible – anyone capturing intact any one of thousands of vehicles in Operation Iraqi Freedom in theory could reach any database linked to it. And penetration is common. In 2001, 16,000 attempts were made to enter the US Navy computer networks, 'of which 400 gained entry, and 40 traveled the networks'.[27] This danger will limit the significance of intelligence easily reached through SIPRnet, and force intelligence agencies to shelter their best material behind secure gates or else on separate intranets. The 'intelsphere' must stand apart from the 'infosphere', while still being linked to it through secure and flexible procedures, which allow information to be pushed from the top and pulled from below, and more co-ordination between databases, and between analysts and users. These links may be more rich, thick, flexible and fast than ever before, or alternately below the standards of 1944 or even 1918. Everything depends on the relationship between the techniques of cyber attack and defence. At worst, C4ISR may follow the classic downward spiral of C3I over radio, where jamming and the need for security sapped most of its flexibility and power.

The mechanisation of intelligence and command has also transformed the dilemma of security. The new killer applications are spies to steal information and cyberwar to corrupt databases. The key danger from hackers is the threat not of an ULTRA but of a nuclear strike on data. An agent in place, conversely, could betray one's entire database of intelligence and command. In the Cold War, sergeants turned spies pillaged storehouses of paper secrets; now, a Walker family could loot 'knowledge warehouses', or corrupt them; and already this has happened. During 1985–2000, the mid-level counter-intelligence officer and traitor, Robert Hanssen, raided FBI computer systems, including 'thousands of searches' on its Automated Case Support (ACS) database in 1999–2001. He sold Soviet/Russian intelligence much material from many agencies on US strategy, estimates and agents in Moscow, devastating US espionage, as well as monitoring information on himself. The FBI concluded its ACS system had elementary security problems – officers posted secret material which should not have been there, and failed to monitor people who accessed material they did not need to know. These problems had been known since ACS's inception in 1995, and ignored – they continued after Hanssen's treachery was discovered, and still did so in August 2003![28] Had an 'intelsphere' existed, Hanssen would have inflicted even more damage than he did. Cyber defence must be geared to handle every possible enemy everywhere all of the time; and its strength will be defined by the weakest link of an 'intelnet'. For the United States, mercenary hackers rather than hostile nations may be the greatest problem for decades – at least until the rise of a peer competitor. Other states, meanwhile, will have to reckon with peers, or superiors. US authorities recognise these threats and have taken action to meet them. Thus, in 2002, a 'layered cyber-defense system' protected the Defense Information Infrastructure, combining 'local DoD intrusion detection systems' with an NSA-controlled 'computer network defense intrusion detection system…a network of sensors that are strategically placed within the DoD infrastructure, providing analysts the capability to identify anomalous cyber activities traversing the network'. The Pentagon hosts annual cyberwar competitions which, in 2003, included 'a so-called rogue box in each network that the red team could use to simulate insider attacks'.[29] Though no US headquarters ever may feature signs reading 'He who uses the computer is a traitor!', this will happen to smaller states. The electron is a weapon. You can use it, but so may your enemy.

Compared to C4ISR and NCW, Information Operations is a less novel and less problematical concept. It describes its subject better than any extant term, like 'covert action'. IO embraces many 'disciplines' – deception, operational security, electronic warfare and psychological operations, but also civil and public affairs (public and press relations). Initially, the latter were added to IO to meet the Army's distinct problems with peace keeping, but the relationship has grown to include political warfare, both defensive and offensive. During the campaign in Afghanistan, in order to inoculate its media against hostile IO, the Pentagon briefed journalists about the techniques of Serb and Iraqi propaganda and press manipulation, or 'enemy denial and deception'.[30] This concern shaped its media policy during the 2003 war in Iraq, and also led to the short-lived 'Office of Strategic Influence' of 2002, a military organisation established to shape international media coverage. Due to bad publicity, that office closed a day after its existence was announced – and no doubt reopened the next under a new title. That US doctrine about IO fuses in one category matters once treated as 'black' (psyops) and 'white' (public relations) and regards their combined practice as normal presents problems for journalists, the public and the military itself. With the significant exception of Computer Network Attack (CNA), IO is less a matter of old wine in new bottles than new labels on old bottles. Functions which intelligence officers once might have conducted in a General Staff, perhaps with operations, security and signals personnel in secondary roles, are now treated as a combat arm, controlled by the senior Operations officer, with intelligence personnel first among equals of specialist elements. This rise of Operations and decline of Intelligence is marginal and reasonable. IO are operational matters, but they require a close relationship with intelligence and other elements. The basic doctrine for IO is sound, and close to the best practices of the best practitioners of two world wars. IO should be controlled by an officer directly responsible to a commander, guided by a small 'cell' of specialists, able to provide expertise and liaison. They should be deliberately organised in an ad hoc manner, cut to fit the cloth; the various 'disciplines' of IO should be 'fused'; not merely co-ordinated, but combined.[31]

Thus, US doctrine on deception regards all aspects of intelligence as force multipliers, to be integrated into every aspect of planning and operations. It defines sound principles: 'centralised control'; 'security'; 'timeliness' in planning and execution; 'integration' of deceit with an operation; and, above all, 'focus' and a clear objective, aiming to influence the right decision makers and to affect their actions. The overall aim is therefore to treat the manipulation of intelligence and ideas merely as means to an end. In order to achieve these ends, practitioners must understand their foe's psychology. They must 'possess fertile imaginations and the ability to be creative'. They must also pass a story through many sources which an adversary will find believable, ideally by reinforcing its expectations. Finally, they must fuse intelligence, psychological warfare and operations security with deception. This doctrine is powerful, but it has weaknesses which stem from the roots of its strength, the influence of the British tradition of deception.

The campaigns of 1943–44 which culminated in FORTITUDE stem from so many unique circumstances that they are a poor guide to the average. To treat them as normal is to assume deception is precise and predictable, that one will have edges equivalent to ULTRA and the 'double cross system', while the enemy's intelligence is castrated. These are tall assumptions. Again, 'focus' and 'objective' are fine principles: but in order to make key decision makers act as one wishes, one must know who they are, what they expect, how to reach them and how to know whether one has succeeded. This is not easy. Deceivers wrestle with uncertainties and pull strings they hope are attached to levers in a complex system they do not understand. Deception rarely has just the effect one wants and nothing else. The unintended cannot be avoided. American doctrine urges that this difficulty and others be resolved through risk assessment. But this is to mistake a condition for a problem. Reason is good, war games are fun; but when assessment concludes, risks will remain.[32]

IO doctrine has been easier to write than to test. US experience with its components since 1989 ranged in quality from poor (Somalia) to decent but uninspired (Panama; the 1991 Gulf War; Kosovo). In 1998, one IO colonel with experience in Bosnia and at Fort Leavenworth, Craig Jones, noted 'much confusion remains – IO is still many different things to many different people'. This was because it lacked measures of effectiveness. 'A commander has the right and the responsibility to ask his IO staff officer this simple question: "How do we know this IO stuff is helping me achieve my overall objectives?".' Between the conception of the idea and 2003, the US military had no experience with IO in war, except in Kosovo, where Serbs matched Americans; its theory was drawn from history, where good examples did abound, some still better than Operation Iraqi Freedom. The theory was good – the problem was praxis. In 2000 the IO Franchise, Battle Command Battle Lab, at Training and Doctrine Command, admitted the need for basic studies on IO in war, including 'good, reliable means' to assess its impact. 'Intelligence doctrine addressing IO remains to be produced, and training remains concentrated on the traditional functions of locating and identifying opposing forces', with 'intelligence products…designed to support force-on-force, kinetic, lethal engagements'. Again, in 'numerous Army Warfighter Exercises…attrition-focused command and staff training exercises', time was too short 'to employ the less tangible aspects of IO in a manner that would influence the operation', and to understand their value and limits. A division or corps headquarters had just hours 'between receipt of mission to course of action selection, allowing as much time as possible for coordination, synchronization, and orders production', and one at theatre level 'out to 120 hours and beyond'. Deception and psyops, however, might take months to work. 'The most important aspect of IO at the tactical and operational levels is execution', yet how far could division or corps staffs 'effectively integrate and execute all elements of IO into their decision-making processes, given the time constraints common to tactical operations?' If not, how should IO be organised? Historical experience, incidentally, including that from Iraq in 2003, suggests deception and psyops can work well even within a month from their start. It also indicates that a theatre-level headquarters should handle these matters for subordinate commands. Again, how should old disciplines like electronic war-fare be adapted to fit new technology, IO and the information age?[33]

Even experts were unsure how to apply IO. It was practised only in exercises, peace keeping, and Kosovo, all experiences with limits. Bosnia illuminated IO's use in peace keeping but not in war, and perhaps provided some counter-productive lessons: a directing committee of 20-plus members possibly is too bureaucratic for operations. In 2000, reflecting on experience with IO in divisional work at the Exercise and Training Integration Center, one IO analyst, Roy Hollis, noted 'All too often, IO is associated with rear area or force protection operations only... This is only a part of what IO is capable of doing, and we have to unlearn this.' Since 'many staffers do not fully understand or appreciate the value of IO', without effective 'IO staff huddles', 'strong leadership' from the IO officer and a supportive Chief of Staff, 'the staff will focus on what they already know and give minimal attention to Information Operation requirements'. Personnel 'lacked actual subject matter expertise in the various disciplines or elements, plus intelligence support, that make up Information Operations', and spent too much time in too many meetings.[34] Amateurishness and bureaucracy are common problems in military intelligence; but for IO, a focus on form may turn revolution into a checklist. Until 2003, these problems characterised US efforts to apply their IO doctrine.

Properly handled, IO are powerful tools, but they do not necessarily work as one hopes. And they can also be used by one's adversary. Defence matters as much as attack; it is simply more difficult. The power of IO will be multiplied in an unpredictable way by the rise of a new discipline. Unclassified material rarely refers to Computer Network Attack but the topic has not been ignored, simply treated with secrecy, just as armies did deception and signals intelligence between 1919–39. One USAF intelligence officer notes 'offensive IO weapons... remain shrouded in limited-access programs'. The Joint Chiefs of Staff's doctrine on IO discusses CNA in a classified annex. In 2000–01, the USAF sponsored research into specialist 'Cyber-Warfare Forces', 'potential targeting issues' and 'how to mitigate or minimize collateral damage effects'. This research will consider how CNA might affect 'the full-spectrum of Information Attacks'. It will also con-sider how to create and fuse new 'broadly defined multi-disciplinary activities, such as: cyber-based deception, Electro-Magnetic Interference (EMI), Web Security, Perception Management'.[35] The Pentagon's Command and Control Research Program describes CNA as 'a rapidly evolving field of study with its own concepts and technology'.[36] Anyone able to employ a hacker for love or money can hope to gain from CNA, while attack somewhere is easier than defence everywhere. The entry costs are small, the potential payoff large, and the con-sequences uncertain. Sooner or later some state will let slip the bytes of cyberwar, with uncertain effect. CNA may revolutionise IO by incapacitating computer sys-tems, or replacing true data with false; or it may prove Y2K revisited. A first strike may be so advantageous that it creates an imperative to move first, adding a new twist to deterrence. Even when not used, CNA creates, one veteran noted, 'built-in paranoia' – the need to fear that hostile states or non-state actors are attacking and to react on that assumption to anything which looks like a threat.[37] This is doubly the case as CNA may be indistinguishable from accident, its authors are undetectable and it can inflict mass destruction (consider the consequences of wrecking the computers controlling air traffic control at Heathrow Airport, or of a nuclear power plant). So too, the nature of CNA power is unknown: 'How do you measure IO power?', asks the USAF's Institute for National Security Studies; 'How would one calculate Correlation of Forces à la past Soviet/Russian approaches?'; what are the 'units of IW force' or their structure 'e.g. squadrons of IW computers'?[38] These are imponderables at the centre of all thinking about IO as a force multiplier.

At the same time, IO is a known commodity; not so, C4ISR and NCW. How will reachback, intelnets, an IDC or 'knowledge warehouses' affect the normal working of intelligence, and its use in crises or operations? Certainly, they will not end uncertainty, but instead create new kinds of uncertainty. They will increase what Michael Handel called 'Type B uncertainty' – the problem of decision making in a context of too much and too constantly changing information.[39] Uncertainty is not just about what is seen, but how we see; not merely what we know, but how we know that we know what we know. It is a problem of too few facts, but also too many. It is a condition linked to problems. The problems can be eliminated. But attempts to end one problem often create another. A condition of uncertainty is that one can never solve all problems at any one time. One merely chooses which problems to avoid and which to embrace. This condition must be endured. One can increase one's certainty and reduce that of an adversary. The resulting gains may be great. But none of this is easy to achieve. When facing a serious foe, uncertainty will remain sizable. Even against a weak enemy it can never vanish. Chess players, knowing their foe's dispositions, remain uncertain about his or her intentions and the clash of their own strategies. C4ISR and 'Dominant Battlespace Knowledge' (DBK) will increase uncertainty precisely through the way they reduce it; they will have the same effect with friction. In time of routine, they will provide more data than a general needs. In time of crisis they will produce less intelligence. How far will the ability to collect and process information under routine circumstances affect ideas of what intelligence can do when it matters? Will such a routine not merely hide pathologies and paradoxes and make them even more debilitating when they strike, when it matters most? How will a machine accustomed to relying on the receipt of facts in hosts react when deprived of them? How will information junkies behave when thrown into cold turkey – just when battle starts?

A fluid but hardened information and command system will not be easy to achieve. The aims must be to simplify the flood of data and direct it where needed, so avoiding the classical problem with satellite imagery, which is that one knows what to look for only after the start of a crisis. It will be hard to gain full access to data about known unknowns and impossible even to know what questions to ask about unknown unknowns. Nor can such systems work unless doctrine and training prepares people to use them. Still, one can reduce these new forms of uncertainty through old-fashioned means. One must start by putting intelligence in its place. It does not make or execute decisions, people do. More fundamental issues, such as their education, intuition, doctrine, character, courage, openness of mind, wisdom, attitudes toward risk, determine how information of all kinds is understood and applied. Moreover, knowledge is only as useful as the action it inspires. Decision makers should listen to intelligence, yet they must remember that intelligence cannot answer every question. They cannot wait for the last bit of information to be received and for data processing to make their decisions. They must know when to act without intelligence or knowledge – that is why they are leaders. Soldiers need to know well enough so that they can act well enough when they must, and to understand when that moment is, nothing more and nothing less.

The key questions are: what information is essential? When and how does one know that one has sufficient information to act upon? All shades of opinion recognise that C4ISR and DBK have magnified problems like information overload, micromanagement and the fruitless search for certainty. A range of solutions have been proposed, all related to changing the culture of command. Units must be able to operate in harmony without command, through some new version of 'marching to the sound of the guns' (what the revolutionaries term 'swarming'). Commanders must learn to act when they have a good enough picture of events – even when this picture is imperfect and new information is arriving – and to understand when they have achieved that condition. Sometimes this process is called 'to opticise'. Clausewitz termed a similar process the 'imperative principle'.[40] When combined, these means have power but they also have limits. They can solve many problems of command, perhaps most of them, but not all. C4ISR will be a function of a complex system manned by many people. It will suffer from all of the things natural to both humans and complex systems, including uncertainty, friction, unachieved intentions, unintended consequences, unexpected failures and unplanned successes.

Operation Iraqi Freedom provides the first serious test of these ideas. But using it as a case study is not straightforward. Care must be taken in extrapolating from this unbalanced war. At the time of writing, data on the role of intelligence in the conflict is limited, if indicative. To a rare degree, this operation was intelligence driven. US authorities aimed to apply their doctrine and concepts, to follow all best practices, and to harness these matters to command and control warfare (C2W). The success of C4ISR and IO was overwhelming at the operational level but mixed at the strategic–political ones. In other words, the system was better at action than calculation, at target acquisition than knowledge. Everything based on machines achieved unparalleled power, all things focused on humans were mediocre, with the exception of IO. Authorities got Iraqi politics wrong. They exaggerated their ability to topple Saddam Hussein's regime through subversion, they overestimated its possession of weapons of mass destruction, and they misjudged the difficulties of post-conflict occupation. These failures stemmed from policy makers, but such errors are a fact of life. C4ISR has changed neither net assessment nor the politicisation of intelligence. Coalition intelligence worked better in military spheres, if less so on the more difficult issue of quality as

opposed to quantity. Its picture of the enemy order of battle and tactical characteristics was good. It appreciated fairly well the strength needed to destroy its
foe, though it overrated the enemy's quality. In technical terms these may have
been major errors. Yet such mistakes are probably unavoidable and, in this case,
they were of minor practical import. The Coalition could hardly have attacked
with fewer forces than it did, or any earlier than it did. Even seasoned analysts
had grounds for uncertainty about Iraqi capabilities, and thought it safer to
believe some units were mediocre instead of all being bad. Nonetheless, the First
Marine Division noted,

> we remained largely ignorant of the intentions of enemy commanders...
> This shortcoming was especially critical as much of the war plan was either
> based on or keyed to specific enemy responses. When the enemy 'failed' to
> act in accordance with common military practice, we were caught flat-footed
> because we failed to accurately anticipate the unconventional response. This
> was primarily due to a dearth of HUMINT on the enemy leadership. In trying
> to map out the opposition's reactions we were largely relegated to our
> OSINT sources and rank speculation based on our own perceptions of the
> battlefield to make our assessments...Our technical dominance has made us
> overly reliant on technical and quantifiable intelligence collection means.
> There is institutional failure to account for the most critical dimension of the
> battlefield, the human one.[41]

C4ISR multiplied some forms of power more than others. At theatre level,
reachback worked, national agencies distributed intelligence well, and a near-NCW
system existed (all of which is common at this level). The theatre commander,
General Franks, noted generals had 'much more precise technology-based
information' than ever before.[42] This multiplied the ability to direct centralised
firepower, and for aircraft to learn of targets of opportunity and to conduct inter-
diction. Airpower was directed with unprecedented speed, power, precision and
reach. It mattered more to ground warfare than ever before, perhaps as much as
did ground forces. Web-based air tasking orders let officers change missions at
will. Fleeting chances which once would have been lost in the shuffle led to
precise strikes.

Little, however, seems to have changed below the corps level in land warfare.
The Marine Division faced every standard problem of bottlenecks and overload
in information, and the failure of every technique touted to manage them. It often
'found the enemy by running into them, much as forces have done since the
beginning of warfare'.[43] Failings in distribution at the national and theatre level,
along with Frank's praiseworthy efforts to avoid over-centralisation of command,
meant that regimental and divisional commanders often took the key actions on
the ground without access to intelligence. Frank was cautious in sending orders
or information to his subordinates, leaving them the initiative, at the price of often
dividing intelligence from operations.

IO, meanwhile, was conducted with more skill and energy than the US military has shown for decades. Deception aimed to pin the Iraqi forces in Kurdistan, by drawing attention to the possibility of a Turkish front, and then to indications the war could not start until the Fourth Division was redeployed to Kuwait. This campaign was creative, though its effect is hard to determine. IO attempts to mobilise civilians in Iraq miscarried, but the Coalition had more success with a 'fused' attack on enemy epistemology. This approach involved the destruction of command and communication targets, and more. The air attacks on Saddam, and the claims they rested on reports from agents in Baghdad, were publicised, to shock his subordinates. His trust in his officers, and their mutual confidence, was sapped by announcements that the Americans were subverting Iraqi officers, and systematically contacting via e-mail those with access to computers. This effort, combining psyops, deception and a human form of cyberwar, manipulated the characteristics of a Stalinist regime and a paranoid political culture, with effect.

Operation Iraqi Freedom demonstrates a new standard for conventional war. How far this success can be repeated is unsure – NCW, C4ISR and IO worked less well in Kosovo. So one-sided was this war that intelligence served primarily for target acquisition rather than ONA. If ONA was practised, it failed, raising questions about the validity of 'Rapid Decisive Operations' as a workable concept. C4ISR, IO and NCW worked as planned because Coalition forces had the initiative and followed their plan, while the enemy was passive, overwhelmed, unable to strike Coalition forces or C4ISR. Had the Iraqis jammed communications, they would have broken most of the Coalition's enhanced power in intelligence and precision of attack or its command. Could this near-NCW system work in complex operations against an able and aggressive enemy? In Afghanistan and Iraq, after all, precise strikes often have failed, showing they work only when the machine performs without friction. Any friction yields failure and no system can always be perfect. An enemy which fights by its own rules, such as light infantry willing to die or to steal away in silence, has caught US forces at a disadvantage. What straws can be pulled from this wind?

NCW or C4ISR will not revolutionise events on the strategic level of war, or the strategic–diplomatic dimensions of peace, which are dominated by human rather than technological matters. Often they will affect these areas in counter-productive ways, by increasing confusion in and between levels of command for example. The US Navy's 'Global 2000' war games tested the application of NCW. It found both the power of C3I and its classic problems multiplied. With every member of the net able to post and edit notes, information overload paralysed command. Officers had so much data that they could make little use of any of it. Bad coin drove out good. One witness questioned the validity of 'visions of a command-and-control structure akin to the civilian internet... that the natural creativity, spontaneity, and adaptability of war fighters can be unleashed by freedom from constraint analogous to that of the civilian Internet in commercial settings'.[44] Experience in the Kosovo campaign led Air Commodore Stuart Peach to sombre conclusions. He observed that 'the drive to streamline procedures and handle ever more data has had an important side effect; airmen have become driven by process not strategy'. Hence, 'in reality, theory, doctrine and practice collide with process. Airmen claim one thing (centralized command and decentralized execution) and in fact practice another (centralized command and centralized execution).' The result was that 'refining the process of airspace control orders, air tasking orders and air task messages became the performance criteria, rather than creative and bold operational ideas or campaign plans'.[45]

According to one USAF officer, during this campaign the Supreme Allied Commander Europe, 'had in his office a terminal that allowed him to view what Predator unmanned aerial vehicles in the air were seeing'. Once, when Wesley Clark viewed three vehicles he thought tanks, 'he picked up a telephone, called the joint forces air component commander, and directed that those tanks be destroyed. With a single call, based on incomplete information, all the levels of war, from strategic to tactical, had been short-circuited.'[46] Similarly, during March 2002 in Afghanistan, officers in superior headquarters at home and abroad bombarded commanders with questions and advice based on live pictures transmitted from Predators in flight.[47] A case of friendly fire in that month showed that information overload, friction between layers of command and inexperienced personnel, had swamped the USAF's premier operational command, in western Asia. So much information was available that USAF squadrons could not circulate much material in ATOs to their pilots, while staff officers would not change their procedures, ensuring confusion between all layers of command.[48] The system processed and circulated far more information faster than ever before, but in this high tempo environment, the need to spend just 30 seconds in retrieving data could produce tragedy. It is so fast moving, fragile and complex that system errors are inevitable even without an enemy; the only questions are how often, at what cost, and crucially, how much an enemy will multiply them.

C4ISR and NCW sometimes will revolutionise tactics and operations where, all too often, friction at the systematic level has reduced the value of intelligence. The problem has always been that one actor has had information another might have used but did not receive in time to act, or that knowledge available in time could not be used with effect; failures by any one cog prevent the whole machine from working well, or at all. In conventional war, NCW and C4ISR may ensure that every cog of the machine works well at the same time, reducing friction to the lowest level possible. All national intelligence assets will focus on giving every unit every chance to exploit every fleeting opportunity; one's forces will be used for asking for or receiving such information and using it instantly, and well. In 1917, British signals intelligence constantly located U-Boats, prompting immediate air or surface strikes, which failed because units were slow and their ordnance weak. By 1943, intelligence on U-Boats was little better but allied forces far more able to kill. In 1944–45, allied air forces, using the cab rank system, could strike any target reported immediately, if not accurately; in the 2003 Iraq war, aircraft launched instant, precise and devastating strikes based on information acquired ten minutes earlier by headquarters 10,000 miles away. C4ISR and NCW will raise the bar on the best use of intelligence, and the frequency of optimum uses, in conventional war. It will multiply any form of firepower relying on rapid, precise and long-distance strikes. Perhaps this system would fail against a serious enemy or a real war, but for whom is this a concern? The point is not just one of transformation, or the quality of forces, but also one of quantity, or one's power relative to one's enemy. When Americans draw lessons from Iraq, they can apply them to a special case of conventional conflict pitting a giant against a dwarf. Other states must think of war as a whole.

Little will change where equals engage, or the weaker side evades one's strength or strikes one's C4ISR, or against guerrillas. If NCW fails in any instance on which it is relied, disaster will be redoubled because of that reliance. And fail NCW ultimately must, in part and in whole. If successful, it will force one's adversaries to find solutions by evading its strength and exploiting its weaknesses. NCW will always be convenient when one's enemy chooses to be foolish or weak (or foolish *and* weak). But not all enemies will make such poor choices and it would be foolish to assume that they will. A smart but weak foe may refuse any game where you can apply your strengths, and play instead by his own rules. Terrorism is an obvious case in point. A tough and able foe might turn the tables by attacking any precondition for NCW and then by imposing a different set of rules. The Revolution in Military Affairs has changed many things, but not everything. It has multiplied American strengths but not reduced American weaknesses. It has increased the value of high technology and firepower in conventional war but the basic nature of war is otherwise unchanged. As a result, where these things have always mattered, they now matter more than ever. But where they have not, nothing has changed. Iraq shows that the United States will aim to practice intelligence, command and war at a higher level than ever achieved before. When it can play to its strengths, it will succeed.

Notes

I am indebted to Michael Handel for discussions on these topics.

1 'Joint Vision 2010' and 'Joint Vision 2020', www.dtic.mil/doctrine.
2 Marine Corps Combat Development Command, Draft 'Information Operations', 25 September 2001, USMC, Doctrine Division Home Page; FM 100-6, 27 August 1996, 'Information Operations', www.adtdl.army.milcgi-bin/adtl.dll; FM 3-0, Operations, 14 June 2001, 5.75, 6.38, 11–47.
3 David Alperts, 'The Future of Command and Control with DBK', in Martin C. Libicki and Stuart E. Johnson (eds), *Dominant Battlespace Knowledge* (Washington, DC: NDU Press, 1995).
4 General Ronald Fogleman, speeches, 25 April 1995, 'Information Operations: The Fifth Dimension of Warfare', *Defense Issues*, 10, 47, www.defenselink.mil/speeches/1995 and 'Fundamentals of Information Warfare – An Airman's View', 16 May 1995, www.af.mil/news/speech/current.
5 George Stein, 'Information Warfare', *Airpower Journal* (Spring 1995), Richard Szafranski, 'A Theory of Information Warfare, Preparing for 2020', *Airpower Journal* (Spring 1995), emphasis in original.
6 Joint Pub 3-13.1, *Joint Doctrine for Command and Control Warfare (C2W)*, Joint Chiefs of Staff, 7 February 1996.

7 Department of Defense, *Transformation Planning Guidance*, April 2003, APP 4, 'Joint Concept Guidance, www.oft.osd.mil/; US Joint Forces Command, *A Concept for Rapid Decisive Operations, RDO Whitepaper*, J9 Joint Futures Lab, 2.3, 4.1, 4.3.1.3.

8 Colonel John A. Warden III, 'Air Theory for the Twenty-first Century', *Aerospace Power Chronicles, 'Battlefield of the Future': 21st Century Warfare Issues* (1995).

9 Williamson Murray, 'Transformation: Volume II', in Williamson Murray (ed.), *Transformation Concepts for National Security in the 21st Century* (Carlisle, PA: Strategic Studies Institute, 2002). pp. 10–17. The US Army War College, September 2002; an untitled briefing paper by Michael Handel, copy in my possession, c. 2000. These papers offer fundamental critiques of assumptions about intelligence in the RMA; cf. John Ferris, 'The Biggest Force Multiplier? Knowledge, Information and Warfare in the 21st Century', in Wing Commander Alistair Dally and Ms Rosalind Bourke (eds), *Conflict, The State and Aerospace Power: The Proceedings of a Conference Held in Canberra by the Royal Australian Air Force, 28–29 May 2002* (Canberra: Aerospace Centre, 2003), pp. 149–65.

10 Cf. n. 2, 6 and 30.

11 Defense Writers' Group, 22 January 2003, interview with General Richard Myers.

12 Arthur Cebrowski, speech to the Heritage Foundation, 13 May 2003.

13 Arthur Cebrowski, 17 June 2003, 'The Path not taken . . . Yet', www.oft.osd.mil/.

14 Briefing Paper by Joe Mazzafro (2002), 'Operation Enduring Freedom, Intelligence Lessons Learned, An Unofficial Quick Look', JWAD Mini-Symposium, 7 May 2002, www.maxwell.af.mil/au/awc/awcgate/awc-lesn Jim Garamone, 'Myers says Joint Capabilities, Transformation Key to 21st Century War', American Forces Information Service, 5 February 2002, www.defenselink.mil/news/Feb2002/n020520002_200202054.

15 'Preface', '2025 In-Time Information Integrations System (I3S)', 'The Man in the Chair: Cornerstone of Global Battlespace Dominance', 'Wisdom Warfare for 2025', *Air Force 2025*, 1996, www.au.af.mil/au; Thomas K. Adams, 'Future Warfare and the Decline of Human Decisionmaking', *Parameters* (Winter 2001–02).

16 *Vector 21, Defense Intelligence Agency Strategic Plan, 1999–2000*; www.loyola.edu/dept/politics/milintel; NCS-21 (*National Cryptological Strategy for the 21st Century*), www.nsa.goc/programs/ncs21/index.; Director of Central Intelligence, *The 2002 Annual Report of the United States Intelligence Community*, 1.03, www.cia.gov/cia/publications/Ann_Rpt_2002/index.; 'Statement for the Record by Lieutenant General Michael V. Hayden, USAF, Director, National Security Agency/Chief, Central Security Service, Before the Joint Inquiry of the Senate Select Committee on Intelligence and the House Permanent Select Committee on Intelligence, 17 October 2002', www.nsa.gov/releases/speeches, emphasis in original.

17 Dan Caterinicchia, 'NIMA, NSA increasing collaboration', *Federal Computer Weekly*, 30 January 2003.

18 Dawn S. Onley, 'Success in Iraq due to Better Info Sharing, Tenet Says', *Government Computer News*, 11 June 2003.

19 *Vector 21, Defense Intelligence Agency Strategic Plan, 1999–2000*; Frederick Thomas Martin, *Top Secret Intranet: How US Intelligence Built Intelink, the World's Largest, Most Secure Network* (New York: Prentice Hall, 1998); speech by A. Denis Clift, President, Joint Military Intelligence College, at Yale University, 27 April 2002, 'From Semaphore to Predator, Intelligence in the Internet Era', www.DIA.MIL/Public/Testimonies/statement06; 'Joint Intelligence Virtual Architecture JIVA', www.fas.org/irp/program/core/jiva.

20 Dawn S. Onley, 'Intelligence Analysts Strive to Share Data', *Government Computer News*, 28 May 2003.

21 ADCI/AP 2000–01, 'Strategic Investment Plan for Intelligence Community Analysis', www.cia.gov/cia/publications/pub.

22 Lt. Gen. Robert W. Noonan, Jr, and Lt. Col. Brad T. Andrew, Retired, 'Army Intelligence Provides the Knowledge Edge', *Army Magazine* (April 2002).

23 Bruce Berkowitz, 'The DI and "IT", Failing to Keep Up With the Information Revolution', *Studies in Intelligence*, 47/1, (2003), www.cia.gov/csi/studies/vol47/no1/article07.

24 Wilson P. Dizzard III, 'White Houses Promotes Data Sharing', *Government Computer News*, 28 June 2002 and Onley, 'Intelligence Analysts Strive to Share Data'.

25 *External Team Report, A Management Review for the Director, NSA*, 11 October 1999; *New Enterprise Team (NETeam) Recommendations, The Director's Work Plan for Change*, 1 October 1999, www.nsa.gov/releases/reports.html.

26 Richard Lardner, 'Leadership streamlined, chief of staff created, NSA Chief Pushes Ahead with Overhaul of Agency's Culture, Operations', inside *Defence Special Report*, 16 October 2000.

27 Charles L. Munns, 'Another View: Navy's Network Services Buy Pays Off', *Government Computer News*, 3 July 2003.

28 Office of the Inspector General, The Department of Justice, 'A Review of the FBI's Performance in Deterring, Detecting, and Investigating the Espionage Activities of Robert Philip Hanssen', 14 August 2003, www.usdoj.gov/oig/special/03-08/index.

29 Director of Central Intelligence, '2002 Annual Report'; William Jackson, 'Cyberdrill Carries Over to Real War', *Government Computer News*, 19 May 2003.

30 'Background Briefing on Enemy Denial and Deception', 24 October 2001, www.defenselink.mil/news/Oct2001/t10242001_t1024dd.ht.

31 Joint Chiefs of Staff, Joint Pub 3-58, *Joint Doctrine for Military Deception*, 31 May 1996 (under revision as of time of writing, June 2003); Joint Pub 3-54, *Joint Doctrine for Operations Security*, 24 February 1997; Joint Pub 3-13, Joint Doctrine for Information Operations, JCS, 9 October 1998; Joint Publication 2-01.3, 24 May 2000, Joint Tactics, Techniques, and Procedures for Joint Intelligence Preparation of the Battlespace.

32 John Ferris, 'The Roots of FORTITUDE: The Evolution of British Deception in the Second World War', in T.G. Mahnken (ed.), *The Paradox of Intelligence: Essays in Honour of Michael Handel* (London: Frank Cass, 2003).

33 Center for Army Lessons Learned (CALL) 2 October 2000, Information Operations Franchise, Research Project Proposals 4, 5.9, 10 and 12, www.call.army.mil/io/research.

34 CALL, 'The Information Operations Process'; 'Tactics, Techniques and Procedures for Information Operations (IO). Information Operations, Observations, TTP, and Lessons Learned. www.call.army.mil/io/ll.

35 Research Topics proposed by INNS, 25 July 2000, 'Information Operations (IO) 5.16', Computer Network Warfare, 'Information Operations (IO) 5.23, and 5.29; and Air Force Materiel Command, 8.28.01, 'Effects Based Information Operations', www.research.maxwell.af.mil/js_Database; Colonel Carla D. Bass, 'Building Castles on Sand, Underestimating the Tide of Information Operations, *Aerospace Power Journal* (Summer 1999).

36 'CCRP Initiatives', Office of the Assistant Secretary of Defense Command, Control, Communications and Intelligence, 26 September 2001, www.dodccrp.org.

37 Dan Caternicchia (2003), 'DOD forms cyberattack task force', *Federal Computer Weekly*, 10 February 2003.

38 Research Topics proposed by INNS, 25 July 2000, IO 5.48 and IO 5.24.

39 J.R. Ferris and Michael Handel (1995), 'Clausewitz, Intelligence, Uncertainty and the Art of Command in Modern War', *Intelligence and National Security*, 10, 1 (January 1995), pp. 1–58.

40 Ibid.

41 'Operation Iraqi Freedom, 1st Marine Division, Lessons Learned, 28 May 2003'; accessible from the website of the *Urban Operations Journal*, Operation Iraq Freedom, AARs, Observations, Analyses and Comments.

42 Joseph L. Galloway, 'General Tommy Franks Discusses Conducting the War in Iraq', 19 June 2003, Knight Ridder Washington Bureau, www.realcities.com/mld/krwashington/6124738.h.

43 'Operation Iraqi Freedom, 1st Marine Division, Lessons Learned, 28 May 2003'; ibid.

44 Kenneth Watman, 'Global 2000', *NWCR* (Spring 2000). For a more optimistic reading of this exercise, and others, cf. Network Centric Warfare, Department of Defense Report to Congress, 27.7.01, pp. E-24, www.c3i.osd.mil/NCW/.

45 Air Commodore Stuart Peach, 'The Airmen's Dilemma: To Command or Control', in Peter Gray (ed.), *Air Power 21: Challenges for the New Century* (London: Ministry of Defence, 2001), pp. 123–4, 141. A US Army observer, Timothy L. Thomas, offered similar views in 'Kosovo and the Current Myth of Information Superiority', *Parameters* (Spring 2000).

46 Major William A. Woodcock, 'The Joint Forces' Air Command Problem – Is Network-centric Warfare the Answer?', *Naval War College Review* (Winter 2003), p. 46; the words are Woodcock's, but his source is Michael Short, the Joint Air Force commander in Kosovo.

47 Anthony H. Cordesman, *The Lessons of Afghanistan, Warfighting, Intelligence, Force Transformation, Counterproliferation, and Arms Control* (Washington, DC: Center for Strategic and International Studies, 2002), pp. 63–4.

48 Verbatim Testimony of Colonel David C. Nichols and Colonel Laurence A. Stutzreim, Tarnack Farms Enquiry. 1.03, www.barksdale.af.mil/tarnackfarms/rosenow.

5   Some Concepts that may be Useful in Understanding the Myriad Forms and Contexts of Surveillance

Gary T. Marx

We are at any moment those who separate the connected or connect the separate.

G. Simmel

'You ought to have some papers to show who you are.' The police officer advised me.
'I do not need any paper. I know who I am,' I said.
'Maybe so. Other people are also interested in knowing who you are.'

B. Traven, The Death Ship

In *Strategic Interaction* Erving Goffman (1972) demonstrated how the activities of intelligence agencies could be related to other social settings of information control. Whether the setting is one of electronic transmissions, smoke signals or facial expressions, seekers of intelligence must attend to the possibility that their rivals are engaged in impression management. Goffman suggests concepts applicable across a variety of settings, although his primary concern was with the face-to-face interaction which occurs when individuals are in each other's immediate presence.

Recent developments in surveillance and communication give the study of remote interaction increased salience as well. There is need for concepts that also include the distance-mediated forms of observation and interaction associated with new technological forms. Concepts are also required that can characterise not only the interaction of individuals and organisations, but that between organisations as with industrial espionage and between individuals as with voyeurism and exhibitionism.

As part of a broad enquiry growing out of an initial study of undercover police practices, I seek to surface the variables that help shape surveillance practices and our evaluation of them, regardless of their specifics. I cast a wide net that includes political, economic and personal contexts. Traditional government political intelligence gathering can be compared to other forms. Governments are hardly the only players in seeking secrets and information of low visibility. Intelligence gathering can be viewed as a general process that crosses a variety of social settings whether involving national security, business intelligence, commerce or families. The behaviour of government actors, or any specific historical instance, can be located within a more inclusive analytical framework.

I seek an empirical, analytic and moral ecology (or geography or mapping) of surveillance.[1] Of particular interest are data which are involuntarily collected and recorded from individuals, whether through intrusive and invasive methods – prying out what is normally withheld, or using technology to give meaning to what the individual offers (for example, appearance, emissions unrecognised by the unaided senses, or behaviour which traditionally was ignored and unrecorded). As noted by Foucault[2] and some more myopic ideological fellow-travelers, this often involves power and goal differences between the watcher and the watched, but it can go far beyond these to also include shared goals and co-operative and reciprocal forms of surveillance.

We can identify at least five broad aspects of surveillance systems. The first involves the *structures of the setting* in which the surveillance is used.[3] The second involves the *characteristics of the means* applied. A third set of factors involves the *content* or the *kind of data* gathered. A fourth involves the *application of the means* including the collection of data and its subsequent treatment.[4] This encompasses traditional data protection principles. A final factor involves the goals sought.[5]

Such classifications identify variation and permit systematic comparisons. They are an initial step in setting research agendas and in explanation, evaluation and the creation of policies sensitive to the richness of the empirical world. In this paper I discuss the second and third items – dimensions of surveillance techniques and of the kinds of personal information they may gather. All five classification systems are treated at greater length in a future work.[6]

What is surveillance?

The dictionary definition of surveillance as it is applied to many contemporary new forms such as video, computer dossiers, electronic location and work monitoring, drug testing and DNA analysis is woefully inadequate or worse.[7] For example in the *Concise Oxford Dictionary* surveillance is defined as 'close observation, especially of a suspected person'. Yet today many of the new surveillance technologies are not 'especially' applied to 'a suspected person'. They are commonly applied *categorically*. In broadening the range of subjects the term 'a suspected person' takes on a different meaning. In a striking innovation, surveillance is also applied to contexts (geographical places and spaces, particular time periods, networks, systems and categories of person), not just to a particular person whose identity is known beforehand.

The dictionary definition also implies a clear distinction between the object of surveillance and the person carrying it out and a non-co-operative relationship. In an age of servants listening behind closed doors, binoculars and telegraph interceptions, that separation made sense. It was easy to distinguish the watcher from the person watched. Yet self-surveillance, co-surveillance and reciprocal surveillance have emerged as important themes, often blurring the easy distinction between agent and subject of surveillance.

Well-publicised warnings that surveillance might be present seek to create self-restraint. A general ethos of self-surveillance is also encouraged by the availability of home products such as those that test for alcohol level, pregnancy, AIDS and other medical conditions.

Nor does the traditional definition capture contemporary cases of 'co-operative' parallel or co-monitoring, involving the subject and an external agent in which the former voluntarily sends a remote message (as with location and some implanted physiological monitoring devices). Individuals may agree to wear badges and have transmitters for toll roads or as anti-theft means installed on their cars. They may join programmes that invite police to search their vehicles if driven late at night. Many bio-metric forms involve some degree of co-operation, or at the least, implicit co-operation by the failure to take steps to block transmission.

The border between the watched and the watcher may also be blurred in that there can be a continuous transmission link between sender and receiver as with brain waves or scents. The sender and receiver are in one sense electronically joined. It may be difficult to say where the subject stops and the agent begins. As with questions of copyright and electronic media, new issues of the ownership and control of property appear. Such transmissions are 'personal' but leave the person's body and control. The line between what is public and private is hazy in such settings.

The term 'close observation' also fails to capture contemporary practices. Surveillance may be carried out from afar, as with satellite images or the remote monitoring of communications and work. Nor need it be 'close' as in detailed – much initial surveillance involves superficial scans looking for patterns of interest to be pursued later in greater detail. It is both farther away and closer than the conventional definition implies.

The dated nature of the definition is further illustrated in its seeming restriction to visual means as implied in 'observation'. The eyes do contain the vast majority of the body's sense receptors and the visual is a master metaphor for the other senses (for example, saying 'I see' for understanding or being able to 'see through people'). Indeed, 'seeing through' is a convenient short-hand for the new surveillance.

To be sure the visual is usually an element of surveillance, even when it is not the primary means of data collection (for example, written accounts of observations, events and conversations, or the conversion to text or images of measurements from heat, sound or movement). Yet to 'observe' a text or a printout is in many ways different from a detective or supervisor directly observing behaviour. The eye as the major means of direct surveillance is increasingly joined or replaced by hearing, touching and smelling. The use of multiple senses and sources of data is an important characteristic of much of the new surveillance.

A better definition of contemporary forms of surveillance is needed. The new forms of surveillance involve, *scrutiny through the use of technical means to extract or create personal data, whether from individuals or contexts.* The data sought may or may not be known by the subject, who may be willing or unwilling to have it discovered or revealed. It may involve revealed information for which verification is sought.

The use of 'technical means' to extract and create the information implies the ability to go beyond what is offered to the unaided senses or voluntarily reported. Many of the examples involve an automated process and most extend the senses by using material artifacts or software of some kind, but the means for rooting out can also be sophisticated forms of deception as with undercover operations, ruses and pretexts. The use of 'contexts' along with 'individuals' recognises that much modern surveillance also looks at settings and patterns of relationships. Systems as well as persons are of interest.

This definition excludes the routine, non-technological surveillance that is a part of everyday life such as looking before crossing the street or seeking the source of a sudden noise or of smoke. An observer on a nude beach or police interrogating a co-operative suspect would also be excluded, because in these cases the information is volunteered and the unaided senses are sufficient.

I use the more neutral and broader verb 'scrutinise' rather than 'observe' (with its tilt toward the visual) in the definition because the nature of the means (or the senses involved) suggests sub-types and issues for analysis that ought not to be foreclosed by a definition. For example how do visual, auditory, text and other forms of surveillance compare with respect to factors such as intrusiveness or validity? In addition much surveillance is automated and hence 'observation' (if that is what it is by a machine, is of a different sort).

While the above definition captures some common elements among new sur-veillance means, contemporary tactics are enormously varied.[8] There is need for a conceptual language that brings some parsimony and unity to the vast array of old and new surveillance activities and which can permit more systematic com-parisons and explanations. The next section suggests dimensions that can be used to categorise the means aspect of surveillance.

Dimensions of surveillance means

The dimensions in Tables 5.1 and 5.2 focus on the means themselves as classified by the observer. They draw from the characteristics of the technology and the data collection process (including the ways it must, or can be applied). They offer a way of classifying and contrasting surveillance. Table 5.1 highlights differences between the new and traditional surveillance means. Table 5.2 suggests criteria that are relevant to surveillance, but which I am hesitant to see as being more characteristic of either the new or traditional forms. These are useful for comparing types of surveillance apart from the issue of change.

For simplicity these are arranged in a series of discrete possibilities (for example, gathered by a human or a machine, visible or invisible). But there may be continuous gradations between the values at either end of the continua (for

Table 5.1: Surveillance dimensions.

Dimension	Traditional Surveillance	New Surveillance
senses	unaided senses	extends senses
visibility	visible (the actual collection, who does it, where, on whose behalf)	less or invisible
consent	lower proportion involuntary	higher proportion involuntary
cost	lower cost per unit of data	higher cost per unit of data
location of data collectors/analysers	on scene	remote
ethos	harder (more coercive)	softer (less coercive)
integration	data collection as separate	data collection activity folded into routine activity
data collector	human, animal	machine (wholly or partly automated)
data resides	with the collector, stays local	with third parties, often migrates
timing	single point or intermittent	continuous (omnipresent)
time period	present	past, present, future
data availability	frequent time lags	real time availability
availability of technology	disproportionately available to elites	more democratised, some forms widely available
object of data collection	individual	individual, categories
comprehensiveness	single measure	multiple measures
context	contextual	acontextual
depth	less intensive	more intensive
breadth	less extensive	more extensive
ratio of self to surveillant knowledge	higher (what the surveillant knows the subject probably knows as well)	lower (surveillant knows things subject does not)
identifiability of object surveillance	emphasis on known individuals	emphasis also on anonymous individual, masses
emphasis on	individuals	individual, networks, systems
realism	direct representation	direct and simulation
form	single media (often narrative or numerical)	multiple media (often audio)
who collects data	specialists	specialists, role dispersal, self-monitoring
data analysis	more difficult to organise, store, retrieve, analyse	easier to organise, store, retrieve, analyse
data merging	discrete non-combinable data (whether because of different format or location)	easy to combine visual, auditory, text, num. data
data communication	more difficult to send, receive	easier to send, receive

example, between visible and invisible). Some dimensions involve mutually exclusive values (for example, single *vs.* multiple measures), but many do not. In some cases classification reflects an inherent property of the technology (for example, infra-red and sound transmission devices go beyond the unaided senses). In other cases where a means is classified depends on how it is used.

Table 5.2: No clear historical surveillance trend.

	Traditional Surveillance	New Surveillance
resistance	easy to neutralise	difficult to neutralise
specificity	laser-like focus on specific person or attribute	sponge-like abosrbency, non-differentiated
invasiveness	less invasive	more invasive
reliability and validity	lower	higher
honesty	deceptive	non-deceptive
knowledge that tactic is used	more likely to be known	less likely to be known
specific knowledge regarding where/when used	more likely to be known	less likely to be known

A technology may seem to lend itself well to a value (for example, a video lens can be easily used covertly relative to traditional 35 mm cameras), but a policy announcing that a video camera is in use or a camera that is easily identifiable would lead to it being classified as visible.

Traditional surveillance tends to be characterised by the left-hand side of Table 5.1. This has been supplemented by the new forms which tend to fall on the right-hand side of the table. Of course there is no bright time-line separating the new from the traditional forms of surveillance. There was, of course, even tapping of telegraph lines during the Civil War. But in broad outline the new surveillance became more prominent during the Second World War (for example, signals intelligence) and rapidly expanded with the increased computerisation of recent decades. What is striking is how much rarified forms of surveillance once episodic and restricted to the military or police have become commonplace across social institutions and settings.

The values on the right-hand side of Table 5.1 do not cleanly and fully characterise every contemporary surveillance tactic that has appeared since the development of the microchip and advances in microbiology, artificial intelligence, electronics, communications and geographic information systems. Nor do the values on the left-hand side perfectly apply to every instance of the old surveillance prior to this. Social life is much too messy for that. There is some crossing over of values (for example, informers, a traditional form, have low visibility, drug testing, a new form, is discontinuous). These are, after all, ideal types whose virtue of breadth often comes with the vice of combining elements that show significant variation at a less abstract level. The dimensions can also be combined to yield sub-types. But if the categories are useful in analysing big variation (or more useful than the descriptive ad hoc naming we presently have), they will have done their job.

The new surveillance relative to traditional surveillance extends the senses and has low visibility, or is invisible. It is more likely to be involuntary. Data collection is often integrated into routine activity. Manipulation as against direct coercion has become more prominent. Data collection is more likely to be automated involving machines rather than (or in addition to) involving humans. It is relatively inexpensive per unit of data collected. Data collection is often gathered through remote means, rather than directly on the scene. The data often resides with third parties. Data is available in real time and data collection can be continuous and offer information on the past, present and future (such as statistical predictions). The subject of data collection goes beyond the individual suspect to categories of interest. The individual as a subject of data collection may also become the object of an intervention. There may be only a short interval between the discovery of the information and the taking of action.

The new surveillance is more comprehensive often involving multiple measures. But since it is often mediated by physical and social distance (being more likely to be acontextual) it is not necessarily more valid. It is more intensive and extensive. The ratio of what the individual knows about him or herself relative to what the surveilling person knows is lower than in the past, even if objectively much more is known. That is, experts, often using sophisticated data collection and analysis means, 'know' things about a person, often of a predictive nature, which the individual does not know. Consider for example various risk profiles involving health, insurance, credit and employment.

Relative to the past, the anonymous individual, a mass or an aggregate have become more prominent as objects of surveillance. The emphasis is expanded beyond the individual to systems and networks. The data often go beyond direct representation to simulation and from narrative or numerical form, to also include video and audio records. The monitoring of specialists is often accompanied (or even replaced) by self-monitoring. It is easy to combine visual, auditory, text and numerical data and to send and receive them. It is relatively easier to organise, store, retrieve and analyse data. Traditional surveillance is the reverse of the above.

Table 5.2 lists factors which appear not to have changed significantly over the last century, such as the extent of deception and the ease or difficulty of neutralising a technique. It also lists factors where the case for a change might be made, but so might its opposite. For example the new surveillance is in some ways more, and in other ways less, invasive. To reach an overall conclusion it is necessary to have agreement on how these general concepts will be operationalised. While the greater invasiveness of many tactics is obvious, one trend is toward less invasive techniques (for example, drug testing from a strand of hair, rather than from a urine sample or X-ray or thermal rather than literal searches, machines seeking matches rather than a human reviewer).

Types of personal information

Beyond the means aspects involving the *way* surveillance is carried out, there is the question of the kinds of data gathered. With respect to content, what are the major kinds of information that can be known about a person and how is the seeking and taking of this evaluated by the culture? There is no easy answer to the question 'What is personal information?', or to how it connects to perceived assaults on our sense of dignity, respect for the individual, privacy and intimacy.

This is very much context dependent. However, even giving due consideration to the contextual basis of meaning and avoiding the shoals of relativism as well as reification, it is possible to talk of information as being more or less personal. There is a cultural patterning to behaviours and judgements about kinds of personal information.[9]

Surveillance involving information that is at the core of the individual and more 'personal' is likely to be seen as more damaging than that involving more superficial matters.[10] But what is that core and what radiates from it? What other attributes effect attitudes here? The concentric circles in Table 5.3 show information that is individual, personal and private, and intimate and sensitive with a unique core identity at the centre.

Table 5.3: Some types of descriptive information connectable to individuals.

1   Individual identification (*the 'who' question*)
      Ancestry
      Legal name
      Alpha-numeric
      Biometric (natural, environmental)
      Password
      Aliases, nicknames
      Performance

2   Shared identification (*the typification question*)
      Gender
      Race/ethnicity
      Age
      Education
      Occupation
      Employment
      Wealth
      DNA
      General physical characteristics (blood type, height)
      Organisational memberships
      Folk characterisations by reputation – liar, cheat, brave, strong, weak,
         addictive personality

3   Geographical/locational (*the 'where', and beyond geography, 'how to reach' question*)
      A   Fixed
            Residence
            Telephone number (landline)
            Mail address
            Cable TV
      B   Mobile
            e-Mail address
            Cell phone
            Vehicle and personal locators
            Wireless computing

4   Temporal (*the 'when' question*)
      Date and time of activity

Table 5.3: (Continued)

---

5   Networks and relationships (*the 'who else' question*)
    Family members, married or divorced
    Others the individual interacts/communicates with, roommates, friends, associates
    Others co-present (contiguous) at a given location or activity including neighbours

6   Objects (*the 'whose is it' question*)
    vehicles
    weapons
    animals
    contraband
    land, buildings and businesses

7   Behavioural (*the 'what happened' question*)
    Communication
        Fact of using a given means (computer, phone, cable TV, diary, notes or library)
            to create, send, or receive information (mail covers, subscription lists, pen reg-
            isters, e-mail headers, cell phone, GPS)
        Content of communication (eavesdropping, spyware, web page surveillance,
            library use, book purchases)
    Economic behavior – buying (including consumption patterns and preferences),
        selling, bank, credit card transactions
    Work monitoring
    Employment history
    Web browsing
    Norm and conflict related behaviour – bankruptcies, tax liens, small claims and civil
        judgements, criminal records, suits filed

8   Beliefs, attitudes, emotions (*the inner or backstage and presumed 'real' person
    question*)

9   Measurement characterizations (predictions, potentials+) (*the kind of person
    question, predict your future question*)
    credit ratings (and limits?)
    insurance ratings
    SAT and college acceptability scores
    Civil Service scores
    Drug tests
    Truth telling
    Psychological profiles, tests and so on
    Medical
    Occupational placement tests

10   Media references (yearbooks, newsletters, newspapers, TV, internet) (*the 15 minutes
    of fame question*)

Concentric circles of information

We can think of information about persons as involving concentric circles. The
outermost circle is that of *individual information* which includes any data/category
which can be attached to a person. The individual need not be personally known,
nor known by name and location by those attaching the data to the person. Nor
need the individual be aware of the data linked to their person.

Individual information varies from that which is relatively impersonal (being widely shared and available, with minimal implications for self-hood) such as being labelled as living in a flood zone or owning a four-door car, to that which is more personal such as illness, sexual preference, religious beliefs, facial image, address, legal name and ancestry. Such information has clearer implications for how individuals view themselves and may be of lower visibility and likely to more distinctly reflect the individual.

Individual information can be imposed onto the person by outsiders as with statistical risk categories, or taken directly from the person and recorded (for example, remote health sensors or a black box documenting driving behaviour).

The next circle refers to *personal* or *private information*. Absent special circumstances to compel disclosure as with social security number for tax purposes or a subpoena or warrant for a search, such information is defined by normative expectations offering the individual discretion about whether or not to reveal it. An unlisted telephone number or a credit card number, and non-obvious or non-visible biographical and biological details ('private parts') are examples.[11]

The next circle is that of *intimate* and/or *sensitive* information. Intimate comes from the Latin *intimus*, meaning inmost. Used as a verb the word intimate means to state or make known, implying that the information is not routinely known. Several forms can be noted.

Some 'very personal' attitudes, conditions and behaviours take their significance from the fact that they are a kind of currency of intimacy selectively revealed (if then), only to those we trust and feel close to. Such personal information is not usually willingly offered to outsiders, excluding the behaviour of exhibitionists and those seen to be lacking in manners. The point is not that the behaviour that might be observed is personal in the sense of necessarily being unique (for example, sexual relations), but that control over access affirms respect for the person and sustains the value of intimacy and the relationship. We can differentiate an intimate relationship from certain forms of information or behaviour which can be intimate independent of interaction with others.

In *Where Angels Fear to Tread*, E.M. Forster observes that we 'radiate something curiously intimate when we believe ourselves to be alone'. This suggests a related form – protection from intrusions into solitude or apartness. Whether alone or with trusted others, this implies a sense of security, of not being vulnerable, of being able to let one's guard down which may permit both feelings of safety and of being able to be 'one's self'.

A central theme of Erving Goffman's work is that the individual, in playing a role and in angling for advantage, presents a self to the outside world that may be at odds with what the individual actually feels, believes or 'is' in some objective sense. Through manners and laws, for most purposes, modern society acknowledges the legitimacy of there being a person behind the mask.

Consider also moments of vulnerability and embarrassment observable in public. For example, the expression of sadness in the face of tragedy – as with a mother who has just lost a child in a car accident. Here manners and decency require disavowing, looking the other way, not staring, let alone taking a news photograph of the individual's grief.

Another rationale for information control is sensitive not in revealing intimate moments, but in revealing information useful for an opponent in a conflict situation, or a stigma that would devalue the individual in other's eyes.

Two final circles at the centre involve a person with various identity pegs. These (whether considered jointly or individually) engender a *unique identity* ('only you' as the song implies) in being attached to what Goffman refers to as an 'embodied' individual who is usually assumed to be alive, but need no longer be. Knowing unique identity, answers the basic question raised by 'Sesame Street', 'Who is it?'.[12] It is from, and to, this identity that many other sources of potential information are derived or attached (radiating outward from as well as being added) to the person.

The elements that make up the individual's uniqueness are more personal than those that do not and as degree of distinctiveness increases so does the 'personalness' of the information. Yet general characteristics such as race or religion may also be seen as personal, particularly when they are not obvious (for example, are hidden, involve atypical appearance or distance mediated interaction). Context is also relevant. Thus to seek to know a person's religion as part of a census, or in order to sell them food or religious objects is different from seeking it to persecute, convert or approach them when they are in prayer.

Traditionally, unique identity tended to be synonymous with a *core identity* based on biological ancestry and family embedment. Excluding physically joined twins, each individual is unique in being the off-spring of particular biological parents, with birth at a particular place and time. Parents of course may be shared, as may time and place of birth. Yet the laws of physics and biology generate a unique *core identity* in the conjunction of these two factors.[13]

For most persons throughout most of history, discovering identity was not an issue. In small-scale societies, where there was little geographical or social mobility and people were rooted in very local networks of family and kin, individuals tended to be personally known. Physical and cultural appearance and location answered the 'Who is it?' question. Names may have offered additional information about the person's relationships, occupation, or residence for example, Josephson, Carpenter, Frankfurt. Names are still often presumed to be clues to ethnicity or national origin, and first names usually reflect gender.[14] Titles such as Mrs or Dr convey additional information.

However, the literal information offered by a name is of little use when the observer, neither personally knowing, nor knowing about the individual in question, needs to verify the link between the name offered and the person claiming it.

With large-scale societies and the increased mobility associated with urbanisation and industrialisation core identity came to be determined by full name and reliance on proxy forms such as a birth certificate, passport, national identity card and driver's license.[15]

Yet given adoption of children, the ease of legally changing or using fraudulent names in the United States, and the frequent sharing of common names, name is not necessarily an indication of unique ancestry. Nor given technologies for forgery and the theft of identification is the mere possession of identity documents sufficient for determining this.

The conventional paper forms of identification have been supplemented by forms more inherent in the physical person. With the expansion of biometric technology a variety of indicators presumed to be unique and harder to fake are increasingly used (for example, beyond improved fingerprinting, we see identification efforts based on DNA, voice, retina, iris, wrist veins, hand geometry, facial appearance, scent and even gait).

Even when validity is not an issue,[16] biological indicators are not automatic reflections of core identity, although they may offer advantages such as always being with the individual and never forgotten, lost or stolen. To be used for identification there must be a record of a previously identified person to which the indicator can be matched.

These need not lead to literal identification, but rather whether or not the material presumed to reflect a unique person is the same as that in a database to which it is compared that is, 'is this the same person?', *whomever* it is. Police files are filled with DNA and fingerprint data that are not connected to a core legal identity. With data from multiple events, because of matching, police may know that the same person is responsible for crimes but not know who the person is.

The question, 'who is it?' may be answered in a variety of other ways that need not trace back to a biologically defined ancestral core or legal name. For many contemporary settings what matters is continuity of identity (is this the *same* person) or being able to locate the individual, not who the person 'really' is as conventionally defined.

A central policy question is just how much and what kind of identity information is necessary in various contexts. In particular: (1) whether identification of a unique person is appropriate; and if it is, (2) what form it should take. Beyond ancestral, legal name and biometric forms of identity, other elements subject to surveillance include location, various forms of anonymity and pseudo-anonymity, composite identity and cultural patterns. Space limitations means that brief mention will be made only of location.

Location refers to a person's 'address'. It answers a 'where', more than a 'who' question. Address can be geographically fixed as with most residences and workplaces, landline phones and post office boxes. Or the address may be geographically mobile (if always located *somewhere*), as with a cell phone, implanted GPS chip or e-mail.

Two meanings of address are 'reachability' involving an electronic or other communications address or the actual geographical location in latitude and longitude. These may but need not be linked, nor do they require core identification. Recent developments in the rationalisation of postal addresses and the linking of census block data to GPS co-ordinates mean that the actual location of every address is now known to within a limited number of metres.

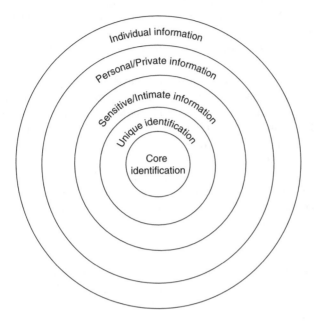

Figure 5.1: Types of information on the embodied.

Actual geographic location form is interesting in revealing where some one *is not*, as well as where they *are* or *were* at a given time, such information may help as well as hurt the individual.

The 'where' question need not be linked with the 'who' question. The ability to communicate (especially remotely) may not require knowing who it 'really' is, only that they be accessible and assessable. Knowing location permits taking various forms of action such as communicating, blocking, granting or denying access, penalising,[17] rewarding, delivering, picking up or apprehending.

Figure 5.1 offers a descriptive listing of ten kinds of personal information most commonly subject to surveillance. This includes:

1   Individual identification (the 'who' question).
2   Shared identification (the typification question).
3   Geographical/locational (the 'where', and beyond geography, 'how to reach' question).
4   Temporal (the 'when' question).
5   Networks and relationships (the 'who else' question).
6   Objects (the 'whose is it' question).
7   Behavioural (the 'what happened' question).
8   Beliefs, attitudes, emotions (the inner or backstage and presumed 'real' person question).

9　Measurement characterisations (the kind of person question, predict your future question).

10　Media references (yearbooks, newsletters, newspapers, TV, internet) (the 15 minutes of fame question).

Form

Beyond content another aspect involves the form in which information is collected and presented. These may initially be connected (for example, video lenses gather images). But they can be subsequently disconnected. Video[18] or audio recordings are likely to be most powerful and convincing if directly communicated the way they were recorded. However, their information can also be communicated in other ways – a written narrative of events or a transcript of conversations. Conversely observations and written accounts can be offered as visual images – as with a sketch of a suspect or a video reconstruction of a traffic accident for court presentation.

Many new surveillance forms are characterised by some form of conversion from data collection to presentation. Thus physical DNA material or olfactory molecules are converted to numerical indicators which are then represented visually and via a statistical probability. The amount of heat is shown in colour diagrams. The polygraph converts physical responses to images in the form of charts. Satellite images convert varying degrees of light to computer code which are then offered as photographs.

With respect to form, the visual and audio, in conveying information more naturalistically, are more invasive than a more abstract written narrative account or numerical and other representations relying on symbols.[19] The visual in turn is more invasive than the audio. The Chinese expression 'a picture is worth a thousand words' captures this, although it must be tempered with some scepticism about the conditions under which, 'seeing is believing'.

Some implications

I have suggested some concepts involving characteristics of the means of surveillance and of the kind of information collected. This can help understanding by making clearer what is distinct about contemporary surveillance means and practices and more broadly in permitting comparisons among techniques and contexts.

Given the nature of perception, lists imply an egalitarianism among terms that is often unwarranted. The dimensions in Table 5.1 are hardly of equal significance. They can be clustered or ranked in various ways. Among those on the new surveillance side with the clearest social implications are extending the senses, low visibility, involuntary nature, remoteness and lesser cost. These create a potential for a very different kind of society and call for stringent vigilance.

Thus with respect to the dimensions in Table 5.1, the new surveillance in extending the senses (the ability to see in the dark, into bodies, through walls and over vast distances and so forth), challenges fundamental assumptions about personal and social borders (these after all have been maintained not only by values and norms and social organisation, but by the limits of technology to cross them). Low visibility and the involuntary and remote nature of much contemporary surveillance may mean more secrecy and lessened accountability, less need for consent and less possibility of reciprocity. Lesser costs create a temptation to, in Cohen's terms, both widen the net and thin the mesh of surveillance.[20]

Independent of the means used we need to consider the kind of information collected. The multi-dimensional nature of personal information, the extensive contextual and situational variation related to this and the dynamic nature of contested surveillance situations[21] prevents reaching any simple conclusions about how the information gathered by surveillance will (empirically) and should (morally) be evaluated. Such complexity may serve us well when it introduces humility and qualification, but not if it immobilises. Real analysts see the contingent as a challenge to offer contingent statements. Consider for example the kind of information collected.

The sense of violation or privacy invasion is likely to be greater when the values on the left side of Table 5.4 are present.[22] These combine in a variety of ways. They might also be ranked relative to each other – the seriousness of a perceived violation seems greatest for items 1–8. But such fine-tuning is a task best left for future hypothesising.

Now let us simply note that there is an additive effect and the more the values on the left-hand side of the table are present, the greater the perceived wrong in the collection of personal information, other factors being equal. The worst possible cases involve a core identity, a locatable person, and information that is personal, intimate, sensitive, stigmatising, of strategic value, deceptive, extensive, biological, naturalistic,[23] predictive, attached to the person, involves a documentary record that endures and is unalterable.

Determining the characteristics of an information gathering technique and the nature of the data gathered are pieces of a broader ecology of surveillance across cultures, time periods and institutional settings. When the above are joined with other dimensions for characterising surveillance – such as the structure of the situation and the nature of the goals we have a fuller picture and a framework for systematic analysis and comparison at the micro and middle ranges.

The question may be raised as to whether the concepts and examples I offer apply broadly, or are distinct to the North American continent or the United States. Given common features and functional needs of industrial democracies, globalisation and export/import of control technologies and tactics, the increased internationalisation of surveillance, and mimicry and fashion, I think the congruence across diverse states is noticeable. Certainly the empirical contours will vary to some degree across national contexts, but I think the concepts have broad applicability and can be helpful in identifying the variation that does exist.

The ethics of surveillance by individuals, private organisations and governments

I have argued that for purposes of scholarly classification and explanation a common set of categories (Tables 5.1–5.4 and Figure 5.1) can be used to order

Table 5.4: Some dimensions of individual information.

1	personal		
	yes		no (impersonal)
2	intimate		
	yes		no
3	sensitive		
	yes		no
4	unique identification		
	yes (distinctive but shared)		no (anonymous)
	core		non-core
5	locatable		
	yes		no
6	stigmatising (reflection on character of object)		
	yes		no
7	reveals deception (on part of object)		
	yes		no
8	strategic value to gatherer		
	yes		no
9	amount and variety		
	extensive, multiple kinds of information		minimal, single kind
10	documentary (re-usable) record		
	yes (permanent?) record		no
11	biological		
	yes		no
12	attached to or part of person		
	yes		no
13	naturalistic (reflects 'reality' in obvious way, face validity)		
	yes		no (artifactual)
14	information is predictive rather than reflecting past and present		
	yes		no
15	shelf life		
	enduring		transitory
16	alterable		
	yes		no

and eventually explain surveillance activities across an array of contexts involving individuals and organisations and the public and private sector.

The above deal with empirical matters. Their worth lies in whether they are useful in parsimoniously capturing variation and in linking elements that seem unrelated, or separating elements that seem to be related.

Questions involving values are of a different order. It is less certain, although certainly debatable, whether a standard set of categories applies in practice (and should apply) to the surveillance actions of persons acting in a private capacity, to organisations pursuing their own ends and to government, particularly when the latter is acting with respect to issues of security and order. For governments the extent to which different standards ought to apply to citizens and non-citizens, domestic and foreign and peace- and wartime surveillance is also a question of great importance.

With respect to questions of ethics and policy for governing domestic surveillance in other than criminal or national security matters, at least 18 underlying values or principles can be noted.

Many of these were first expressed in the Code of Fair Information Practices developed in 1973 for the US Department of Health, Education and Welfare. They are also now found in various European Community directives.

The Code offered a *principle of informed consent* in which the data collection is not to be done in secret, individuals are to be made aware of how it will be used, and where appropriate, consent to it; a principle of *inspection and correction* in which individuals are entitled to know what kind of information has been collected and to offer corrections and emendations; a *principle of data security* in which the information will be protected and precautions taken to prevent misuses of the data; a *principle of validity and reliability* in which organisations have a responsibility to ensure the appropriateness of the means used and the accuracy of the data gathered and *a principle of unitary usage* in which information gathered for one purpose is not to be used for another without consent.

As new surveillance technologies and problems have appeared additional principles have emerged. These include a *sanctity of the individual and dignity principle* in which there are limits (even with consent) on the taking, volunteering and commodification of personal information; a *golden rule principle* in which those doing the surveillance would agree to be the subjects of information gathering under comparable circumstances; a *principle of consistency* such that the broad ideals rather than the specific characteristics of a technology should govern surveillance practices; a *principle of morality* in which the fact that a tactic is legal is not sufficient justification for using it apart from broader ethical considerations; a *principle of minimisation and relevance* such that only information that is directly relevant and necessary for the task at hand is gathered; a *principle of restoration* such that in a communications monopoly context those altering the privacy status quo should bear the cost of restoring it; *a safety net or equity principle* such that a minimum threshold of information protection should be available to all; a *principle of equal treatment* such that surveillance deemed to be invasive, but appropriate, is applied to all members of an organisation not just the least powerful members; a *reciprocity or equivalence of tactics principle* in which in situations of legitimate conflict of interest all parties can use the same tactics; a *principle of timeliness* such that data are expected to be current and information which is no longer timely should be destroyed; a *principle of joint ownership of transactional data* such that both parties to a data-creating transaction should agree to any subsequent use of the data, including the sharing of benefits if appropriate; a *principle of human review* such that an automated decision is always subject to review by a person; and a *principle of redress* such that those subject to inappropriate surveillance or unfairly hurt by it have adequate mechanisms for discovering and being compensated for the harm.

Certainly these principles cannot be automatically transferred to the actions of national intelligence agencies in foreign settings and to actions taken for national security or criminal investigation purposes against non-citizens and even citizens, domestically. Yet common sense and common decency argue for some of them – whether procedural or substantive.

The reality of the events of September 11, 2001 and related actions intrude into our lofty conceptions of fairness, non-violence, avoiding harm to innocents, due process, transparency and the appropriate relationship between means and ends. A pragmatic survival ethos informed by notions of efficiency, prevention and turn-about-as-fair-play takes centre stage. Yet, as has often been noted, if in fighting our enemies we fail to be guided by anything more than pragmatism, we become less distinguishable from our enemies. Yet if we are rigidly guided only by the highest moral standards when opponents do not follow these, we may risk grave harm and even being destroyed.

There are of course national laws and policies and international treaties, agreements and informal understandings controlling what states are to do. Within democratic societies the lines are generally looser for foreign activities than is the case for domestic intelligence and security. Even within most countries citizens are granted rights not accorded non-citizens. And, at least until recently with the Patriot Act, in the United States, domestic intelligence involving foreign agents was held to a different and lower standard than were conventional criminal investigations.

In the current climate the familiar distinctions between foreign and domestic, national and international, intelligence gathering and criminal prosecution, the military and the police, and the public and the private are increasingly blurred.

With increased internationalisation and globalisation of crime, terror and social control, the meaning of national borders and foreign and domestic actions is less clear.[24] The links now made between dealing in contraband (drugs, weapons) and terror weakens the traditional distinction between crime and political activities. The previous separation of the military from domestic police, and intelligence from operational units, is also weakened by new legislation and new forms of co-operation. The emphasis on prevention blurs the line between intelligence and crime-fighting activities and weakens the tradition of a predicate before invasive surveillance is undertaken.

Government intelligence and security contracting with the private sector and greater government access to what had been private and private sector data (for example, communications, credit card transactions, library usage) muddies the line between the public and the private.[25]

Within this conceptual haze it is clear that there is a major need to elucidate new meanings for many of our traditional concepts and to study the consequences of these changes.

Beyond changing practices and meanings, there are enduring value conflicts and ironic, conflicting needs and consequences which make it difficult to take a broad and consistent position in favour of, or against, expanding or restricting surveillance, apart from public discussion and careful analysis and consideration of the context. For example, we value both the individual and the community. We want both liberty and order. We seek privacy and often anonymity, but we also know that secrecy can hide dastardly deeds and that visibility can bring accountability. But too much visibility may inhibit experimentation, creativity and risk taking.

In our media-saturated society we want to be seen and to see, yet also to be left alone. We value freedom of expression and a free press but do not wish to see individuals defamed or harassed. We desire honesty in communication and also civility and diplomacy. We value the right to know, but also the right to control personal information. The broad universalistic treatment citizens expect may conflict with the efficiency driven specific treatment made possible by fine-honed personal surveillance.

Whatever action is taken there are likely costs, gains and trade-offs. At best we can hope to find a compass rather than a map and a moving equilibrium rather than a fixed point for decision making.

Notes

1 A number of articles on this are at garymarx.net. On the ecology of communication more generally see D. Altheide, *An Ecology of Communication: Cultural Forms of Control* (Hawthorne, NY: Aldine de Gruyter, 1995). For a related approach emphasising the need to consider the local situational character of privacy in designing legal protections see D. Solove, 'Conceptualizing Privacy', *California Law Review*, 90 (2002).

2 M. Foucault, *Discipline and Punish: The Birth of the Prison* (New York: Vintage, 1977).

3 Here I include factors such as organisational and non-organisational surveillance, type of surveillance role – agent, subject, third party; and reciprocal and non-reciprocal surveillance.

4 Thus is the procedure seen to be fair and is it competently applied, are trust and confidentiality sustained, or are personal and social borders inappropriately violated, are undesirable consequences minimized or otherwise mediated? (G.T. Marx, 'An Ethics for the New Surveillance', *The Information Society*, 14, 3 (1998)).

5 I identify 12 major goals and a series of sub-goals including compliance, organisational functioning, strategic advantage, prevention, documentation, discovery, symbolism and self-knowledge.

6 G.T. Marx, *Windows Into the Soul: Surveillance and Society in an Age of High Technology* (Chicago, IL: University of Chicago Press, forthcoming).

7 This section draws from G.T. Marx, 'What's New About the New Surveillance?: Classifying for Change and Continuity', *Surveillance and Society*, 1, 1 (2002).

8 Consider for example a parent monitoring a baby on closed circuit television during commercials or through a day-care centre webcast; a database for employers containing the names of persons who have filed workman compensation claims; a video monitor in a department store scanning customers and matching their images to those of suspected shoplifters; a supervisor monitoring employee's e-mail and telephone communication; a badge signalling where an employee is at all times; a hidden camera in an ATM machine; a computer program that monitors the number of keystrokes or looks for key words or patterns; a thermal imaging device aimed at the exterior of a house from across the street; analysing hair to determine drug use; a self-test for level of alcohol in one's

system; a scanner that picks up cellular and cordless phone communication; mandatory provision of a DNA sample; the polygraph or monitoring brain waves to determine truthfulness; caller ID; brain scans for lie detection and computer matching, data merging and mining.

9 This holds for non-objectionable forms as well, for which failure to ask/collect is itself a failing. It also holds for the kind of information that can be offered the individual from a loquacious bearer of personal health details one does not wish to hear, as well as information a male might wish to hear. Regarding the latter note Emily Post's advice: 'women frequently ask whether they should call an unzipped fly to the wearer's attention, unless you are a total stranger do' (Post, *Emily Post's Etiquette* (New York: HarperCollins, 1992), p. 242). These issues tie to the broader sociology of information questions regarding norms about concealing and revealing information (G.T. Marx, 'Murky Conceptual Waters: The Public and the Private', *Ethics and Information Technology*, 3, 3 (2001)).

10 Yet such information is not only personal. Implications for groups matter as well, even if rarely acknowledged or studied (S. Alpert, 'Protecting Medical Privacy: Challenges in the Age of Genetic Information', *Journal of Social Issues*, 59, 2 (2003); O. Gandy, *The Panoptic Sort* (Boulder, CO: Westview Press, 1993); P. Regan, *Legislating Privacy: Technology, Social Values, and Public Policy* (Chapel Hill, NC: University of North Carolina Press, 1999)). Our language, which gives us ready concepts regarding the individual and privacy, leads us away from seeing the social and shared components and how groups may be harmed or helped.

11 Note that here we treat personal information as that which the individual is aware of (regardless of whether the category is imposed from the outside or is more naturally connected to the person). Labelling by the judicial or mental health system may involve imputed identities (for example, a recidivism risk category) which the individual is aware of. A related issue has to do with a classification imposed by an organisation of which the individual may be unaware. We can refer to information about the self not known by others communication of which the individual can control as existentially private. In contrast information that an organisation or another individual has about a person of which that person is unaware (whether of the information's existence or its content) is better seen as secret than private. This may be information which would be considered personal and even sensitive were it known by the individual.

Another distinction is whether, once known, an organisation's information corresponds to how a person sees themselves. This raises fascinating questions involving the politics of labelling and measurement validity. The disparity between technical labelling and self-definition may increase and become increasingly contested as abstract measurements claiming to predict the individual's future based on comparisons to large databases become more prominent.

12 The question assumes the point of view of an outside observer trying to be honest, since individuals may prevaricate, or in rare cases not know 'who' they are.

13 This may of course be muddied by unknown sperm and egg donors, abandonment and adoption.

14 Names popular in one time period that go out of fashion also may offer unwitting clues to age.

15 J. Caplan and J. Torpey, *Documenting Individual Identity* (Princeton, NJ: Princeton University Press, 2001).

16 Validity varies significantly here from very high for DNA and fingerprinting (if done properly) to relatively low for facial recognition. There also are many ways of thwarting data collection efforts.

17 Consider a means used against theft of cable TV signals. A New York City cable provider used a roving truck with a remote sensor to identify homes illicitly using its services. It then sent a signal that damaged the television set. The core identity of the violators was not known. When sets were brought to be repaired persons faced arrest.

18 We need to differentiate the video means of data collection from the visual as one of the senses. In considering how surveillance is viewed, both the means of data collection and the sense used in comprehending it matter. For example reading a purloined document is visual, but not pictorial, regardless of whether or not it is a photocopy. Sound in contrast seems conceptually less complicated.

19 In absolute terms however the latter have the potential to reveal far more information given the vast number of things that can be measured. They can also pierce the veil of deceptive appearances. However, I am considering perceptions here, rather than a presumed literal correlation between invasiveness as measured in some objective way and the evaluation of it. The representational closeness of surveillance data to the way we perceive data from others (absent technical aids) would seem more important to evaluation than the absolute amount of data.

20 S. Cohen, *Visions of Social Control* (Cambridge: Polity Press, 1985).

21 G.T. Marx, 'A Tack in the Shoe: Neutralizing and Resisting the New Surveillance', *Journal of Social Issues*, 59, 1 (2003).

22 There is an obvious need to study cultural variation, not only within national sub-cultures, but across societies as well. In China, to judge from the questions I was asked when I taught there, it is appropriate and perhaps even a sign of respect to ask how old a person is and there seems no inhibition on asking a stranger how much money he earns. In Europe it is much less common to ask those one has just met about their family status such as married, divorced, or if they have children. The information that is required or prohibited from a vitae offers another striking contrast. A nice comparative study could be (and most likely has been) done of 'Miss Manners' type books across cultures.

23 The logic here is that the unwarranted taking of information in actually reflecting the person would be seen as worse than an abstract category applied by others about which the individual can say, 'that's not me'. However, one could as well argue the opposite. The latter in being artificial and in less realistically, or at least less self-evidently, claiming to represent the person is worse than the seeming more real natural information.

    This is an aspect of backstage behaviour. The individual's sense of a unique self is partly to be found in the less than perfect fit between cultural expectations and the situation (regarding both attitudes and behaviour). Goffman's role distance and the idea of identity lying in the cracks of the roles we play fit here.

24 M. Deflem, *Policing World Society* (New York: Oxford University Press, 2002); W. McDonald, *Crime and Law Enforcement in the Global Village* (Cincinnati, OH: Anderson Publishing, 1997).

25 Beyond changes in policies, the enhanced power of the new surveillance technologies is blurring our conventional understanding of the public and private. Consider technologies that break through barriers such as walls, distance, darkness, skin, time and the compartmentalisation of data from various parts of the individual's life. Previously these physical and logistical limits helped protect the private, for both good and ill. Consider for example night vision technology, the reading of brain waves, scent, or gait or the case of a video camera (and images) operating from private space but pointed at the public or quasi-public space of a parking lot or a person within the private space of a car. Or take the case of thermal imaging technology in which heat from inside a house is picked up by a device 'outside' the protected area of the house.

6 'Who Profited from the Crime?' Intelligence Failure, Conspiracy Theories and the Case of September 11

Robert Alan Goldberg

In statecraft and commerce, secrets can be the talismans of power. No wonder that so much effort has been devoted to the study of intelligence, its acquisition, disclosure and influence. Scholars, usually maintaining an institutional focus, have concerned themselves with the methods of gathering secrets, the dynamics of their dissemination within a bureaucracy, and their role in the decision-making process. Less well explored is the impact of intelligence work beyond the bureaucratic arena. If valuable intelligence can safeguard a nation, how does intelligence failure affect domestic politics and public faith in authorities? This essay, using the lens of the terrorist attacks on September 11, 2001 against the World Trade Center and the Pentagon, considers the symbiotic relationship between intelligence failure and conspiracy thinking. This inter-action not only influences public debate, but meets psychological needs induced by national trauma. In making their scenarios believable, the con-spiracists who weave events into plots quickly discovered that government leaders came to be their unwitting partners.

In the immediate aftermath of the terrorist attacks of September 11, 2001, Americans rallied around their President and rekindled a faith in the federal government that had grown cold since the 1960s. Observers noted this renewed trust and compared it favourably to the 1990s when counter-subversives had found large audiences for their claims that aliens, or Jews, or globalists, or Satanists had penetrated the highest levels of the national government and taken control of the future of the United States. If faith had been restored, the attack also demonstrated the resilience of the conspiracy theorists. Official admission of failure to predict or intercept the strikes encouraged them to incorporate September 11 into their plot lines. The conspiracist clamour in the United States, Europe and the Middle East soon became so insistent that it raised concerns among high-level government officials in Washington. Just two months after the terrorist blow, President George Bush addressed the General Assembly of the United Nations and warned:

We must speak the truth about terror. Let us never tolerate outrageous conspiracy theories concerning the attacks of September the 11th, malicious lies that attempt to shift the blame away from the terrorists themselves, away from the guilty. To inflame ethnic hatred is to advance the cause of terrorism.[1]

Conspiracy thinking is not American born. The Latin word *conspirare* – to breathe together – suggests both drama and a deeply rooted past. The fear of conspiracy was a prominent feature on the mental maps of the first English settlers in Massachusetts and Virginia. Early colonists suspected both neighbours and strangers of secret alliances and dangerous plots. Subsequent generations entertained visions of vast conspiracies that targeted their religion, race and nation. Salem witches, British ministers, Catholic priests, slave holders, Wall Street bankers, Jews, Bolsheviks and black militants, all in their turn and among other suspects, have been cast in the plotter's role. If a national tradition, Europeans have long cued their American kin about the means and ends of conspiracy and its perpetrators.[2]

The conspiracist's script is familiar: individuals and groups, acting in secret, move and shape history. Driven by a lust for power and wealth, they practice deceit, subterfuge, and even assassination, sometimes brazenly executed. The conspiracy-minded suspend reality, for their protagonists move in lockstep unhampered by miscalculation, institutional process and chance. Ambiguity finds no place in their explanations for all events and actions take meaning from the single cause of conspiracy. The cry of conspiracy is not easily silenced. Not only is conspiracy thinking dramatic and rigorously integrated, but it finds occasional grounding in historical experience.

Prominent among recent American conspiracy theories are those rooted in intelligence failures. The Japanese attack on Pearl Harbor on 7 December 1941 brought the United States into the Second World War and unleashed decades of conspiracist speculation. Did President Franklin Roosevelt back-door the United States into the war against Germany by manipulating the Japanese into firing the first shot in the Pacific? Why did Washington delay in warning Pearl Harbor of the impending attack? Were Hawaii commanders Admiral Husband Kimmel and General Walter Short dismissed to cover up the plot? Military comrades of Kimmel and Short came to their defence and blamed Washington for withholding vital information from Pearl Harbor despite having broken the Japanese diplomatic code. They also found it curious that US aircraft carriers were conveniently away on manoeuvres and out of harm's way on the day of the attack. By mid-May 1946, nine separate, official investigations had been conducted with suspicious revisionists still convinced that important information had been either ignored or suppressed. During the Cold War, critics who accused Roosevelt of being soft on communism alleged that Pearl Harbor had been sacrificed to ensure US involvement in Europe and to save his Russian pals. Most recently, author John Toland has claimed that 'the comedy of errors on the sixth and seventh [of December 1941] appears incredible. It only makes sense if it was a charade, and Roosevelt and the inner circle had known about the attack.'[3] Japanese intentions surprisingly are insignificant to these conspiracy scenarios, and the Empire's burden of guilt has shifted to US shoulders. The US Senate offered conspiracy theorists some consolation in 1999. It voted to overrule military authorities and clear Kimmel and Short of all charges of dereliction of duty.[4]

The intelligence failure that was the assassination of President John F. Kennedy in November 1963 may be the most intensively studied event in US history. It is flush with details and offers hundreds of eyewitnesses, extensive ballistics evidence and autopsy results, and even a film that frames action to the split second. Bibliographies now count more than 3,000 entries, including films, plays, television programmes, and a dozen newsletters. Conspiracy thinking permeates most of these efforts. Born of bereavement and drawing strength from the memory of a lost Camelot, conspiracy theories challenge the official conclusion that indicted a lone gunman. Once conspiracists were convinced that they had exposed the cover-up, new theories and a counter-history appeared. The assassination, they contend, was actually a coup d'état that robbed the nation of its future. Filmmaker Oliver Stone made the case in his motion picture *JFK*, released in 1991. Stone has the furtive character 'X' reveal the conspiracy, tracing its tracks to the White House, CIA, FBI and the 'military-industrial complex'. Kennedy had to go because 'he wanted to call off the moon race in favor of cooperation with the Soviets. He signed a treaty with the Soviets to ban nuclear testing, he refused to invade Cuba in '62, and he set out to withdraw from Vietnam. But this all ended on November 22, 1963.'[5] Opinion surveys repeatedly testify to the success of the conspiracy theorists, showing that for the large majority of Americans an assassination conspiracy is the conventional wisdom. The 'magic bullet' and the 'grassy knoll', conspiracy's short-hand terms, remain fixed in the national lexicon.[6]

In the wake of the terrorist strikes on September 11, 2001, a variety of conspiracy theorists were certain that they had uncovered the hidden plots behind events. On talk radio, through the internet, and in press they connected the dots of conspiracy, usually following well-known paths to the usual suspects. Thus, word spread from the Middle East and Europe and was echoed by American right-wing groups that the attacks were a Jewish conspiracy and had 'all the earmarks of Zionist agents provocateurs'. According to Edward Hendrie, the CIA had joined with its Israeli counterpart the Mossad to lure 'unwitting' Arabs into a plot that would galvanise Americans in a jihad against the Muslim world.[7] Declared the anti-Jewish National Alliance, 'Let's Stop Being Human Shields for Israel.'[8] Not only did Mossad agents orchestrate the assault, they had contacted the Jews working in the World Trade Center and ordered them not to go to work on September 11. Such belief, of course, required the denial of the many men and women with Jewish names listed among the casualties. This first 'salvo' of the Third World War had allegedly been outlined in the *Protocols of the Elders of Zion*, an early twentieth-century, fabricated account of a Jewish plot to destroy Christianity and rule the world.[9] Americans were also alerted to the Jews' next operation, a conspiracy to blow up the Dome of the Rock Mosque in Jerusalem. Reverend V.S. Herrell observed: 'This may turn out to be like the death of John F. Kennedy, now clearly linked to the involvement of Jews and the Jewish Mossad.'[10]

While end-times minister Texe Marrs was concerned about the Jews, his eyes were on a more formidable foe. In the smoke that billowed from the World Trade Center, some evangelical Christians bore witness that they had seen the face of Satan.[11] The terrorist attack, declared Marrs, was the work of the anti-Christ and the secret brotherhood of the Illuminati, a sect seeking global power. Their impressive organisation chart included the Masonic Order, the Vatican, the Mafia, the Trilateral Commission, the Mossad, the CIA and the United Nations. He warned Christian patriots that this was just another step in their 'master plan of world domination' and that such 'manufactured terrorism' would 'drive us into accepting tyranny'.[12] Marrs, using the Bible as his guide, found proof that Satan and his minions were similarly plotting a cashless society, microchip implants, mind-control experiments, crematoria and guillotines. Concentration camps had 'already [been] built'.[13] Mainstream Christian leaders also discerned the cosmic implications of the attack. Baptist minister Jerry Falwell condemned abortionists, feminists, gays and lesbians for provoking God and causing him to lift his protection from the United States: 'All of them who have tried to secularize America, I point the finger in their face and say, "You helped this happen."'[14] In support, internet websites and bulletin boards focused Christians on the meaning of events and announced the events of September 11 as the 'latest harbinger' on the prophetic time-line.[15]

For those fearful of a coming New World Order, September 11 was an obvious globalist ploy for power. Leaders of the right-wing John Birch Society charged that federal authorities had prior knowledge of the terrorist attack, yet did nothing to prevent it. Resembling Pearl Harbor conspiracy theorists, they asked why did Attorney General John Ashcroft travel by leased jet aircraft and avoid commercial airplanes? Who gave the order to ignore FBI warnings of an impending attack? Why did officials fail to scramble Air Force jet interceptors after the airliners were hijacked? The answers were obvious to them. Writing in the Birch Society's *New American*, William Jaspar accused 'subversives', long engaged in weakening the United States from within, of having 'scripted' the failure to respond.[16] Like the Nazis' burning of the Reichstag in 1933, they conjectured that the 'ruling elite' made September 11 its pretext to initiate secret plans creating a 'police state' with 'Gestapo-like powers'.[17] The Constitution of the United States would be overturned and the Bill of Rights destroyed. In the end, patriots would be disarmed and left defenceless as the United States became a province of the global New World Order. The failure to proceed with a truly independent investigation convinced them that a 'cover-up' was securely in place.[18]

Conspiracy theories also came from the left side of the political spectrum. Congresswoman Cynthia McKinney, a liberal Democrat from Georgia, accused President Bush of having advance warning yet allowing 'innocent people' to be 'needlessly murdered'. The President failed to act, she surmised, because he wanted his father and cronies in the oil and defence industries 'to make huge profits' from the subsequent war on terrorism. Replaying the refrain heard during the Watergate investigations during the 1970s, she asked: 'What did the administration know and when did it know it ... What do they have to hide?'[19]

Richer in detail is Thierry Meyssan's book *9/11: The Big Lie*. Meyssan, a French investigative journalist and the director of the Voltaire Network, a prominent left-wing think tank, was drawn to the events of September 11 by 'contradictions in the official version'. Studying the photographic evidence, he failed to see plane wreckage at the Pentagon crash site. Meyssan also dismissed the administration's assertion that amateur pilots had sufficient skill to strike the World Trade Center towers without ground assistance. Convinced that the cover story was merely 'propaganda', he asked, who had the expertise to plan and execute the attacks and 'who profited from the crime'? Meyssan surmised that the attacks were an inside job: 'Only a missile of the United States armed forces transmitting a friendly code could enter the Pentagon's airspace without provoking a counter-missile barrage.' Curiously, he offers no evidence of the existence of a Pentagon missile defence. Nor is he concerned about the whereabouts of the missing American Airlines flight that he denies crashed into the Pentagon. Military precision similarly characterised the strike at the World Trade Center. Meyssan believes that strategically placed radio beacons guided the planes automatically to their targets. Neither Osama bin Laden nor al-Qaeda, he continues, had the ability or resources to engineer the attacks. Rather, bin Laden is a 'patsy' of the US government, who worked for the CIA since 'at least 1998'. As proof, he reports that bin Laden was seen in the company of a CIA operative at the US hospital in Dubai as late as July 2001. The FBI, meanwhile, 'has applied itself to making clues disappear and silencing testimony'.[20]

For Meyssan, the conclusion is inescapable. The events of September 11 were 'masterminded from inside the American elite apparatus'. Mirroring Oliver Stone's version of the assassination of President John Kennedy, Meyssan accuses representatives of the oil companies, defence industries, the intelligence community and military establishment of plotting September 11 and 'cynically sacrific[ing]' thousands of American lives to pursue 'a classic colonial expedition'. Oil companies demanded that the Taliban be subdued so that a pipeline across Afghanistan could be built that would deliver the oil and gas resources of the Caspian Sea region into American hands. The Pentagon needed an excuse to scrap the ABM treaty, open outer space to militarisation, and increase its budget. The CIA sought release from Congressional oversight and authority to pursue a world-wide campaign against terrorism. Meyssan could not resist adding that Kennedy defied the military–industrial complex and 'probably paid for it with his life'. Like Stone, Meyssan must rely on circumstantial evidence or no evidence and leaps of logic to make his case. Nevertheless, with more than 50 pages of official documents and 26 pages of notes and references, the book appears authoritative. It remained on the top ten bestseller list for three months in France and in the United States, amazon.com ranked it high in customer sales while readers gave it a five-star rating.[21]

Knowing that the devil is in the details, other conspiracy theorists fleshed out Meyssan's scenario with additional information. Nafeez Ahmed's *War on Freedom*, another bestseller on amazon.com, sets the September 11 attacks in a broader geopolitical perspective, noting that the United States had long desired 'to secure hegemony over Central Asia as a means to the control of Eurasia'. With this economic base secured, 'unrivaled global hegemony' was within reach.[22] Former Los Angeles police officer Michael Ruppert, whose website at one time attracted 6,000 visitors per day, connected the Bush administration plot to efforts by Texaco, Shell, Enron and ExxonMobil to secure oil reserves in Kazakhstan during the 1990s. Unusual stock market activity also caught his attention. Prior to September 11, large sums were speculated on United and American Airlines stocks, betting that their value would plummet. Following the money, Ruppert found that a German bank, once managed by a 'current executive director of the CIA', was a key player. Others tried to fix precisely the source of the bin Laden–CIA connection in Dubai with both an Italian and a French newspaper in competition for the scoop.[23]

A tale well told may disguise its weaknesses. Conspiracy theorists ignore mundane tests of logic and evidence for explanation based on circumstance, rumour and hearsay. Thinking magically, they create antagonists who exercise power without constraints. Human error, chance and bureaucratic process have no place in their narratives. Proximity in time and location are bent to create collusion; common interests define guilt. Similarly, casual accusations of high crimes and mass murder sell books, but their credibility demands testimony based on more than innuendo. The plot weavers, working from a premise of conspiracy, focus with a vengeance on their suspicions and reject inconsistencies and more plausible alternatives. Thus, al-Qaeda plays a minor and supporting role, always lost in the shadow of US power brokers. Meanwhile, as in the execution of the Pearl Harbor attack, Washington is callously and flawlessly able to plan, perform and conceal its role in another day of infamy. Fast-paced writing suitable to the adventure genre augments the prosecutorial style of the conspiracists and disguises logical leaps and gaps in evidence. Most readers, captivated by the sensational, do not hold the conspiracy theorist to exacting criteria of proof and are quick to believe. Interconnected and reinforcing, the message grows more credible through repetition. The result is a seamless web of subversion that is suspended from history. This kind of thinking about the unthinkable is not merely wrong. Conspiracy theories are dangerous for they demonise public officials and erode faith in national institutions.

Despite their weaknesses, conspiracy theories offer much to believers. If slippery in their logic and often careless of facts and assumptions, they order the random and make consistent the paradoxical. In the face of national crisis and human failure, conspiracy theorists rush to find purpose in tragedy and clarity in ambiguity. They also respond to the traumatised who cry for vengeance and demand the identities of those responsible. Conspiracy thinking thus becomes an antidote to powerlessness. It lifts the despair of vulnerability by arming believers with tantalising, secret knowledge to understand and defeat the enemy. Whether men and women act on this intelligence is less important than their security in knowing the truth.

These theorists do not, by themselves, nourish US conspiracy thinking. Also stoking public apprehension are federal actions that legitimise conspiracy cries, erode accountability and tarnish those who claim authority. Since the origins of the Cold War, federal officials have mobilised the home front with the rhetoric of conspiracy. Politicians cried conspiracy for Partisan advantage, and bureaucrats used it to leverage power. In the 1950s, conspiracy charges were made against US communists; in the 1960s, against New Left activists; and more recently, against militia group members. In addition to radicals, federal prosecutors have used the conspiracy charge repeatedly and successfully against men and women accused of racketeering, murder, drug trafficking and financial fraud, among many other crimes. The message is clear from the official record. Conspirators never rest; their plots to betray the nation or prey upon the innocent are a constant reminder of the fragile nature of the US mission.

Opinion polls since the 1960s have tracked a decline in popular trust in federal authorities. The Vietnam War not only drained the United States of blood and resources but deepened cynicism and eroded faith in government leaders. Mistrust crept into the debate at the very beginning, with many convinced that President Lyndon Johnson had duped the nation into war. Candour did not return to the White House during Richard Nixon's tenure. Public support and faith in the President ebbed with a long series of discoveries that became the Watergate scandal. The decade of the 1970s was a season of disclosures with revelations that the CIA and FBI had repeatedly betrayed the trust of the US Congress and the American people. The election of Ronald Reagan in 1980 ushered in a brief period of renewed faith that was squandered in the Iran–Contra scandal. 'Contragate' returned the United States to the Congressional hearing room to witness high-ranking government officials caught in lies and rogue operations. The spiral of mistrust accelerated in the 1990s. Sexual improprieties tore at Bill Clinton's credibility and draped the Oval Office in duplicity. Poll takers surveyed the damage. In 1964, they found that 75 per cent of the American people trusted the federal government 'to do what is right always or most of the time'. In 1976, only one in three Americans expressed similar thoughts. In 1995, public trust hit an all-time low. In mirror image of the 1964 findings, 75 per cent of Americans expressed no faith in the government's ability to do what is right.[24]

Such historical flares illuminate conspiracist nightmares, but even the standard operating procedures of the federal government can inflame distrust. For more than half a century, a cult of secrecy has dominated the bureaucracy in Washington and distanced federal authorities from the governed. Bred in the Second World War and nurtured in the Cold War, the secrecy state was driven by national security fears and a determination to preserve the American way of life. The results were predictable. By 1995, 3 million men and women were tasked with classifying as many as 10,000 documents per day. The secrets piled up, and by the end of the century an estimated 10 billion pages have secrecy stamps, with 1.5 billion of them at least 25 years old. Behind this veil, laws were broken and democratic values subverted. Even without the taint of malevolence, suppression of information aroused concern. Essayist Susan Griffin was insightful: 'Wherever there is a secret, there is a rumor.'[25] Drawing sustenance from America's resilient fear of centralized authority, perceptions of sinister design became truth. As outsiders, the conspiracy-minded only intensified their gaze and watched for confirmation of their worst suspicions.

Even before September 11, the Bush administration validated such suspicions. Federal officials reversed Clinton-era efforts to relax secrecy requirements and tightened restrictions on the public release of information. This 'sea change in government openness' became more obvious after the terrorist attacks and was designed not only to increase security, but strengthen the authority of the executive branch. Attorney General Ashcroft thus directed that Freedom of Information Act requests be denied if 'there were any legal basis to do so'.[26] Since September 11, three additional agencies were given the authority to stamp materials as secret and the number of documents classified increased by 18 per cent over the previous fiscal year. Consistent with these efforts, in 2003, President Bush delayed for three additional years the declassification of documents 25 years and older.[27]

Washington's legal response to intelligence failure did much to convince conspiracists that there was a hidden agenda in the events of September 11. The Patriot Act, passed in October 2001, reified fears of a police state and a gutted Bill of Rights by easing long-time restrictions on police and intelligence forces. The law authorised federal officers without showing warrant or probable cause to conduct secret searches; infiltrate anti-war and religious groups; spy electronically on e-mail and internet communication; and gather confidential financial, educational and business information in pursuit of the war on terrorism. Bank accounts, credit data, medical records, library acquisitions and even video store rentals were now under the jurisdiction of federal agents. This, of course, ignored the possibility that the events of September 11 were a failure not because of a lack of information, but the inability to sift important intelligence from a surfeit of 'noise'. By the end of 2001, nearly 1,200 foreign nationals were under arrest, held incommunicado, denied legal counsel, and subjected to, what internal Justice Department watchdogs would latter describe, as 'a pattern of physical and verbal abuse'.[28] Those US citizens who fell into the federal net also found that their claims to constitutional protection were moot. Conspiracists no longer had to imagine their fears. Daily newspapers and Washington press conferences now provided the grist for their theories. Moreover, in justifying their actions, federal authorities used the rhetoric of conspiracy. Calling for a holy war, President George Bush condemned the 'evil doers' and an 'axis of evil'. Conspiracy thinkers were well acquainted with the script.[29]

To the conspiracy-minded, Washington was soon even more obvious in showing its hand. Operationalising the Patriot Act, the Department of Defense created the Information Awareness Office (IAO) in January 2002 (Figure 6.1). This agency was tasked with the creation of a super databank that would compile, without warrant, information about an individual's website and e-mail logs; credit card purchases; magazine subscriptions; medical prescriptions; and employment, financial and travel records. Another anti-terrorist project in planning called for subjects to be fitted with monitors that produced a daily 'LifeLog'. This 'cyberdiary' would record everything a 'user' smelled, touched, saw, tasted and heard.[30] Reverend Texe Marrs was quick to condemn 'the Gestapo-like IAO' and its 'Big Brother

Figure 6.1: The now discarded emblem of the Information Awareness Office.

Source: http://geocities.com/totalinformationawareness/.

plot for a global central command'. The 'scheme exceeds anything that Hitler, Stalin and Mao ever dreamed about'.[31] If the IAO's purpose was not sufficient to arouse counter-subversives, its official seal stunned anyone with even a casual knowledge of conspiracy theory. The agency's website showed an occult pyramid with an all-seeing eye that fixed its gaze upon the world. Beneath it was the motto *Scientia Est Potentia*, meaning Knowledge is Power. Seemingly taunting its prey, the IAO had chosen for a shield the symbols of the ancient anti-Christ/ Illuminati/Masonic Conspiracy. Making matters even worse, Retired Navy Admiral John Poindexter, who had been in the thick of the Iran–Contra Affair and indicted for lying to the US Congress, was charged to command the agency. To the conspiracy-minded, the New World Order's conquest of Washington appeared complete. Nevertheless, in 2003, the US Senate unanimously voted to bar deployment of the project without specific Congressional authorisation. Later, the IAO removed the logo from its website and also took down the biographies of its senior staff. Conspiracists knew, however, that the price of liberty was constant vigilance. The Information Awareness Office, if deactivated, remained on organisational charts and still claimed its anti-terrorism mission.[32]

In their dance with the authorities, conspiracy theorists always take the lead. Relieved of the responsibilities of evidence and logic, they make their adversaries into men of supreme power, in absolute command of all essential information, with no limit to their will to move events. Poor judgement, conflict in the inner circle, bureaucratic culture and incompetence never figure into their scripts. Nor could the ordinary workings of government compete with dramatic conspiracy scenarios of malevolent men bent on conquering the world. Understandably, such plots are necessary for they spur book and video sales, the life blood of professional counter-subversives. At the same time, government leaders may become the partners, even if reluctant ones, of conspiracists. While candour and openness deter rumour and allegation, an unthinking and imperious practice of secrecy instinctively raises suspicion. Overreaction, official deception and explanations that intentionally obscure provide opportunities for the conspiracy theorists. They thrive on public disillusionment and the loss of faith in national leaders and institutions. In such an atmosphere, intelligence failure readily mutates into conspiracy. Leaders then find that even the shield of national security proves unwieldy and offers no shelter. When authorities mimic their critics and sound the alarm of conspiracy, they further condition citizens to its premises and conclusions. Opponents become traitors; enemies are stripped of their humanity. The world divides between good and evil. Fearing their vulnerability in the face of such plots, men and women acquiesce in the erosion of traditional liberties and rights for the promise of security. This only gives heart to the conspiracy-minded. With suspicion officially aroused and sanctioned, their claims become more convincing. In a cycle of action and reaction, they have also found new fodder for their fears.

Like the Japanese attack on Pearl Harbor and the assassination of John F. Kennedy, September 11 has become a conspiracy born in intelligence failure. Seeking meaning and justice in trauma, men and women entertain thoughts of hidden hands and evil minds. Professional conspiracists are eager to supply the details, plotting their scenarios with standard themes and framing the traditional suspects. If the burden of proof rests on the conspiracy theorists, they must rely on national authorities to make their cases credible. Secrecy, manipulation of facts, and self-serving explanations create the culture that makes conspiracy thinking the conventional wisdom.

Notes

The author would like to thank Paul Allen, Anne Freed Goldberg, David Goldberg, L. Ray Gunn and Jim Sheldon for reading and commenting on earlier drafts of this essay.

1 www.usinfo.state.gov/topical/pol/terro.011100.htm, 15 May 2003.
2 See Robert Alan Goldberg, *Enemies Within: The Culture of Conspiracy in Modern America* (New Haven, CT: Yale University Press, 2001); Mark Fenster, *Conspiracy Theories: Secrecy and Power in American Culture* (Minneapolis, MN: University of Minnesota Press, 1999); Peter Knight, *Conspiracy Culture: From Kennedy to the 'X-Files'* (London: Routledge, 2001).
3 John Toland, *Infamy: Pearl Harbor and Its Aftermath* (New York: Doubleday, 1982), p. 321.
4 Robert A. Theobald, *The Final Secret of Pearl Harbor: The Washington Contribution to the Japanese Attack* (Greenwich, CT: Devin-Adair, 1954), pp. 192–6; George Morgenstern, *Pearl Harbor: The Story of the Secret War* (New York: Devin-Adair, 1947), pp. ix, 327, 329; Gordon W. Prange, *Pearl Harbor: The Verdict of History* (New York: McGraw Hill, 1986), pp. 36–42; Toland, *Infamy*, p. 321; *New York Times*, 26 May 1999.

5 Oliver Stone and Zachary Sklar (eds), *JFK: The Book of the Film* (New York: Applause, 1992), p. 112.

6 Goldberg, *Enemies Within*, pp. 105–49.

7 Edward Hendrie, 'Anti Christ Conspiracy: Inside the Devil's Lair', www.antichristconspiracy.com, 5 June 2003, pp. 286–7.

8 Kelly Patterson, 'The Unbelievers', *Ottawa Citizen*, 1 September 2002.

9 Hendrie, 'Anti Christ Conspiracy', p. 297.

10 David Irving, 'Jews Warned in Advance', www.fpp.co.uk, 25 November 2001; V.S. Herrell, 'Have the Jews Started World War III?', www.publiceye.org, 3 June 2003; Chip Berlet, 'Post 9/11 Conspiracism', www.publiceye.org, 3 June 2003.

11 According to the tabloid *Weekly World News*, the face of Satan appeared in bomb clouds over Baghdad during US air attacks in the recent Iraqi war. In addition, US troops were reported to have uncovered a 'demon' on the battlefield near Najaf. *Weekly World News*, 29 April 2003.

12 Texe Marrs, *Power of Prophecy* (February 2003), p. 3.

13 Texe Marrs, 'Concentration Camps in America', www.texemarrs.com, 20 December 2002.

14 *Washington Post*, 14 September 2001.

15 Kevin Sack, 'Apocalyptic Theology Revitalized by Attack', *New York Times*, 23 November 2001.

16 William F. Jaspar, 'What can be Done' and 'The Action is in the Reaction', *New American*, 7 October 2002, www.thenewamerican.com, 20 December 2002.

17 Ibid.

18 William Norman Grigg, 'Did We Know What was Coming?' 11 March 2002, 'Foreknowledge and Failure', 17 June 2002, 'Burying the Truth', 30 December 2002, *New American*, www.thenewamerican.com, 23 January 2003; Des Griffin, 'Homeland Security: Stars and Stripes or – Bars and Stripes', *Emissary Publications* (Winter 2003), pp. 1, 20–1; 'The Masters of Terror', www.infowars.com, 5 June 2003.

19 Dennis Bernstein interview with Congresswoman Cynthia McKinney, KPFA, 25 March 2002. www.rise4news.net/mckinney.html. See also McKinney's revised statement made on 13 April 2002, www.house.gov/mckinney, 20 April 2002.

20 Thierry Meyssan, *9/11: The Big Lie* (London: Carnot, 2002), pp. 13, 22, 24, 25, 27, 33–4, 59, 105–6; amazon.com, 15 April 2003; *Salt Lake Tribune*, 26 June 2002.

21 Meyssan, *9/11*, pp. 118, 122, 139, 145, 147, 153.

22 Nafeez Mosaddeq Ahmed, *The War on Freedom: How and Why America Was Attacked, 11 September, 2001* (Joshua Tree, CA: Tree of Life Publications 2002), pp. 16, 18.

23 Michael C. Ruppert, 'A Timeline Surrounding 11 September – If CIA and the Government Weren't Involved in the 11 September Attacks What Were They Doing?', www.fromthewilderness.com, 3 June 2003, Christopher Bollyn, 'Who Profits? Examining 'Fortuitous' 9–11 Stock Trades Could Expose Real Terrorist Mastermind', *American Free Press*, 10 June 2002; Johann Hari, 'Who *Really* Downed the Twin Towers?', www.mindcentral.com; James Rosen, 'Conspiracy Theories Arise from 11 September Attacks', *Nando Times*, www.nandotimes.com, 30 April 2002.

24 Seymour Martin Lipset, *American Exceptionalism: A Double-Edged Sword* (New York: Norton, 1996), p. 282; *Salt Lake Tribune*, 1 August 1995.

25 Susan Griffin, *A Chorus of Stone: The Private Life of War* (New York: Anchor Books, 1993), p. 16.

26 Adam Clymer, 'Government Openness at Issue as Bush Holds onto Records', *New York Times*, 3 January 2003.

27 *New York Times*, 26 March 2003.

28 *New York Times*, 3 June 2003.

29 Stephen J. Schulhofer, *The Enemy Within: Intelligence Gathering, Law Enforcement, and Civil Liberties in the Wake of 11 September* (New York: The Brookings

Institution, 2002), pp. 1, 3, 11, 17–19, 32, 39, 50–1, 66; Jane Mayer, 'Lost in the Jihad', *New Yorker* (10 March 2003), pp. 57–8.

30 '"Big Brother" Watching new Super Diary?', www.fas.org, 3 June 2003, William Safire, 'Digital Diary could Become a High-Tech Government Snoop', *New York Times*, 5 June 2003.

31 Marrs, *Power of Prophecy* (February 2003), pp. 3, 6.

32 Hendrik Hertzberg, 'Talk of the Town', *New Yorker* (9 December 2002), pp. 45, 48; *New York Times*, 24 January 2003; www.darpa.mil/iao/, 5 December 2002.

7 Bletchley Park and the Holocaust

Michael Smith

This chapter examines the truth behind claims that British codebreakers knew Nazi police operating behind the German troops invading the Soviet Union were murdering thousands of Jews but that they and the British wartime Prime Minister Winston Churchill, who read their messages, did nothing about it. These claims were first published in 1998 in the book *Official Secrets: What the Nazis Planned, What the British and Americans Knew* by Professor Richard Breitman. He argued that instead of using the intelligence to show the world the plight of the Jews the British 'simply hoarded' it. Churchill should have told the world, warning the Jews in countries like Romania and Bulgaria, which were as yet not under German occupation, of what was going on. Professor Breitman also criticised the British for failing to provide the intelligence reports as evidence to the International Tribunal at Nuremberg at which those Nazis accused of war crimes were tried. His allegations were repeated in a number of newspaper articles publicising the book, and often based on interviews with him, which carried headlines such as: 'Britain Accused of Hiding Facts on Holocaust'; 'Should Churchill have Acted?'; and 'MI6 Concealed Extermination of Jews'.[1]

The British knowledge of the killings, derived from messages broken by the Government Code and Cipher School at Bletchley Park, was first published in 1981 in an appendix to the second volume of the official history of *British Intelligence in the Second World War*.[2] In the mid-1990s, Professor Breitman, a professor of history at American University, Washington, and a specialist in Holocaust Studies, obtained copies of the documents from the National Security Agency (NSA), the US codebreaking organisation, through the Freedom of Information Act. He succeeded in April 1996 in getting the documents released in the United States and shortly afterwards they were released to the Public Record Office. Professor Breitman's book *Official Secrets* incorporated them into what else we know about the Holocaust.

Professor Breitman is one of the leading authorities on the Holocaust. *Official Secrets* is a powerful, compelling and thoroughly depressing narrative of what by any measure must count among the foulest of deeds ever committed by man on his fellow men. Its central theme was that the British knew far more about what are now recognised as the beginnings of the Holocaust than previously realised and that they, and in particular Churchill, did not do enough to make this more widely known. 'Do I think he personally should have spoken out?' Professor Breitman said. 'Yes, I do.'[3]

There are clear risks involved in speaking openly about information obtained from secret intelligence; sources are all too easily revealed and this was undoubtedly the main argument against talking openly about the intelligence produced by breaking the German Enigma machine ciphers. Professor Breitman argues that the relevant German police messages were not enciphered using the Enigma machine and that as a result this argument does not apply. He writes that 'it appears that Britain could have publicised Nazi killings of Jews in the East without in the least impairing its code-breaking success.' But I believe that his interpretation of the Bletchley Park records was hampered by a lack of understanding of how British intelligence and Bletchley Park operated at the time and that, in short, both the Bletchley Park code breakers and Churchill are innocent of the charges laid against them.

On 22 June 1941, German troops invaded the Soviet Union in an operation that was given the rather apt codename Barbarossa. Behind the frontline more German troops carried out 'mopping-up' operations. These were conducted by the *Waffen SS* and German police regiments, mostly made up of members of the *Ordnungspolizei* or *Orpo*, the ordinary uniformed police officers in whom most normal law-abiding people in civilised countries place their trust.

There were three main formations, roughly speaking, one was designated to carry out mopping up operations in the Baltic republics to the north, one through Belorussia at the centre of the front and one through the Ukraine in the south. At the heart of each formation was an *Einsatzgruppe* made up largely of members of the Gestapo and *Sicherheitspolizei*, the *Sipo*, the Security Police and split into four separate *Einsatzkommando*. It was the *Einsatzgruppe* of each formation that was expected to orchestrate the bulk of the killings.[4] But messages deciphered by Bletchley Park very soon showed that the ordinary police units, as well as of course the SS troops, were heavily involved in the killings.

The first that Western intelligence knew of what was going on behind the Eastern Front was on 18 July 1941, army special wireless operators at Chicksands Priory in Bedfordshire[5] picked up a message from SS *Gruppenführer* Erich von dem Bach-Zelewski, commander of the SS and police troops in occupied Belorussia. It was addressed to Heinrich Himmler, the head of the SS, and to Kurt Daluege, head of the *Orpo*, the *Ordnungspolizei*, the basic uniformed police in Berlin. The cipher in use was a basic double transposition cipher broken relatively easily by Bletchley Park. The message read: '1,153 Jewish plunderers were shot dead by Police Regiment Centre in yesterday's mopping up activities in Slonim.'[6]

On 4 August von dem Bach-Zelewski reported that in further mopping-up operations in an area south of the Belorussian town of Pinsk his men had shot dead '90 Bolsheviks and Jews'. Later the same day, he reported that his SS Cavalry Brigade was still putting down opposition in the region north-northeast of Lake Sporowski. 'As at the evening of 3 August the SS Cavalry Brigade had liquidated 3,274 Partisans and Jewish Bolsheviks. Police Battalion 306 has shot dead 260 guerrillas', he said.[7] Three days later von dem Bach-Zelewski reported that the SS Cavalry Brigade was now pushing further forwards. 'By midday today a further 3,600 had been executed, so that the complete total for those executed by the brigade is now 7,819. This brings the total in my area to more than 30,000.'[8] His apparent determination to make as much of the killings as possible was such that one Bletchley Park analyst noted: 'The tone of this message suggests that word has gone out that a definite decrease in the total population of Russia would be welcome in high quarters and that the leaders of the three sectors stand somewhat in competition with each other as to their scores.'[9]

There had, as yet, been no indication in the messages intercepted at Chicksands that the police units in the north and the south were killing Jews. Although there was no doubt that ruthless brutality was being inflicted on the local population throughout the occupied areas of the Soviet Union. On 24 August, clearly angered by the intercepts, Churchill made a BBC broadcast in which he denounced the 'most frightful cruelties' that were being carried out in those parts of the Soviet Union occupied by German forces. 'Whole districts are being exterminated', the British Prime Minister said.

Scores of thousands – literally scores of thousands – of executions in cold blood are perpetrated by the German police troops upon the Soviet patriots who defend their native soil. Since the Mongol invasions of Europe, there has never been methodical, merciless butchery on such a scale or approaching such a scale. We are in the presence of a crime without a name.[10]

Churchill did not mention anywhere in his speech that large numbers of those killed were Jews. Sir Martin Gilbert, in his magisterial history of the Holocaust suggests that Churchill did not do so for reasons of security. He did not want to give away the fact that Britain was reading Germany's codes and ciphers.[11] Professor Breitman dismisses this suggestion, rightly pointing out that Churchill mentioned the police troops, which he could only have known from the intercepts. He also makes the point that the Nazi persecution of the Jews was already well known, so Churchill could have mentioned the Jews. Confusingly, Professor Breitman also suggests Churchill's speech was not sparked off by the killings of the Jews since at this stage there was not, in his opinion, 'enough clear information' to indicate the Nazi focus on killing Jews.[12] I shall come back to the arguments surrounding this issue later.

On 23 August 1941, the day before Churchill made his speech, Bletchley Park deciphered a message from SS *Gruppenführer* Friedrich Jeckeln, commander of the SS and police troops in the south which confirmed that he was also busy killing Jews. In a report sent not only to Himmler and Daluege but also to Reinhard Heydrich, head of the Security Police, Jeckeln said 314 Battalion of the Police Regiment South had shot dead 367 Jews in the area around the Ukrainian towns of Belokorovichi and Luginy, southwest of Kiev.[13] This was an important message. It confirmed the analysis of the Bletchley Park intelligence reporter that there was more to the killings of Jews than just von dem Bach-Zelewski misinterpreting his orders, or portraying his actions in a way likely to curry favour with his superiors. It was very clear that Jews were being killed simply because they were Jews. Its content may have been relayed verbally to Churchill by Menzies. They discussed intelligence matters each morning and the Prime Minister was very clearly interested in the activities of the police troops operating behind the Eastern Front. It would be strange indeed if Churchill had not discussed them with Menzies prior to making his BBC broadcast.

The first message deciphered by the British on 24 August, the actual day that Churchill made the broadcast, found Jeckeln telling Himmler, Daluege and Heydrich that the 10th Infantry Regiment of the 1st SS Brigade had taken 29 prisoners and shot dead 65 'Bolshevik Jews'. His *Einsatzgruppe* had 'shot dead 12 bandits and guerrillas and 70 Jews' while 314 Battalion of the Police Regiment South had shot dead 294 Jews; 45 Battalion had shot dead 61 Jews and the Police Squadron (possibly members of the small police air force accompanying the police troops) had shot dead 113 Jews.[14]

The item was the first to be decoded that day by Bletchley Park's military section so it is possible that it was sent on by teleprinter to MI6 in time for Menzies to have discussed it with Churchill before the Prime Minister made his 'crime without a name' broadcast. But the evidence appears to suggest that, at the very least, Churchill had not seen the full details of either of the two Jeckeln messages, because a few days later, on 27 August 1941, Bletchley Park issued the first of a special series of Most Secret reports concerning the activities of the police troops and specifically prepared for Churchill.[15]

These reports, which were released to the Public Record Office in 1993, were written out on good quality paper, in stark contrast to the normal, poor quality, flimsy paper that was so common at Bletchley Park. There is only one copy, to be kept on file at Bletchley Park. The report itself goes to Menzies, who as well as being head of MI6 is also the official Director of the Government Code and Cypher School (GC&CS), and he passes it on to Churchill in his daily bundle of intelligence, singling it out in the covering letter. This of course suggests very firmly that Churchill was very interested in the police and had asked specifically to be informed about their activities. The reports are concise and to the point and signed personally by Nigel de Grey, the head of research in Hut 3. de Grey was an experienced code breaker who had worked for Room 40, the Admiralty's First World War codebreaking unit, and had joined GC&CS at its inception in 1919. He would later become Deputy Director of GC&CS and, for five years after the war, GCHQ.[16]

de Grey's first report in this series covers Jeckeln's message of 23 August announcing that his men operating in the Luginy area had shot dead 367 Jews. It was seen by Churchill on 28 August and the Prime Minister signified his particular interest in the killings of the Jews by circling the figure 367.[17] The second on 30 August began with the words: 'Further light on the use being made of the Police Forces in the back areas on the Russian front is shed by some of the daily reports received.' It went on to recount the details of Jeckeln's message of 24 August and the killing of a total of 603 Jews.[18]

In this second report, de Grey added new information on further killings from another report to Berlin by Jeckeln, this time on 25 August, in which he reported that his men operating south of Kiev had killed 1,625 Jews. The 1st SS Brigade had taken 85 prisoners and shot dead 283 Jews while the Police Regiment South had shot dead 1,342 Jews. Churchill circled the latter figure, the largest figure so far for a single massacre. Also on 25 August, von dem Bach-Zelewski broke what for him appears at first sight to have been a period of silence on the killings, to say that the SS Cavalry Brigade, which was operating in the Pripet marshes, had killed 92 Soviet soldiers and 150 Jews.[19]

Another similarly carefully compiled report in the same series on the same day contained totally innocuous information about the activities of German police forces in Yugoslavia. It was produced by de Grey on the same high quality paper, again this suggests that Churchill had demanded that he be sent any reports on the activities of the German police troops in the occupied territories.[20]

I think that at this point we need to recap and make a number of points. First, the code breakers have received, and passed on, reports of killings of Jews from von dem Bach-Zelewski and now from Jeckeln. They do not have any from SS *Gruppenführer* Hans-Adolf Prützmann, the commander of the SS and police troops in the north. This does not mean that his men have not been carrying out any killings, any more than the fact that our first report from Jeckeln came on 23 August means that prior to that period his men had not done so either.

In fact, we know they were all carrying out massacres – murdering large numbers of people, the majority, by no means all, but the majority Jews – because there is a wealth of evidence from a number of other sources telling us that they were:

- Human witnesses.
- German written reports produced as evidence during the International Military Tribunals at Nuremburg.
- A collection of Himmler's radio messages held in the Military Archive in Prague and on microfilm at the US Holocaust Museum.
- German Operational Situation Reports for the Russian Campaign held in the archives of Yad Vashem, the Holocaust Memorial Museum just outside Jerusalem.

There may be a number of reasons why the killings that we know were going on are not reflected in full in the Bletchley Park files released to the Public Record Office, the most likely being that they were simply not intercepted. The northern SS and Police forces were having communications problems. Prützmann was almost certainly sending his reports on the killings of the Jews, which were designated as 'state secrets', via the more secure landline. Before the fall of France, Bletchley Park had largely relied on German police messages intercepted in France and deciphered by its mission to the French Deuxième Bureau east of Paris, because coverage in Britain was so patchy.

By now the interception of German police messages was an army responsibility and was mainly taking place at the RAF station at Chicksands Priory – a temporary measure caused by German bombing of the original army intercept site at Chatham in Kent.[21] Reception was not good enough to give complete coverage of the different radio nets involved – given the frequencies in use for the lower level nets, even in ideal conditions, this would not have been possible – and the Bletchley Park analysts frequently mention gaps in interception. There were also signs that radio security was being tightened up – almost certainly as the result of a signals security investigation set in train by Churchill's speech. The cipher in use was now changing twice daily instead of only once and this was making it more difficult to decipher the messages that were being intercepted.[22] This is almost certainly why a message sent by Jeckeln on 26 August 1941 and in which he reports that his units had shot a further 1,246 Jews, was not included in the 30 August report to Churchill.[23] It was issued separately on 1 September and seen by Churchill a day later. Again the Prime Minister circled the figure for the number of Jews shot.[24] The slaughter was unremitting. Jeckeln reported on 30 August that the Police Regiment South had shot dead 45 Jews in the central Ukrainian town of Slavuta[25] and von dem Bach-Zelewski reported that his men had shot dead 84 Jews in the Belorussian town of Gorodishche.[26] A day later, on 31 August, Jeckeln reported that 911 more Jews had been shot dead in Slavuta and a further 2,200 Jews shot dead in Minkowzky.[27] This was reported to Churchill on 6 September simply as 'over 3,000 Jews shot by various units'.[28]

On 2 September Jeckeln reported that his men had shot dead a further 60 Jews and 15 Partisans in the Kaments-Podolsky region of the southern Ukraine.[29] Four days later, on 6 September, they had shot dead 494 Jews and two Partisans.[30] On September 11 Jeckeln reported that Police Regiment South had liquidated 1,548 Jews 'according to the usage of war'.[31] This euphemism was commonly used. The victims were variously 'disposed of'; 'liquidated'; 'executed'; 'shot dead'; or sometimes simply 'evacuated'. The upshot was, of course, always the same.

The next day, 12 September, the German Police changed their cipher, starting with the ciphers in use by the police troops in the occupied areas of the Soviet Union. Previously they had used a double transposition system. In a transposition cipher, the letters that make up the text of the message are shuffled in some pre-determined way. As the name suggests, in a double transposition system, the order of letters produced by the initial process is shuffled a second time. Now the Germans used a system known as Double Playfair, a fairly sophisticated substitution system, albeit one that Bletchley Park was able to break again with relative ease.[32]

Also on 12 September, Churchill sees his final report on the killing of Jews during this initial period. There were very clear decryption difficulties with this report. It is only shown to Churchill on 12 September, although it dates back to 27 August, when Jeckeln reported that the 1st SS Brigade had killed 16 Jews and Partisans; Police Regiment South had shot dead 914 Jews; and the 'Special Handling Staff' with 320 Police Battalion had shot dead 4,200 Jews. At the bottom of the report, de Grey notes: 'The fact that the Police are killing all Jews that fall into their hands should by now be sufficiently appreciated. It is not therefore proposed to continue reporting these butcheries specially, unless so requested.' The use of the word 'specially' confirms that the reports were specially commissioned, and the way in which the note is phrased suggests that they were commissioned by Churchill himself.[33]

The day after the ciphers were changed General Daluege sent the following message to Jeckeln, von dem Bach-Zelewski and Prützmann; it was either not intercepted in full at Chicksands or could not be completely deciphered at Bletchley Park, but the gist of what it said was clear: 'The danger of decipherment by the enemy of wireless messages is great', Daluege warned. Information containing state secrets, 'which includes precise figures for executions' should not be sent by radio. 'Any references to these are to be sent by courier.' At this point the messages from the Eastern Front dry up as the German commanders obey Daluege's orders.[34]

There can be no coincidence that the speech by Churchill, which made clear that police troops were being used in the massacres in the German-occupied areas of the Soviet Union, was followed within a few weeks by increased signals security measures. First, there was the move from changing the cipher keys daily to twice daily. Then there was a switch to a different, more complex cipher and a day later there is a warning from Daluege not to send the totals of those killed with the limited security provided by what was only a medium-grade cipher. This bears all the hallmarks of a classic response to a communications security breach. The Bletchley Park intelligence analyst compiling the summary of police activity for this period appears to agree, preceding the transcript of Daluege's warning with the suggestion that he may have been 'alarmed perhaps by our evident awareness of the unspeakable activities of his police in Russia', an apparent reference to the Churchill broadcast.[35]

Which brings us back to the differing conclusions of Sir Martin Gilbert and Professor Breitman. Why did Churchill not refer to the Jews? Was he concerned about cipher security? If he discussed the broadcast with Menzies – and given its content and the subsequent special series of reports on police activities, it seems likely that he would have done – then the MI6 chief would certainly have reminded him of the dangers. Possibly there was a compromise made. The mention of both Jews and the police would have left absolutely no doubt as to how Churchill had acquired the information. Possibly he did not mention the Jews because they were not the only ones being killed. Partisans, homosexuals, gypsies, communists, even on occasion captured Soviet soldiers. They were all likely to become the victims of the German police troops.

Menzies would have been fighting all the way to try to remove any references from the broadcast that might give away the fact that the cipher had been broken. MI6 was extremely concerned to protect the security of the intelligence coming out of Bletchley Park and controlled it with what some regarded as too much rigour.[36] During the 1920s the politicians had given away codebreaking secrets with disastrous results (Churchill had been a party to one of those errors) but since he was determined to speak out a compromise had to be made.[37]

Professor Breitman points out that the reports of the killings were not sent using an Enigma cipher and at first sight that is an apparently strong argument against those who specify the protection of the Enigma secret as a reason for Churchill to leave out any mention of the Jews. But similar messages were no doubt being sent by the SS using their operational Enigma cipher, which was codenamed Orange II by the code breakers. The British had broken Orange I, an SS administrative cipher which contained nothing on the killings of the Jews. But at this stage they had not broken Orange II.[38] What would have happened if the Germans had decided that the British had broken this cipher? It would have taken only a few changes to the Enigma machine ciphers to ensure they were unbreakable. The advantage the British had through their breaking of Enigma, which is estimated to have taken as much as two years off the end of the war, would have been lost. The other thing the Germans could have done was precisely what the Soviets did in 1927 after Stanley Baldwin, the then Prime Minister resorted to reading out deciphered Soviet telegrams in Parliament, change the hand-cipher to a one-time pad system, which when properly used would have been unbreakable. The medium-grade ciphers used by the police and the German army were an invaluable aid to deciphering Enigma.[39] If the Germans replaced their medium-grade ciphers with a one-time pad system, it would have been a disaster for Bletchley Park.

For all of these reasons, I am afraid I cannot accept Professor Breitman's attack on Churchill. But while that made the headlines, it was not the only attack Professor Breitman made. Statements made by British officials on the plight of the Jews in the 1930s and early 1940s were frequently crass. But it is important not to take them out of context. Professor Breitman takes one Bletchley Park analyst to task for a note appended to the 12 September 1941 report to Churchill in which he states that

> the execution of 'Jews' is so recurrent a feature of these reports that the figures have been omitted from the situation reports and brought under one heading. Whether all those executed as 'Jews' are indeed such is of course doubtful; but the figures are no less conclusive as evidence of a policy of savage intimidation if not of ultimate extermination.[40]

The note is written several months before the Wannsee Conference. Yet Professor Breitman appears to regard the Bletchley Park analyst as a holocaust-denier. 'Perhaps this analyst was...not particularly familiar with Nazi racial thought', Professor Breitman writes. 'Whereas it was quite conceivable that the Nazis wanted to get rid of large numbers of people, there was something uncomfortable about concluding that they were isolating and executing Jews – hence the use of quotation marks and the note of doubt.'[41] But the Bletchley analyst was simply stating the truth. Large numbers of people were being killed; there is no doubt that a large majority of them were Jews but there were many others. The analyst's point was that the killing of Jews was not simply sanctioned, the police commanders in the field knew that the more Jews they killed the better it would look for them. Hidden among the numbers of 'Jews' would have been many non-Jews. With that in mind, the note is nothing more than a common sense rider that took into account the vagaries of war before pointing out that the evidence of extermination was nonetheless overwhelming. As we have already seen, only the day before, de Grey was telling Churchill that 'the fact that the Police are killing all Jews that fall into their hands should by now be sufficiently appreciated'.[42]

Where then did Bletchley Park or MI6 fall down in response to the killings? Was there an intelligence failure with regard to the German police messages? The academic study of intelligence focuses on what is known as 'the intelligence cycle', which divides the production of intelligence into three main processes: collection, analysis/interpretation and dissemination. As we have seen, the intelligence was collected in that, where atmospheric conditions made it possible, the German police messages were intercepted. Although Professor Breitman has cast doubt on some of the code breakers' interpretation of the messages, we have seen that this is unfounded. The messages were analysed as being precisely what they were, evidence of a policy of widespread slaughter on the Eastern Front with Jews being the main, although by no means the only, target. The only remaining process is dissemination and we know the content of the messages was sent to Churchill. There is therefore no intelligence failure. Bletchley Park reacted properly and in a very timely fashion, providing very early evidence of what we now know as the Holocaust.

What did the British do with that evidence? On 8 October 1942, Victor Cavendish-Bentinck, Chairman of the Joint Intelligence Committee (JIC), wrote to Sir Alexander Cadogan, the head of the Foreign Office, suggesting that two officials be tasked with collecting evidence of atrocities. He pointed out that 'two of our most reliable sources on intelligence cannot be used until after the war'. These were signals intelligence, the decrypts of the reports from the German police mopping up behind the Eastern Front, and the transcripts of bugged conversations among German PoWs.[43]

Roger Allen, a Foreign Office official, and a trained lawyer, would oversee the collection of the evidence from the Bletchley Park decrypts and the transcripts of the bugged conversations, assisted by another Foreign Office official, a Mr Campbell. Menzies wrote to de Grey telling him to have a dossier of the killings in occupied parts of the Soviet Union compiled and sent to MI6 so that it could be passed on to the Foreign Office. The dossier could be kept up to date by monthly supplementary reports. de Grey had three thick files of the messages detailing the killings compiled – the most important of the messages are marked out with a red crayon line alongside them. There was also a fourth file containing working aids to assist in the understanding of the files and they were sent to the Foreign Office, via MI6, sometime in 1943.[44]

At the meeting of the JIC on 22 December 1942, Allen briefed the members on the work to collect evidence of war crimes. The Foreign Office was now collecting evidence of war crimes not just against Britons but against other countries' citizens, he said. Those details would be passed on to the countries whose citizens were affected.[45] Why then was the evidence not used as part of the international tribunal set up in Nuremberg to punish Nazi war crimes?

Although Cavendish-Bentinck had suggested that Bletchley Park's evidence of Nazi atrocities could be used after the war, within a few months, he was telling the JIC that 'some of the best evidence on this subject is derived from sources that might make it undesirable to use it'.[46] At the end of the war, there was a blanket ban on the disclosure of any details about what had gone on at Bletchley Park, not just of the Enigma decrypts but of any other intelligence produced there. Nothing that indicated that the British had been intercepting the messages of both its enemies and its allies during the war was to be released. The ban on what could be said about Britain's signals intelligence capabilities was all-embracing.[47] There was no cover-up. Just a determination to ensure that Britain's interception and codebreaking capabilities were not damaged by the release of too much information.

Writing on intelligence issues is a complex business, particularly when the only sources used are official documents, which all too often represent only a snapshot of history rather a considered overview. Very few of those who are not, or have not been, practitioners are able to put themselves into the position of those involved and fully understand the processes taking place.[48] Professor Breitman is undoubtedly one of the leading authorities on the Holocaust. *Official Secrets* is a very important book, pulling together a large number of sources to show the appalling barbarism of the Nazi attacks on the Jews and others as they pushed forward into Russia in the second half of 1941. But Professor Breitman is not an intelligence expert and as a result his book is not based on a proper understanding of the process involved in the collection, analysis and dissemination of the intelligence harvested from the German Police decodes. Its attacks on Churchill and the Bletchley Park code breakers, repeated unquestioningly by journalists around the world, were wrong and a prime example of how anyone, no matter how careful and studious and whether they be a journalist or academic, can get history wrong.

Notes

1 R. Breitman, *Official Secrets: What the Nazis Planned, What the British and Americans Knew* (New York: Hill & Wang, 1998). (All further references to this book will come from the updated British paperback edition published by Penguin Books, London, in 2000); James Bone and Michael Binyon, 'Britain Accused of Hiding Facts on Holocaust', *The Times*, 15 October 1998; Dominic Donald, 'Should Churchill have Acted?', *The Times*, 15 October 1998; Hugo Gurdon, MI6 'Concealed Extermination of Jews for a Year', *Daily Telegraph*, 15 October 1998.
2 F.H. Hinsley, *British Intelligence in the Second World War*, Vol. 2, Appendix 5, the German Police Cyphers, pp. 669–73.
3 James Bone and Michael Binyon, 'Britain Accused of Hiding Facts on Holocaust', *The Times*, 15 October 1998.
4 Ibid., pp. 37–41.
5 Public Record Office, Kew, Surrey (PRO), HW3/165, BP (Bletchley Park) History: Chapter X, Story of the Special Liaison Units, pp. 178–9.
6 PRO, HW16/45, selected reports illustrating GP (German Police) war crimes in Russia and the Ukraine, 18.7.41 item 15. (Slonim is a town in southwest Belorussia, midway between Warsaw and Minsk.)
7 PRO, HW16/45, 4.8.41, item 9.
8 PRO, HW16/45, 7.8.41, item 24.
9 PRO, HW16/6, bound volume of BP GP periodic summaries, p. 4.
10 Winston Churchill, BBC broadcast, 24 August 1941.

11 Martin Gilbert, *The Holocaust* (HarperCollins, London, 1987), p. 186.
12 Breitman, *Official Secrets*, pp. 93–4.
13 PRO, HW16/45, 23.8.41, item 4.
14 PRO, HW16/45, 24.8.41, item 1.
15 PRO, HW1/30, signals intelligence passed to the Prime Minister, messages and correspondence, 28 August 1941, item 12; HW1/35, 31 August 1941, item 13; HW1/40, 2 September, item 13; HW1/51, 6 September 1941, item 6; HW1/62, 12 September 1941, item 9.
16 For de Grey, see M. Smith, *Station X: The Codebreakers of Bletchley Park* (London: Channel Four Books, 1998), pp. 10–11, 179–80.
17 PRO, HW1/30, item 12.
18 PRO, HW1/35, item 13.
19 PRO, HW16/45, 25.8.41, item 9.
20 PRO, HW1/35, item 12.
21 PRO, HW3/165, pp. 178–9.
22 PRO, HW3/155, history of the GC&CS German Police Section 1939–45.
23 PRO, HW16/45, 26.8.41, item 18.
24 PRO, HW1/40, item 13.
25 PRO, HW16/45, 30.8.41, item 1.
26 PRO, HW16/45, 30.8.41, item 4.
27 PRO, HW16/45, 31.8.41, item 1.
28 PRO, HW1/51, item 6.
29 PRO, HW16/45, 2.9.41, item 2.
30 PRO, HW16/45, 6.9.41, item 2.
31 PRO, HW16/45, 11.9.41, item 1.
32 Smith, *Station X*, pp. 74–5; PRO, HW3/155.
33 PRO, HW16/45, 27.8.41, item 1; HW1/62, item 9.
34 PRO, HW16/6, MSGP 28, 12 September 1941.
35 Ibid.
36 M. Smith and R. Erskine (eds), *Action This Day: Bletchley Park from Breaking of the Enigma Code to the Birth of the Modern Computer* (London: Bantam Press, 2001), pp. 288–9.
37 Ibid., pp. 25–6.
38 Hinsley, *British Intelligence*, Vol. 2, p. 669.
39 Ibid., p. 670.
40 Breitman, *Official Secrets*, p. 96.
41 Ibid.
42 PRO, HW1/62, item 9.
43 PRO, CAB 81/90, minutes of JIC meeting on 8 October 1942.
44 PRO, HW16/44, miscellaneous notes and working aids for accompanying batch of German language message decrypts; HW16/45, selected reports illustrating GP war crimes in Russia and the Ukraine; HW16/46, illustrations of war crimes; HW16/47, illustrations of war crimes.
45 PRO, CAB81/90, minutes of JIC meeting on 22 December 1942.
46 Ibid.
47 PRO, CAB103/288, JIC (48) 14 (0), 11 February 1948.
48 For the view of a code breaker who worked on the messages see Smith, *Station X*, p. 76.

8 Fiction, Faction and Intelligence

Nigel West

It is one of the paradoxes of the British intelligence tradition that whereas there is a convention, and now a criminal statute, to prevent intelligence officers from making unauthorised disclosures, more have done so in this country than anywhere else in the world. This paper is intended to be a survey of intelligence literature, concentrating on books published by British Security Service (MI5) and British Secret Intelligence Service (SIS) officers.[1] Its central argument is that, contrary to what has commonly been assumed, the British intelligence community has entered the public sphere often since its creation, primarily in the form of memoirs, fictionalised memoirs and classic spy fiction.[2]

A few definitions are required because, at least in the mind of the public, there are some grey areas in the specialist field of intelligence literature. A case in point is the notorious *A Man Called Intrepid*, the hopelessly unreliable 1974 biography of Sir William Stephenson, which was reclassified as fiction by Macmillan Publishers in the United States following complaints and bad reviews.[3]

And what of MI5's official publications? I recall being told by a senior MI5 molehunter that one of the most interesting MI5 documents in the public domain was not only considered extremely important, but was known within the service to be a work of fiction written by a Soviet spy suspect. The document in question, I later discovered, was the 1955 Burgess and Maclean White Paper written by Graham Mitchell, who was then MI5's Director of Counter-Espionage, and was later to be investigated as a possible Soviet mole in the notorious PETERS enquiry.[4] Bizarrely, one of the items of evidence used against Mitchell was the content of the White Paper, which contained numerous errors of fact but some other quite inexplicable untruths, upon which the molehunters placed the more sinister construction. Accordingly, even what is purported to be copper-bottomed fact, from an ostensibly reliable source, can fall into the realms of fiction, or a potentially confusing mixture of the two, faction.

Most of the books to be considered in this paper are written by authors with intelligence experience and who have drawn on this experience when writing espionage fiction.[5] The cast of characters is rich, and includes Graham Greene, Compton Mackenzie, Somerset Maugham, Ian Fleming, Malcolm Muggeridge, Alec Waugh, Valentine Williams, Kenneth Benton, Geoffrey Household and David Cornwell, all of whom served in the Secret Intelligence Service, and

John Bingham, Maxwell Knight, Derek Tangye and John Dickson Carr, who worked for the wartime Security Service. Furthermore, apart from the very large number of SIS and MI5 officers who have published accounts of their own careers, both with and without permission, there is a parallel convention of both organisations giving covert assistance to individual outsiders who are working on approved subjects. Into this latter category fall authors such as Alan Moorehead, Alan Judd and Gordon Brook-Shepherd, whereas Courtney Young, ghosting for the defector Alexander Foote, received encouragement from their own respective services for their literary endeavour.[6] As well as writing the biography of Sir Mansfield Smith-Cumming, Judd (actually Alan Petty, formerly Personal Assistant to the Chief of the Secret Service Sir Colin McColl) has also ventured into fiction, with the bestseller *Legacy*.[7] Most recently, Andrew Cook has followed Brook-Shepherd into SIS's archive to read Sidney Reilly's file and produce *On His Majesty's Secret Service: Sidney Reilly, Codename ST-1*.[8] While Brook-Shepherd was an early beneficiary of the Waldegrave Initiative to open requested Whitehall classified documents of historical importance to historians, Cook says he exploited his ministerial connections, as an aide to the Secretary of State for Defence George Robertson, to receive a briefing from SIS, and be given access to a dossier known as the Reilly Papers.

There exists a widespread suspicion that selected, trusted outsiders are routinely given the run of MI5 and SIS registries, but this is far from the truth. Certainly Gordon Brook-Shepherd received plenty of official help with two of his books, but one led him into treacherous waters of a threatened defamation action when the files disclosed the identity of a suspected traitor in the Royal Navy, and the other caused panic amongst officialdom when there was an innocent acknowledgement of the assistance he had received while researching Sidney Reilly's adventures in SIS's archive. The co-operation that benefited Alan Moorehead was altogether of a more sinister variety, and its purpose was to conceal the Security Service's blunder over the clearance given to the atom spy Klaus Fuchs. The investigation had been bungled from the very first moment when Fuchs was granted a clean bill of health by MI5 when its own files listed him as a communist. Furthermore, a note on his personal file in 1946 recommending he be the subject of an immediate espionage enquiry had been ignored and, even worse, when finally he was unmasked as a spy in 1949 the Director-General, Sir Percy Sillitoe, was persuaded by his senior staff to conceal MI5's incompetence. As a result, based on Sillitoe's bogus assurances, Clement Attlee made a statement to the Commons in March 1950 containing patently false information, so in 1952 the Director-General authorised Jim Skardon to feed sanitised versions of MI5's files on Allan Nunn May, Klaus Fuchs and Bruno Pontecorvo to the journalist Alan Moorehead, thus ensuring *The Traitors* provided a less than accurate version of the atomic spies. In particular, Moorehead stated authoritatively that Fuchs had been the subject of a routine but detailed investigation while at Harwell in 1946 but it

> happened to coincide with just that period, on his return from the United States, when Fuchs was dormant... This was pure bad luck; had the enquiry

started a month or two later, there was every possibility that he would have been caught nearly three years earlier.[9]

Actually, this was MI5's fiction, peddled to Moorehead as fact, on the explicit instructions of Sillitoe.[10]

Graham Greene never wrote any non-fiction about his own experience in Section V, nor his posting to Freetown between January 1941 and March 1943. But there can be little doubt that his books, which demonstrate a preoccupation with espionage and the issues of loyalty and betrayal, draw on his own knowledge. His first book of espionage, *The Confidential Agent*, was released before he joined SIS, but his sister Elizabeth by then had been employed as one of Stewart Menzies's secretaries, so he knew something of the business. As well as writing humorously about the organisation in *Our Man in Havana*, he dealt with some of the more serious issues in *The Human Factor*, and even contributed a foreword to Kim Philby's memoirs, *My Silent War*.[11] This latter effort was received with dismay by SIS because Greene had asked, 'who among us has not committed treason to something or someone more important than a country?' This rhetorical question was almost certainly calculated to enrage the then current Chief, Sir Dick White, who replied angrily that he had never betrayed anyone. Greene also loftily compared Philby's commitment to communism with Catholics enduring the Spanish Inquisition, a moral equivalence that thereafter served to isolate the novelist from his former colleagues.[12]

It is worth noting, in passing, that Greene was brought into SIS from the *Spectator*, a journal that was also to provide the service with a veritable pool of literary talent, among them Derek Verschoyle, Archie Lyall, Goronwy Rees and Cyril Ray, not forgetting the art critic, Anthony Blunt, who joined MI5 and wrote a short biography of his wartime colleague, *Tomas Harris*.[13]

Compton Mackenzie's contribution to intelligence literature is in part based upon his own notoriety, following the publication in October 1932 of the third volume of his wartime memoirs, *Greek Memories*, in which he gave an account of his work for SIS in the Aegean in 1917. Mackenzie pleaded guilty to a breach of the Official Secrets Act and was fined £100, and subsequently took his revenge on the organisation with the publication of *Water on the Brain*, in which he wickedly mocked SIS and its management.[14] Another of the Chief of SIS's First World War recruits, Somerset Maugham, also found himself threatened with the Official Secrets Act, and was obliged to destroy his second volume of *Ashenden*, his collection of short stories about a British agent on the continent, clearly drawn from his own adventures in wartime Switzerland.[15] The treatment received by Maugham was certainly unusual, for his fiction could hardly be described as a work of disclosure, whereas Sir Paul Dukes (*The Story of ST-25*), Samuel Hoare (*The Fourth Seal*), William Gibson (*Wild Career*) and George Hill (*Go Spy the Land*) seem to have received a measure of official approval despite revealing a good deal about SIS's clandestine operations during the Great War.[16]

One of the pre-war SIS officers to establish the organisation's strong literary tradition was Valentine Williams, creator of the *Clubfoot* series of thrillers writing as Valentine Douglas, and a close friend of the first Chief, Sir Mansfield Smith-Cumming. Williams served at SIS's Broadway headquarters before being transferred to Washington, DC, in 1941, and thereafter he wrote novels and screenplays in Hollywood.[17]

The post-war literary tradition of British intelligence is dominated by Ian Fleming, David Cornwell (writing as John le Carré) and Kenneth Benton. Fleming's contribution to intelligence literature lies in James Bond, the most famous British agent in the world. Bond was described by a former SIS Chief, Sir Colin McColl, as 'the best recruiting sergeant the service ever had' because half the population of the world has seen a Bond movie and therefore has heard of the British Secret Service. Fleming himself knew about his subject because he had acted as an agent for SIS while reporting for Reuters on a trial in Moscow of Allan Monkhouse in 1933. Furthermore, he had been educated at a finishing school in Kitzbühel run by Major Ernan Forbes-Dennis, formerly the SIS station commander in Vienna, and of course during the war had served in the Naval Intelligence Division as an assistant to the Director, Admiral John Godfrey. The inspiration for his first Bond novel, *Casino Royale*, allegedly originated from a visit to the Estoril Casino in Portugal in 1941. The portable 'Lecta' Russian cipher machine described in *From Russia With Love*, which is at the centre of the plot, sounds suspiciously close to an Enigma.[18] But who inspired Fleming to write about 'the British Secret Service'? His tutor Forbes-Dennis may have played a part in this, but the latter's wife, Phyllis Bottome should not be overlooked, for in 1946 she wrote a spy novel, *The Lifeline*, which doubtless Fleming read, that centred on a 36-year-old British agent, 'Mark Chalmers' – an amateur mountaineer and an 'Eton beak'.[19] Bond, of course, shared the same age and sport, and had been educated in Switzerland. In her autobiography, *The Goal*, Bottome revealed that her husband's post in pre-war Vienna had also given him responsibility for supervising SIS's outposts in Budapest and Belgrade, and that his office had been staffed by Alymer Macartney, from Prague, and 'Miss Margery Bates, who was known, for her skilled and responsible counter-espionage work in Switzerland, as "Sergeant-Major Bill"'.[20] Those who were close to Fleming knew all too well the extent to which he drew on them for his characters. The legendary Caribbean diver Blanche Blackwell, who was his long-time girlfriend, is easily recognisable as the beauty played so memorably by Ursula Andress in *Dr No*.

As for Bond himself, there have been several candidates proposed for Fleming's model, if indeed he did not base the character on himself, or his elder brother Peter. Among them are the dashing diplomat Fitzroy Maclean (author of *Eastern Approaches*), Fleming's pre-war skiing companion Conrad O'Brien-ffrench (*Delicate Mission*), his old friend Ivar Bryce (*You Only Live Once*) who worked for the wartime British Security Co-ordination in New York, and, rather less likely, the wartime double agent Dusko Popov (*Spy CounterSpy*) who, despite his hunchback, exercised a tremendous magnetism for beautiful women, among them the French movie star Simone Simone.[21]

While the Bond novel could never have been mistaken for the real thing, even some of the cognoscenti have accepted George Smiley as an accurate portrayal of a molehunter. David Cornwell's celebrity stems in part from his well-known service with SIS in Bonn and then Hamburg between 1960 and 1964, which is often alleged to have given his novels verisimilitude. Cornwell himself credited Maugham, asserting that 'the Ashenden stories were certainly an influence in my work. I suppose that Maugham was the first person to write about espionage in a mood of disenchantment and almost prosaic reality.'[22] The extent to which *The Spy Who Came in from the Cold*, which was published while the author was operating under diplomatic cover in Germany, and *Tinker, Tailor, Soldier, Spy* bear any relation to reality is probably a suitable subject for detailed analysis, but we do now know that his model for George Smiley was John Bingham, a senior MI5 case officer. Although Maurice Oldfield (whom the actor Alec Guinness met to prepare himself for the role), and others, have been proposed as possible candidates for the humourless counter-intelligence expert, the reality is that Cornwell had a less well-publicised role in the Security Service, dating back to his undergraduate days at Lincoln College, Oxford.[23] Cornwell did not confirm Bingham's identity until after the latter's death, perhaps because his mentor strongly disapproved of the way he misrepresented the intelligence profession, and in particular criticised his portrayal of intelligence officers as 'moles, morons, shits and homosexuals'. He claimed that his approach 'makes the Intelligence job no easier, and he was certainly in a position to know'. Later Lord Clanmorris, Bingham spent his career in the Security Service and wrote many novels, including *The Double Agent*.[24]

To demonstrate the almost incestuous nature of MI5's overlap with novelists, it is worth noting that Bingham was a protégé of that pre-eminent MI5 agent handler, Maxwell Knight, a thriller-writer who wrote *Crime Cargo*, recruited his staff over dinner at the Authors' Club in Whitehall Court, and that one of his books was illustrated by David Cornwell. In addition, Bingham's wife Madeleine and his daughter Charlotte both worked for MI5, and both are distinguished novelists (*Peers and Plebs*, and *Kind Hearts and Coronets*, respectively).[25] Furthermore, Bingham's assistant in the Security Service, Bill Younger, wrote *Skin Trap*, using the nom-de-plume of William Mole, and his mother, Joan, who was also in MI5 and was married Dennis Wheatley, also used the pen-name Eve Chaucer to write *No Ordinary Virgin*. If one pursues these family, literary links within MI5 one might note that Younger's sister also worked for MI5, as did their cousin Kenneth, later a Labour MP, whose 1964 book *Changing Perspectives in British Foreign Policy* cannot, alas, be said to have any direct relevance to intelligence.[26]

The case of Sir John Masterman, however, who chaired the famous wartime 'Double Cross' or 'Twenty Committee', and co-ordinated MI5's double agent operations, is extraordinary in that he not only wrote the definitive account of his committee's work in 1972, he also produced an autobiography, *On The Chariot Wheel*, several murder mysteries including *An Oxford Tragedy* and, more relevant for our purposes, in 1957 wrote *The Case of the Four Friends*.[27] Part of the latter novel was set in wartime Lisbon, which he described as a kind of international clearing-ground, a busy ant-heap of spies and agents where political and military secrets and information – true and false but mainly false – were bought and sold and where men's brains were pitted against each other.

His representation of life as an intelligence operative is equally dramatic: 'The life of the secret agent is dangerous enough, but the life of the double agent is infinitely more precarious. If anyone balances on a swaying tight-rope it is he, and a single slip must send him crashing to destruction.'[28] Having mentioned a character named Chapman (perhaps a reference to the wartime double agent Eddie Chapman, codenamed ZIGZAG, whose case was very familiar to Masterman) the author described a fictional double agent named Bannister 'who was well-known and respected in British and allied diplomatic and business circles'. Like the real ZIGZAG, Bannister had risked a journey to Berlin:

> Through a long and cautious period he had insinuated himself into the confidence of the Germans who, as time went on, believed that they had bought him and that he was firmly attached to them. He gave them information at a high price, and enough of that information was correct and true for them to believe more and more that self-interest bound him to them. Once to my certain knowledge, and, I surmise, on another occasion also, Bannister was smuggled into Germany and visited both Berlin and Hamburg for consultations. It's not necessary to stress the cool, the almost unnatural courage which was necessary for these journeys. I can picture the long interviews with German secret service chiefs – at which a false word or unconscious admission or slip would have meant death . . . [29]

This is a superb illustration of the 'faction' genre. The first-hand knowledge of a practitioner, or former practitioner, is drawn upon in a dramatic fictional account of the work of a wartime intelligence operative. The great difficulty, of course, is determining just how accurately intelligence work is represented in this and Masterman's other works of fiction.

Masterman's controversial decision to publish in the United States an illicitly retained copy of *The Double Cross System of the War of 1939–45*, which he had written for the archives in 1945 while still a serving MI5 officer, in the face of Whitehall's official opposition, set a precedent for the declassification and release of material that had never been intended for general circulation. From the Security Service also came Tomas Harris's *Summary of the GARBO Case*, Robin W.G. Stephens's *A Digest of Ham* (being the history of MI5's interrogation centre, Camp 020, at Ham Common) and Jack Curry's *MI5 1909–45*.[30] In the post-war era Charles Elwell and Ronnie Reed have also produced material that has found its way into the public domain, and several other MI5 retirees have received permission to release their memoirs, among them are David Sutherland (*He Who Dares*), Leonard Burt (*Commander Burt of Scotland Yard*), Bill Magan (*Middle Eastern Approaches*) and Sir William Charles Crocker (*Far From*

Humdrum).[31] It is worth noting, incidentally, with the controversy that surrounded Stella Rimington's memoirs *Open Secret*, that one of her predecessors as Director-General, Sir Percy Sillitoe, not only obtained permission to publish *Cloak without Dagger*, but they were written by his assistant, Russell Lee, as part of his official duties, and the book contained a foreword written by the then Prime Minister, Clement Attlee.[32] Former Director-Generals notwithstanding, perhaps the most distinguished MI5 retirees to have taken up the pen as a profession are the historians Alistair Horne (*Macmillan*), who served in its overseas counterpart, Security Intelligence Middle East, and Hugh Trevor Roper, later Regius Professor of History at Oxford (*The Philby Affair*).[33]

When it came to commissioning official histories of the various components of British intelligence, the Cabinet Office's historical section naturally turned to those who knew their subject well. Accordingly we find Antony Simkins, who served as Deputy Director-General of MI5 under the redoubtable Sir Martin Furnival Jones, as co-author of the fourth volume of the official history, *Security and Counter-intelligence*, and Charles Ransom, formerly SIS's station commander in Rome working on Sir Harry Hinsley's team of official historians.[34]

In addition to those MI5 officers who have written about their professional experiences, there are a few, such as the Earl of Cottenham (*Motoring without Fear*), Herbert Hart (*Liberty and Morality*), Lindsay Jenkins (*Britain Held Hostage*) and Roger Fulford (*Queen Victoria*) whose books did not touch on their professional calling.[35] Rarest of all is the contribution of George Leggett whose post-war study of *The Cheka: Lenin's Political Police* must have been drawn from his professional role as an analyst of Soviet intelligence operations.[36] The list of wartime MI5 officers who have written their memoirs is small, consisting of just Gerald Glover (*125 Park Street*), Derek Tangye (*The Way to Minack*), Stephen Watts (*Moonlight on a Lake in Bond Street*) and Lord Rothschild (*Random Variables*), all of whom exercised various degrees of discretion over their work for MI5.[37] None, however, has gone to the lengths of the MI5 author, as yet unidentified, who adopted a female pen-name to write Mills and Boon novels.

Another Mills and Boon author, Molly Darby, was married to Ellis Morgan, a senior SIS officer who retired in 1973. One of her books, in which she gave a detailed and accurate account of how a Current Intelligence Group conducts its business within the Joint Intelligence Committee, caused some consternation in Whitehall until the source of her information was discovered.

Of those that neatly bridged the gap between fact and fiction in the British intelligence community, among the most elegant was Kenneth Benton, a career SIS officer who had joined SIS in Vienna before the war and worked for the local station. Among his many books was *Sole Agent*, and after his 'twilight tour' in Rio de Janeiro he was elected chairman of the Crime Writers' Guild. Benton was always quite coy about his long service in SIS, a characteristic he shared with Alec Waugh, author of *A Spy in the Family*, whom few realised had run double agents for SIS in the Middle East during the war. The proposition that individual agents, and entire networks, were regarded as mere pawns by MI5 and SIS and manipulated to deceive the enemy is a central theme of *Circle of Deception*, made in 1960 into a movie starring Bradford Dillman and Harry Andrews. A depressing plot, in which Dillman plays an officer parachuted into enemy-occupied territory with the intention that he should disclose deliberately fabricated information, was an idea conceived by Waugh. Although the storyline was considered improbable by the critics, Waugh knew about his subject. He had been a prisoner of war in Germany in 1918, and had rejoined his regiment, the Dorsets, in 1939. After completing the intelligence officers' course at Swanage he was posted to France, and after the evacuation served in the Middle East, returning to London and SIS in 1945.[38]

It was during his service in 'Paiforce', the Persia and Iraq headquarters in Baghdad that Waugh had learned the intricacies of handling double agents, and had realised that the Abwehr's entire network in the region was under the direct control of a sophisticated British deception organisation known as 'A' Force, actually located above a bordello in Cairo, whose objective was to persuade the enemy that a large army was poised for a major offensive in the Balkans. Security Intelligence Middle East, like its counterpart MI5 in London, created a co-ordinating unit, dubbed the Thirty Committee, to liaise with the appropriate authorities in Cairo and manage the day-to-day activities of the double agents who ranged from the entirely notional (and amusingly codenamed) NICOSSOF, ostensibly a Syrian, pro-Nazi businessman of Slavic origins who was also a heavy gambler, to QUICKSILVER, an entirely authentic patriotic officer in the Greek Air Force. In Baghdad Waugh was indoctrinated into the OPTIMIST case, widely regarded as one of the most successful of the war. In fact OPTIMIST was an Indian Army officer, Major Gulzar Ahmed, who had been recruited by SIS's Ronald Croft in January 1943, and transferred to censorship duties at the British Consulate in Istanbul.[39]

While none of the double agents cases run by the Thirty Committee corresponded exactly with Waugh's plot in *Circle of Deception*, there is a resonance in the experience of Renato Levi, an Italian Jew codenamed CHEESE. Levi had reported to SIS in Rome that he had been approached to work for the Abwehr, and in October 1940 he turned up in Istanbul en route for Cairo where he and his wireless operator were arrested for passing counterfeit currency. He finally arrived in Cairo in February 1941 and was supplied by Security Intelligence Middle East (SIME) with the notional Paul Nicossof as his replacement radioman. Having established himself in Egypt, Levi returned to Rome for consultations, but in November was arrested by the Italian authorities for trading on the black market and sentenced to five years' imprisonment, leaving the Abwehr heavily reliant on the fictitious NICOSSOF who maintained contact continuously until February 1945, transmitting a total of 432 messages to Bari. Although SIME had not deliberately despatched CHEESE to Italy equipped with bogus information, and did not learn of his fate until 1943, he is the only example of a double agent being allowed to return to the Axis in the Mediterranean theatre.[40]

Although, as has been demonstrated, SIS personnel have made a robust contribution to spy fiction, there is an impressively strong body of work in the field of non-fiction, including that of Sigismund Best, George Blake, Desmond Bristow, Nigel Clive, John Colvin, John Cross, Brian Crozier, Donald Darling, Nicholas Elliott, Dick Ellis, Richard Evans, Xan Fielding, David Footman, David Smiley, Harford Montgomery Hyde, Philip Johns, Reginald Jones, Henry Landau, Leslie Nicholson, Donald Prater, Hugh Trevor Roper, Patrick Whinney, Fred Winterbotham and Monty Woodhouse, plus two other biographers whose names are not usually associated with the Service. These works of non-fiction fall broadly into two categories. The first concerns those titles that were not written with open publication in mind, and both Brian Crozier and Richard Evans produced original, classified versions of their biographies which included material drawn from classified sources, and were intended as personality profiles.[41] SIS often draws up such analyses for limited consumption within Whitehall, and very occasionally it is possible for these documents to be redrafted so as to allow general publication. There are at least four biographers who fit this description.[42]

The second category, while not uniquely British, is a recognisable genre of personal memoir mixed with disclosure which is to some extent anomalous because of the atmosphere of secrecy which is supposed to prevail. Of course, MI5 has suffered its own humiliations in this minefield, with *Spycatcher*, attributed to Peter Wright but actually ghosted by the filmmaker Paul Greengrass.[43] Another example of this phenomenon is *One Girl's War* by Joan Miller. Miller was actually Joanna Phipps, writing under her maiden name, and she made a rather apposite observation about her work in Maxwell's Knight's section:

> It's easy to see what made Max's department such a literary one; with so much dramatic material to hand, the impulse to make a high-class spy story out of it must have been pretty well irresistible to anyone with the least degree of narrative ability.[44]

However, despite *Spycatcher* and *One Girl's War*, it is SIS which has developed a veritable library of personal memoirs, some authorised, some not. Those that were not sanctioned were *The Venlo Incident* (Sigismund Payne Best), *No Other Choice* (George Blake), *A Game of Moles* (Desmond Bristow), *Secrets of the White Lady* (Henry Landau), *Inside Intelligence* (Anthony Cavendish), *A Greek Experience 1943–48* (Nigel Clive) and *British Agent* (Leslie Nicholson, writing under the pseudonym 'John Whitwell').[45] Although Bristow and Clive did not bother to seek official approval for their texts, their books were uncontroversial and went largely unremarked. Not so Landau and Nicholson, who both proceeded in the face of the strongest official disapproval from SIS, having fallen out with management. Both men emigrated to the United States and took no notice of the British government's demands to remain silent. In the event no action was taken against them, although there was civil litigation against Blake, not to suppress his book, but to seize his profits on the basis that he had breached his lifelong duty of confidentiality, an implied condition of employment with SIS, as confirmed by the House of Lords in the *Spycatcher* case. Since that landmark ruling only one ex-SIS officer, Richard Tomlinson, has attempted to circumvent the law by releasing the first edition of *The Big Breach* in Russia in 2000.[46]

Those who obtained official permission include John Cairncross (*The Enigma Spy*), John Colvin (*Twice Around the World*), John Cross (*Red Jungle*), Nicholas Elliott (*With My Little Eye*), Donald Darling (*Secret Sunday*), Adrian Gallegos (*From Capri to Oblivion*), Xan Fielding (*Hide and Seek*), Richard Evans (*Deng Xiaoping*), David Smiley (*Albanian Assignment*), Harford Montgomery Hyde (*Secret Intelligence Agent*), Philip Johns (*Within Two Cloaks*), Theodore Pantcheff (*Fortress Island*), Reginald Jones (*Reflections on Intelligence*), Sir James Marshall-Cornwall (*Wars and Rumours of Wars*), L.B. Weldon (*Hard Lying*), Pat Whinney (*Corsican Command*), Fred Winterbotham (*The Ultra Secret*) and Monty Woodhouse (*Something Ventured*).[47]

There is a third category of non-fiction, whose authors were SIS officers who published works of non-fiction unrelated to their clandestine roles, and include Donald Lancaster (*The Emancipation of Indo-China*), Rex Fletcher (*The Air Defence of Britain*), Brian Montgomery (*A Field-Marshal in the Family*), Robert Carew Hunt (*The Theory and Practice of Communism*), Robert Cecil (*A Divided Life*), Dick Ellis (*Transcaspian Episode*), Wilfred Hindle (*Foreign Correspondent*), Donald Prater (*A Ringing Glass*), Brian Stewart (*All Men's Wisdom*), Stephen Hastings (*The Drums of Memory*), Stephen de Mowbray (*Key Facts of Soviet History*), Aubrey Jones (*The Pendulum of Politics*), Hugh Seton-Watson (*Neither War Nor Peace*), Robin Zaehner (*Hinduism*) and Ruari Chisholm (*Ladysmith*).[48] None of these authors was writing on behalf of SIS, nor can be detected as having delivered some subliminal message to SIS's advantage, but the sheer number of them show the organisation's literary tradition, which could be said to date back to the first headquarters, which were accommodated in 2, Whitehall Court, directly above the Authors' Club.

Finally, there is a separate, almost elite group of SIS authors who fall into no other obvious category, and regarded themselves as too senior to submit to the clearance system. David Footman wrote both fiction (*Pemberton*) and non-fiction (*The Civil War in Russia*) throughout his long SIS career and afterwards in retirement at St Antony's, Oxford, whereas George Young, briefly Dick White's Deputy Chief, wrote highly combative polemics, such as *Subversion and the British Riposte*.[49]

The foregoing amounts to a reasonably exhaustive survey of British intelligence literature written by insiders and serves to undermine the pretence that MI5 and SIS officers never venture into print, or do so very occasionally, or that those organisations can never countenance disclosure. The evidence suggests that much has been written about the famous British secret services from within, in both fictional and non-fictional terms, with a good deal in between. While it may have suited successive governments to promote an image of reticence and self-discipline, probably more information is available in print about the British secret establishment than about the intelligence agencies of any other country, including that paragon of transparency, the United States.

Notes

1 This chapter therefore excludes material written by individual agents such as John Cross, John Brown, Harald Kurtz and others. Also excluded are books written by defectors to Britain sponsored by SIS such as Grigori Tokaev, Vladimir Rezun, Vladimir Kuzichin, Oleg Gordievsky and Vasili Mitrokhin from the Soviets, and Otto John and Wolfgang zu Pulitz from the Nazis. Nor will this essay consider the work of former members of GCHQ such as Gordon Welchman or Peter Calvocoressi, Foreign Office advisers such as Geoffrey McDermott and Sir Nicholas Henderson and Joint Intelligence Committee personnel such as Sir Percy Cradock and Michael Herman. Another category that has been excluded includes books written by Soviet spies such as Harry Houghton and John Vassal, unless the individuals concerned happened to be intelligence officers, like Kim Philby, John Cairncross and George Blake. Also deliberately omitted are those authors of official histories, including Neil Blair, John Bruce Lockhart and Christopher M. Woods, whose work has yet to be declassified and gain a wider readership, and those who later were elected to the House of Commons and produced non-biographical, political tracts (Dick Brooman-White, Niall Macdermott, Henry Hunloke and Rod Richards from MI5; Cranley Onslow and Paddy Ashdown from SIS).

2 For a useful discussion of these issues which perhaps exaggerates the extent to which the intelligence services have been gagged, see D. Vincent, *The Culture of Secrecy* (Oxford: Oxford University Press, 1997).

3 William Stevenson, *A Man Called Intrepid* (Basingstoke and London: Macmillan, 1976).

4 Public Record Office, ZHC 1, microfiche no. 165.501, 1955, Cmd. 9577, *Report Concerning the Disappearance of Two Former Foreign Office Officials.*

5 This chapter will not consider those 'faction' titles written by Len Deighton, Frederick Forsyth, Jack Higgins and others who have not had first-hand experience of service in one of the security and intelligence agencies. Instead, it will concentrate on those authors who have written espionage fiction, but clearly have drawn from their own knowledge.

6 A. Moorehead, *The Traitors: The Double Life of Fuchs, Pontecorvo and Nunn May* (London: Harper & Row, 1952); G. Brook-Shepherd, *The Iron Maze* (Basingstoke and London: Macmillan, 1999); A. Judd, *The Quest for C* (New York: HarperCollins, 1999), and A. Foote, *Handbook for Spies* (London: Museum Press, 1949).

7 A. Judd, *Legacy* (New York: HarperCollins, 2000).

8 A. Cook, *On His Majesty's Secret Service: Sidney Reilly, Codename ST-1* (Stroud: Tempus Publishing, 2002).

9 Moorehead, *The Traitors*, p. 129.

10 Interview, Russell Lee, PA/DG, 1983.

11 Graham Greene, *The Confidential Agent* (London: Heinemann, 1939); *Our Man in Havana* (London: Heinemann, 1958); *The Human Factor* (London: The Bodley Head); and Kim Philby, *My Silent War* (London: McGibbon & Kee, 1967).

12 Philby, *My Silent War*, p. vii.

13 D. Verschoyle, *The Balcony* (n.p., 1949); A. Lyall, *The Balkan Road* (London: Metheun, 1930); G. Rees, *A Chapter of Accidents* (London: Chatto & Windus, 1972); C. Ray, *From Algiers to Austria* (1952); and A. Blunt, *Tomas Harris* (London: Courtauld Institute, 1975).

14 Compton Mackenzie, *Greek Memories* (London: Cassell, 1932) and *Water on the Brain* (London: Chatto & Windus, 1933).

15 Somerset Maugham, *Ashenden* (London: Heinemann, 1928).

16 P. Dukes, *The Story of ST-25* (London: Cassell, 1938); S. Hoare, *The Fourth Seal* (London: Heinemann, 1934); W. Gibson, *Wild Career* (London: Harrap, 1935) and G. Hill, *Go Spy the Land* (London: Cassell, 1932).

17 V. Williams, *The Man with the Clubfoot* (London: Herbert Jenkins, 1918).

18 I. Fleming, *Casino Royale* (London: Signet Books, 1953); and *From Russia With Love* (London: Jonathan Cape, 1957).

19 Phyllis Bottome, *The Lifeline* (London: Faber & Faber, 1946).

20 Phyllis Bottome, *The Goal* (London: Faber & Faber, 1947).

21 F. Maclean, *Eastern Approaches* (London: Jonathan Cape, 1949); C. O'Brien-ffrench, *Delicate Mission* (London: Skilton & Shaw, 1979); I. Bryce, *You Only Live Once* (London: Weidenfeld & Nicolson, 1975); D. Popov, *Spy CounterSpy* (London: Weidenfeld & Nicolson, 1974).

22 David Cornwell, quoted in N. West (ed.), *The Faber Book of Espionage* (London: Faber & Faber, 1993), p. 47.

23 *Daily Telegraph* obituary, 9 August 1988; West (ed.), *Faber Book of Espionage*, p. 493; John Le Carré, *The Spy Who Came in from the Cold* (London: Victor Gollancz, 1963); and *Tinker, Tailor, Soldier, Spy* (London: Hodder & Stoughton, 1974).

24 Lord Clanmorris quoted in West (ed.), *Faber Book of Espionage*, p. 493. *The Double Agent* was published by Victor Gollancz in 1966.

25 Maxwell Knight, *Crime Cargo* (London: Phillip Allan, 1934); Madeleine Bingham, writing as Eve Chaucer, *Peers and Plebs* (London: Allen & Unwin, 1975) and Charlotte Bingham, *Kind Hearts and Coronet* (London: Heinemann, 1963).

26 William Younger, *Skin Trap* (London: Eyre & Spottiswode, 1957); Eve Chaucer (Joan Wheatley), *No Ordinary Virgin* (London: Victor Gollancz, 1935) and Kenneth Younger, *Changing Perspectives in British Foreign Policy* (Oxford: Oxford University Press, 1964).

27 Masterman's account of the Twenty Committee and British deception is *The Double Cross System of the War of 1939–45* (New Haven, CT, and London: Yale University Press, 1972). *On The Chariot* Wheel was published by Oxford University Press in 1975; *An Oxford Tragedy* by Victor Gollancz (London) in 1933. The quoted passages are from *The Case of the Four Friends* (London: Penguin, 1957).

28 Masterman, *The Case of the Four Friends*, p. 71.

29 Ibid.

30 T. Harris, *Summary of the GARBO Case* (London: Public Record Office, 2000); R. Stephens, *A Digest of Ham* (London: Public Record Office, 2000) and J. Curry, *MI5 1909–45* (London: Public Record Office, 1999).

31 C. Elwell, *Corsican Excursion* (London: The Bodley Head, 1954); R. Reed, *British Intelligence in the Second World War*, Vol. 5 (London: HMSO, 1992); D. Sutherland, *He Who Dares* (Barnsley: Leo Cooper, 1998); L. Burt, *Commander Burt of Scotland Yard* (London: Heinemann, 1967); B. Magan, *Middle Eastern Approaches* (London: Michael Russell, 2001) and C. Crocker, *Far From Humdrum* (London: Hutchinson, 1967).

32 S. Rimington, *Open Secret* (London: Hutchinson, 2001) and P. Sillitoe, *Cloak without Dagger* (London: Cassell, 1955).

33 Among Horne's many publications that have made an important impact on the historical profession are *Macmillan* (Basingstoke and London: Macmillan, 1991) and *A Savage War of Peace* (Harmondsworth: Penguin, 1979). Among the numerous important books published by Trevor Roper are two related directly to his experiences as an intelligence officer: *The Philby Affair* (London: William Kimber, 1968) and *The Last Days of Hitler* (Basingstoke and London: Macmillan, 1947). Trevor Roper worked first in the Radio Security Service (MI8, an MI5 offshoot) then transferred to SIS.

34 A. Simkins, *Security and Counter-intelligence* (London: HMSO, 1995), which is part of the multi-volume official history of British intelligence in the Second World War prepared under Hinsley's direction: *British Intelligence in the Second World War: Its Influence on Strategy and Operations*, 6 volumes (London: HMSO, 1979 *et. seq.*).

35 E. Cottenham, *Motoring without Fear* (London: Metheun, 1928); H. Hart, *Liberty and Morality* (Oxford: Oxford University Press, 1963); L. Jenkins, *Britain Held Hostage*

(London and Washington, DC: Orange State Press, 1997) and R. Fulford, *Queen Victoria* (London: Collins, 1951).

36 G. Leggett, *The Cheka: Lenin's Political Police* (Oxford: Oxford University Press, 1981).

37 G. Glover, *125 Park Street* (London: Gerald Glover, 1982); D. Tangye, *The Way to Minack* (London: Michael Joseph, 1978); S. Watts, *Moonlight on a Lake in Bond Street* (New York: Norton, 1961), and L. Rothschild, *Random Variables* (London: Collins, 1984).

38 K. Benton, *Sole Agent* (London: Collins, 1970); K. Waugh, *A Spy in the Family* (London: W.H. Allen, 1970), *Circle of Deception* (London: W.H. Allen).

39 Alec Waugh, *The Early Years of Alec Waugh* (London: W.H. Allen, 1952), pp. 77–81.

40 Ibid.

41 Ibid.

42 Personal communication.

43 P. Wright and P. Greengrass, *Spycatcher* (London: Heinemann, 1978).

44 Joan Miller, *One Girl's War* (London: Brandon Books, 1986).

45 S. Best, *The Venlo Incident* (London: Hutchinson, 1950); G. Blake, *No Other Choice* (London: Jonathan Cape, 1990); D. Bristow, *A Game of Moles* (New York: Little, Brown, 1993); H. Landau, *Secrets of the White Lady* (London: Putnam, 1933), A. Cavendish, *Inside Intelligence* (London: Collins, 1990); N. Clive, *A Greek Experience 1943–48* (London: Michael Russell, 1985), and J. Whitwell (Nicholson), *British Agent* (London: William Kimber, 1986).

46 R. Tomlinson, *The Big Breach* (Edinburgh: Cutting Edge, 2001).

47 J. Cairncross, *The Enigma Spy* (London: Century, 1997); J. Colvin, *Twice Around the World* (Barnsley: Leo Cooper, 1991); J. Cross, *Red Jungle* (London: Robert Hale, 1957); N. Elliott, *With My Little Eye* (London: Michael Russell, 1993); D. Darling, *Secret Sunday* (London: William Kimber, 1975); A. Gallegos, *From Capri to Oblivion* (London: Hodder & Stoughton, 1959); X. Fielding, *Hide and Seek* (London: Secker & Warburg, 1984); R. Evans, *Deng Xiaoping* (New York: Penguin USA, 1994); D. Smiley, *Albanian Assignment* (London, Chatto & Windus, 1984); H. Montgomery Hyde, *Secret Intelligence Agent* (London: Constable, 1982); P. Johns, *Within Two Cloaks* (London: William Kimber, 1979); T. Pantcheff, *Fortress Island* (London: Phillimore, 1978); R. Jones, *Reflections on Intelligence* (London: Hamish Hamilton, 1978); J. Marshall-Cornwall, *Wars and Rumours of Wars* (Barnsley: Leo Cooper, 1984); L. Weldon, *Hard Lying* (London: Herbert Jenkins, 1925); P. Whinney, *Corsican Command* (London: Patrick Stephens, 1989); F. Winterbotham, *The Ultra Secret* (London: Weidenfeld & Nicolson, 1974), and M. Woodhouse, *Something Ventured* (London: Granada, 1982).

48 D. Lancaster, *The Emancipation of Indo-China* (Oxford: Oxford University Press, 1961); R. Fletcher, *The Air Defence of Britain* (London: Penguin, 1938); B. Montgomery, *A Field-Marshal in the Family* (London: Constable, 1973); R. Carew Hunt, *The Theory and Practice of Communism* (London: Geoffrey Bles, 1950); R. Cecil, *Divided Life* (London: The Bodley Head, 1988); D. Ellis, *Transcaspian Episode* (London: Hutchinson, 1963); W. Hindle, *Foreign Correspondent* (London: George Routledge, 1939); D. Prater, *A Ringing Glass* (Oxford: Clarendon Press, 1986), B. Stewart, *All Men's Wisdom* (River Bank Culture Enterprise, 1985); S. Hastings, *The Drums of Memory* (Barnsley: Leo Cooper, 1994); S. De Mowbray, *Key Facts of Soviet History* (London: Pinter, 1990); A. Jones, *The Pendulum of Politics* (London: Faber & Faber, 1946); H. Seton-Watson, *Neither War Nor Peace* (London: Metheun, 1960); R. Zaehner, *Hinduism* (Oxford: Oxford University Press, 1966); R. Chisholm, *Ladysmith* (London: Osprey, 1979).

49 D. Footman, *Pemberton* (London: Cressett, 1943) and *The Civil War in Russia* (London: Faber & Faber, 1961); G. Young, *Subversion and the British Riposte* (Glasgow: Ossian, 1984).

9   The Geopolitics of James Bond

Jeremy Black

To an unprecedented degree, the world of espionage powerfully grasped the twentieth-century imagination. As with detective fiction, which can be seen not so much as a parallel literature but rather as the seedbed of the espionage novel, Britain played a central role in the new field. The central figure in the fictional world of British intelligence is James Bond, because his success has led not only to longevity but also to a character that has spanned the worlds of novels and films.

Fictional characters that have a long lifespan, such as Bond, who first appeared in 1953, provide an opportunity for the historian to study change, for, at the same time that the use of the character requires consistency, there is also a need to respond to the shifting expectations or concerns of the audience. This can be seen in the most surprising of characters. In the mid-twentieth century, Sherlock Holmes, who had been directed by Conan Doyle against the machinations of Wilhemine Germany, was translated afresh to the screen by Basil Rathbone, and the corpus was brought up to date as Holmes was taken to new destinations – Canada and the United States – and given contemporary concerns and foes, in particular the Nazis. In the film *Sherlock Holmes and the Voice of Terror* (1942), Holmes thwarts a deadly Nazi programme of sabotage and an attempted invasion whose mastermind is the head of the British Intelligence Coordination Committee, Sir Evan Barham. As a reminder of the usual rule of detective fiction – that the detective intervenes to restore a harmony disrupted by the hubristic evil of crime – Barham is not really the Home Counties agent he appears to be, but a long-term German agent who took his place when the real Barham was shot in cold blood while a prisoner in the First World War. Barham is also over-confident: he brings Holmes into the case in order to appear to be doing everything possible to thwart the Nazis, but Holmes thwarts both him and the German invasion plans.

Holmes richly repays a treatment in terms of his politics. In Conan Doyle's hands, he changed; he subsequently was reinterpreted by other writers, for example to include a married Holmes, and he has been extensively interpreted on television and in film, not least with greater interest in his drug addiction.

The same is true of John Buchan's Richard Hannay, Agatha Christie's Hercule Poirot and Ian Fleming's James Bond. Poirot might apparently be a timeless figure well removed from the world of espionage, but he records shifting concerns and assumptions, as well as the details of life, such as the role of servants. In a number of inter-war novels, Christie records the standard fears of affluent society, and adds the paranoid conviction of an underlying conspiracy, although this theme is not one that has been taken up in the television and film presentation of the Christie corpus. This is typical of the modern treatment of inter-war adventure literature, but in fact much of this literature reflected a concern about foreign threats that linked domestic and international challenges. In Christie's *The Big Four* (1927), readers were told about, 'The world-wide unrest, the labour troubles that beset every nation, and the revolutions that break out in some... there is a force behind the scenes which aims at nothing less than the disintegration of civilization... Lenin and Trotsky were mere puppets.'[1]

Technology was seen by Christie as at the service of this force: 'a concentration of wireless energy far beyond anything so far attempted, and capable of focusing a beam of great intensity upon some given spot... atomic energy', so that the Big Four could become 'the dictators of the world'.[2]

This links earlier concerns with the world of Bond. Number one among the 'Big Four' is an all-powerful Chinaman, Li Chang Yen, with his base in the mountain fastness of the Felsenlabyryth, who echoes the sinister orientalism of Dr Fu-Manchu. The creation of the British reporter Arthur Sarsfield, who wrote under the pseudonym of Sax Rohmer, Fu-Manchu, 'the greatest genius which the powers of evil have put on the earth for centuries', and the foe of British civilisation and empire in *The Mystery of Dr Fu-Manchu* (1913) and *The Devil Doctor* (1916), combined great cruelty with advanced scientific research. In the first novel, Fu-Manchu, 'the yellow peril incarnate in one man'[3] is presented as a figure behind anti-Western actions in Hong Kong and Chinese Turkestan, as well as striking at Western politicians and administrators aware of the secret importance of Tongking, Mongolia and Tibet; indeed 'he has found a new keyhole to the gate of the Indian Empire!'. The omnipotence and range of the villain was such that no-one in Britain was safe: 'a veritable octopus had fastened upon England – a yellow octopus whose head was that of Dr. Fu-Manchu, whose tentacles were dacoity, thuggee modes of death secret and swift, which in the darkness plucked men from life and left no clue behind.'[4]

In his account of Macao in *Thrilling Cities* (1963), Fleming referred to his 'Doctor Fu-Manchu days... the adventure books of one's youth',[5] and, in *Dr. No* (1958), he created in Julius No his own Fu-Manchu. Furthermore, like Poirot in *The Big Four*, Bond has to hunt the villain down in his base hidden within a mountain.

Bond's impact on the popular perception of espionage is considerable and multiple: the most successful adventure hero in history, thwarting 'the instruments of Armageddon' in the film, *The Spy Who Loved Me* (1977), saving the world as the seconds tick away in the 1979 film *Moonraker* (other victims saved on different occasions more modestly include London in the novel *Moonraker*), Bond also offers an opportunity to record and reflect on change.

There is an extensive literature on Bond, although most of it is of the exploitation type, and makes scant attempt to consider context and change.[6] This is unfortunate, as the Bond corpus provides many opportunities for considering aspects of the popular perception of the world of intelligence, for example the stress on covert operations and on human intelligence, rather than on signals operations. Furthermore, both novels and films drew on current fears in order to reduce the implausibility of the villains and their villainy, while they also presented potent images of national character, explored the relationship between a declining Britain and an ascendant United States, charted the course of the Cold War, offered a changing demonology, and were an important aspect of post-war popular culture, not only in Britain but also more generally, particularly after the Americans created and financed the filmic Bond.[7]

In the films, Bond dramatically, and frequently, saved the United States. After all, as the seconds ticked away towards the close of the films, he stopped *Dr. No* from 'toppling' a crucial US missile test (1962), prevented Goldfinger from making the Fort Knox gold reserves radioactive (1964), thwarted Largo's attempt to blow up Miami (*Thunderball*, 1965), and Blofeld's to destroy Washington (the villain rejects Kansas – 'the world might not notice', (*Diamonds Are Forever*, 1971), as well as Zorin's plan for the devastation of Silicon Valley (*A View To A Kill*, 1985), and those of other megalomaniacs, some of whom, such as Stromberg in *The Spy Who Loved Me* (1977) and Drax in *Moonraker* (1979), would have destroyed the United States as part of a global cataclysm.

In fact it was the United States that saved Bond. Launched on the world in the novel *Casino Royale* in 1953, Bond was a quintessentially British figure, but he was translated for the film role, and the modern world knows Bond through the films, not the novels. The intentions of Ian Fleming are glimpsed at second hand and even then only fitfully so after the third film, *Goldfinger*, which appeared in 1964, the year of Fleming's early death.

Ironically, the first portrayal of Bond on screen was as an American, 'Jimmy Bond', played as a hard man, in a 1954 CBS hour-long television version of *Casino Royale*. In contrast to the novel, it was the British agent, called Clarence Leiter, who assisted Bond, so that the Anglo-American relationship of the book was reversed for US consumption.

Excluding the parody *Casino Royale* (1967) and *Never Say Never Again* (1983), the films have been the work of Eon Productions, which was established by Harry Saltzman, a Canadian, and Albert Broccoli, an American, who, in 1961, together persuaded United Artists to provide the money needed for the production and agreed a six-picture deal. Broccoli eventually bought Saltzman out, and his family have retained control since. They have established the tone of the series. Fleming had wanted David Niven, a stylish public-school gent, to play Bond, but Broccoli wanted a tougher, mid-Atlantic image, able to appeal to American filmgoers as a man of action without putting them off with jarring British mannerisms. Bond had to be self-contained, not self-satisfied, and thus, with Sean Connery, a star was born.

The Bond stories can be used to consider changing images of Britain, the United States and the world, not least because the clear presentation of evil afoot served to record changing threats. The politics of the novel *Casino Royale* (1953) were located squarely in the Cold War, with an attempt to thwart Soviet influence in the French trade unions. Indeed, in 1947, 'Wild Bill' Donovan, the former head of the OSS, had helped persuade the US government to fund opposition to communist influence in these unions. In the novel, Bond's attempt to out-gamble his communist opponent, Le Chiffre, the paymaster of the communist-controlled trade union in the heavy and transport industries of Alsace, the most vulnerable part of France to Soviet attack, is rescued by Felix Leiter, the CIA observer, who loans him 32 million (old) francs, with which Bond subsequently beats the villain. There was, indeed, considerable sensitivity in Britain at the time about the extent of communist influence in the trade unions. In 1949, the Labour government had sent in troops to deal with a London dock strike that it blamed on communists. The following year, Hugh Gaitskell, the Minister for Fuel and Power, and later the lover of Fleming's wife Ann, claimed that a strike in the power stations was instigated by communist shop stewards and served for them as a rehearsal for future confrontation.

Bond's need for the American money reflected the central role of the United States in the defence of the West. Leiter provides it without difficulty and is happy to rely on Bond's skill, suggesting a far smoother working of the alliance than was in fact the case. The two powers were co-operating in NATO and the UK–USA Security Agreement covering signals espionage, and had fought together in Korea, but there were serious differences of opinion, particularly over the Middle East. Furthermore, US concern over the British spy system had risen greatly after the defections of Guy Burgess and Donald Maclean in 1951, and, in 1952, (correct) distrust of Kim Philby, the Secret Services liaison officer in Washington, led the CIA to insist that he did not return there.

Fleming did not press Anglo-American tensions in his novels, but he was aware of them and, at times, his plots can be seen as efforts to create an impression of the normality of British imperial rule and action, with Bond as the defender of empire.

In the second novel, *Live and Let Die* (1954), Fleming presented the United States as threatened. Responding to interest among British readers in the United States and to the market there, Fleming did not become formulaic by repeating the setting of his first novel. In *Casino Royale*, the use of the fictional Royale, a luxurious European gambling resort modelled on Deauville and Le Touquet, was a throwback to the locations of inter-war novels not least with the villain being a deracinated European: Le Chiffre is described as part Jewish with some Mediterranean, Prussian or Polish blood added into the mix. Instead, Fleming offered the New World, with Britain, in the person of Bond, active in it; and presented his agent as moving by plane, not the liners used so frequently in pre-war novels. In place of the tired, cloying opulence of the casino at Royale at 3 a.m., *Live and Let Die* opened with the movement, energy and luxury of a welcomed arrival at Idlewild (now JFK) airport in New York, a scene based on Fleming's arrivals there in 1941 and 1953. Thanks to the airplane, Bond is able to travel at will and at speed across the globe, and the novels were very much part of the air age. Driving in from Idlewild, Bond remarks that New York 'must be the fattest atomic-bomb target on the whole face of the world',[8] and Black Power is seen as the tool of Soviet subversion. Its leader, the sinister Mr Big, who uses voodoo, has Bond seized in Harlem.

In the fourth novel, *Diamonds Are Forever* (1956), Bond returns to the United States, appealing to British interest in a land of wealth and excitement, as well as America's role as a model for consumer society. Again, however, there is an enemy within. Fighting the Mafia in *Diamonds Are Forever* provides Fleming with an opportunity to express the racist views of the inter-war years: 'They're not Americans. Mostly a lot of Italian bums with monogrammed shirts who spend the day eating spaghetti and meat-balls and squirting scent over themselves',[9] a clear sign of contemporary British views on masculinity.

Live and Let Die concluded in the Caribbean, providing Bond with his first visit (in the novels) to the Empire. An important aspect of the politics and geopolitics of the novels, and one that did not translate to the films, was that Fleming's Bond was in part a defender of empire. This is a strand that tends to be lost with reference to Bond as a figure of the Cold War, and his location in terms of the struggle with the Soviets. That dimension was of course important, but it is necessary also to consider what was being defended. For Fleming and his readers, this was the British Empire. Here, as with the Cold War, it is necessary to move from an abstraction to the specifics of particular moments. The Cold War, for example, meant very different situations throughout the 1950s, let alone over a longer timespan. For example, in 1952, when Fleming was writing *Casino Royale*, Britain was providing the second-biggest contingent in the UN force that had intervened in the Korean War, and the continuation of the conscription introduced for the Second World War meant that the book was being written for readers many of whose friends and relatives were still serving. The situation was different by the end of the decade. Then the burden of defence against communism was largely placed on missiles and, indeed, that was to underline the rocketry that played a major role in three of the first six Bond films (with atomic bombs being central to the plot of another).

Similarly, empire meant different situations in particular years. From the perspective of the 2000s, there is a misleading theme of gradual and inevitable descent from imperial status, and the emphasis is on Britain's willingness to concede independence and on the generally peaceful nature of the process. Indeed, in 1947, Britain had granted independence to India, its most populous colony, and Burma, Ceylon, Palestine and Newfoundland rapidly followed. However, although India had of all the 'non-white' colonies most engaged the imaginative attention of the British, its loss was not seen as part of an inevitable process of imperial withdrawal. On the contrary, there were attempts to strengthen both formal and informal empire in the late 1940s and early 1950s, while it was believed that most colonies were far from ready for independence.

Bond's main beat was not that of imperial policeman, thwarting insurrection in Malaya or Kenya. Instead, Fleming located empire in the wider context of British strategic interests and did so, significantly, with reference to the West's position in the Cold War. This was clearly seen in *Live and Let Die* when, in pursuit of

Mr Big, Bond travels to Jamaica and is briefed by Commander John Strangeways, the chief Secret Service agent for the West Indies, about the Isle of Surprise, an offshore island recently purchased by Mr Big. Readers were offered a defined sense of strategic threat:

> Since 1950 Jamaica had become an important strategic target, thanks to the development by Reynolds Metal and the Kaiser Corporation of huge bauxite deposits found on the island. So far as Strangeways was concerned, the activities on Surprise might easily be the erection of a base for one-man submarines in the event of war, particularly since Shark Bay was within range of the route followed by the Reynolds ships to the new bauxite harbour at Ocho Rios, a few miles down the coast.[10]

Bauxite was necessary for the manufacture of aluminium, a strategic metal, not least for the aircraft industry. Bond is revealed as already knowing Jamaica, as he had spent time there assigned to protect local labour unions from communist infiltration, a sign of the seamless transition from fighting Nazis to combating communism. Fleming was not troubled with detail: as part of the Empire, Jamaica for intelligence purposes came under E Branch of MI5, so the fictional Bond would have had to be seconded to it. Bond returned to the Empire at the close of *Diamonds Are Forever* (1956), killing the last of the villains in Sierra Leone, whose 'great diamond mines' were 'a rich capital asset of the British Commonwealth',[11] and then again in *Dr. No* (1958), where another island off Jamaica holds a dark secret. At the close of the latter, there is a display of imperial power. The brigadier in command of the Caribbean Defence Force, 'a modern young soldier of thirty-five...unimpressed by relics from the Edwardian era of Colonial Governors, whom he collectively referred to as "feather-hatted fuddy-duddies"', pressed for immediate action without waiting from London. He was ready to provide a platoon that would be embarked on HMS *Narvik*,[12] a warship whose name recalled a Second World War British naval success.

The youthfulness and vigour of the brigadier suggested that the Empire was not moribund, but there was also a sense of threat, as when the bastion of colonial rule in Kingston is discussed: 'Such stubborn retreats will not long survive in modern Jamaica. One day Queen's Club will have its windows smashed and perhaps be burned to the ground.'[13]

In *Dr. No*, Bond thwarts a Soviet-backed attempt to bring down US rockets, and a sense of the United States under threat is also clear in the novel *Goldfinger* (1959): the Superintendent at Pennsylvania Station tells Goldfinger that travellers from Louisville report being sprayed from the air by the Soviets. If, in this novel, Bond saves the US gold reserves, the old world coming to the aid of the stronger knew, he is also all that a post-Suez Britain can rely on. By *Goldfinger*, Bond was a representative of a shift from brawn to brains, resources to skill. In October 1957, Harold Macmillan, the British Prime Minister, claimed to have regained the special relationship with the United States, but this position was precarious.

Competition and tension with the United States also echoed in the Bond stories, although this theme was not pushed. In the short story 'Quantum of Solace' there is mention of Anglo-American competition on the Nassau–New York air route and in another short story 'The Hildebrand Rarity', published in 1960, Milton Krest, a villainous American collector of rare species, treats Bond to an account of British inconsequence:

> Nowadays, said Mr. Krest, there were only three powers – America, Russia and China. That was the big poker game and no other country had either the chips or the cards to come into it. Occasionally some pleasant little country...like England would be lent some money so that they could take a hand with the grown-ups. But that was just being polite like one sometimes had to be – to a chum in one's club who'd gone broke.

Bond finds this argument oversimplified and naïve and recalls an aphorism about the United States lacking 'a period of maturity',[14] but Krest's words reflect the growing perception of Britain as weak.

The British need to adapt to the United States was an important, albeit concealed, theme in the politics of the novels and films. Bond's style could barely conceal the diminished British political and military presence in Cold War confrontations. In the person of the wife-beating Krest, who is in fact murdered, wealth and power became insensitivity and sadism, an unsettling account of what British weakness could lead to.

The novel *Thunderball* (1961) represented a new departure with the introduction of SPECTRE (the Special Executive for Counterintelligence, Terrorism, Revenge and Extortion), which is presented as evil unconstrained by ideology. This can be seen as a surrender to fantasy occasioned, in part, by the decline of the British Empire and Fleming's consequent lack of certainty about the country's position. Britain, however, is still presented as playing a major role, with M declaring: 'We've teamed up with the CIA to cover the world. Allen Dulles is putting every man he's got on to it and so am I', as if the two were equal. Bond is given CIA support in the Bahamas, providing an opportunity for probing the unsettled nature of the Anglo-American relationship: he fears he will be sent 'a muscle-bound ex-college man with a crew-cut and a desire to show up the incompetence of the British...to gain credit with his chief'. In fact, he gets the helpful Leiter. In *Thunderball*, Bond is keen to borrow superior US weaponry, while a US atomic submarine plays a role in helping thwart the villain. Its commander tells Bond, 'These atomic weapons are just too damned dangerous. Why, any one of these little sandy cays around here could hold the whole of the United States to ransom – just with one of my missiles trained on Miami',[15] a reflection that pointed the way forward for the espionage/adventure novel.

You Only Live Twice (1964), reflected Fleming's increasing melancholia about Britain, with Bond mirroring the author's moods. Britain is in decline, the Americans are refusing to pass on information, in part because they treat the Pacific as a 'private preserve', and therefore the British seek intelligence information from Japan, and have to earn it by Bond's use on a mission for specifically Japanese ends. Indeed, in his 1959 tour to the region, Fleming had noted Britain's greatly lessened influence in east Asia and the Pacific. In the book, a Soviet scheme to use nuclear blackmail to force the removal of US bases from Britain and British nuclear disarmament is thwarted by Kennedy's willingness to threaten nuclear war; a step taken as a result of British intelligence information. The implication is clear that this is a description of a real episode.

Published posthumously, *The Man with the Golden Gun* (1965), warns about links between the KGB, the Mafia, Black Power, terrorism and drugs, although scepticism is expressed about the likely success of US pressure on Castro: 'If the Americans once let up on their propaganda and needling and so forth, perhaps even make a friendly gesture or two, all the steam'll go out of the little man.' The novel linked the Soviet Union, Cuba, drugs and subversion, in the West Indies and more widely, including 'the big black uprising'.[16]

After Fleming's death, the novels continued. As a character, Bond could not be copyrighted, and the best way to deal with the threat of imitations was for Glidrose, which owned the Bond publishing rights, to commission a sequel. In the first, *Colonel Sun* (1968), by the Bond fan Kingsley Amis, writing under the pseudonym Robert Markham, the Chinese were the villains, seeking to exploit Cold War hostilities to their own ends. Aside from novelisations of film screenplays, the sequence of novels was resumed in 1981 by John Gardner, who produced a whole sequence, closing with *Cold* (1996), the thwarting of General Brutus Clay's attempt to stage a fascist coup in the United States on behalf of the Children Of the Last Days (COLD). His successor, Raymond Benson, was a US board member of the Ian Fleming Foundation, which is based in the United States.

However, it is the films that dominate modern attention. For a decade, it has been claimed that half the world's population has seen a Bond film, ensuring that billions of people have viewed an image of global struggle through Western eyes. Individual films have not done as well, as say, *Star Wars*, but the series as a whole has been more profitable than any other.

Aside from comforting British viewers about their state's continued role and competence, and lacking any of the doubts expressed, for example, in Fleming's novels and, even more clearly, the novels and films of Len Deighton and John Le Carré, the Bond series also charted shifts in the wider world. However improbable the plot, to work as adventure stories, the films had to be able to resonate with the interests and concerns of viewers. This they did, and themes such as the space race, the energy crisis, nuclear confrontation and drugs were all played out. Shifts in the Cold War were also noted. In *Moonraker* (1979), the Americans check with the Soviets when their radar shows the space station from which Drax is planning to fire germ-laden globes at the Earth in order to confirm that it is not a Soviet space vehicle. In *Octopussy* (1983), there are good and bad Soviets, in *A View To a Kill* (1985), the villain Zorin has escaped KGB control, while, in *The Living Daylights* (1987), the KGB head emerges in a positive light, as does the Afghan resistance; the villains being a KGB general and his American partner, who plays at being a military commander.

As a parallel to the theme of placelessness seen with SPECTRE and its willingness to extort from all, in the film *Licence To Kill* (1989), Franz Sanchez, a sadistic drug king based in a thinly disguised Panama, is depositing much of his money in the United States, while he takes American orders for drugs and sets the price under the cover of his employee, Professor Joe Butcher, who operates as a television evangelist seeking pledges over the television. Sanchez sees money as the universal solvent, and there is a 'death of history' in the sense of the absence of competing grand ideologies.

The wider search for political meanings and echoes in the films need not detract from an appreciation of the adventure, but there are serious problems for the future. If he remains British, Bond must appear an anachronism. As Blofeld had already mocked in *Diamonds Are Forever* (1971): 'Surely you haven't come to negotiate, Mr. Bond. Your pitiful little island hasn't even been threatened.' Nevertheless, this Britishness is part of the frame of reference that ensures continuity for the films.

If Britishness and the desire to resonate with the US market (seen for example in making North Korea the source of the villainy in the latest film *Die Another Day* (2002)) provide the geopolitical axis of the Bond films, displacing the Britain-Empire axis of the novels, there is, in both, a common tendency to treat the rest of the world as a lesser sphere vulnerable to the activities of villains and therefore requiring the actions of Bond and his British and US allies. Thus, in the film *Thunderball* (1965), SPECTRE is based in Paris and SPECTRE No. 2, Largo, is shown being able to park illegally and being saluted by a policeman; while in *You Only Live Twice* (1967), both novel and film, Bond is needed in order to defeat Blofeld in Japan: the Japanese cannot achieve the task, and in the novel cannot even contribute assistance.

In western Europe, intelligence services play no major role. Thus, in the pre-credits adventure in *Thunderball* (1965), Bond is assisted by a female agent from the French section in killing SPECTRE No. 6; the Deuxième Bureau is nowhere to be seen. Similarly, in Italy, Greece, Spain and Germany, national intelligence services are absent. Geopolitically, there is a vacuum that is contested between Britain, sometimes with US support, and either SPECTRE or the Soviets or dangerous megalomaniacs, such as Stromberg. Although Fleming wrote a homage to the Levantine espionage of Eric Ambler in his novel *From Russia, With Love* (1957),[17] the world of Royale and Piz Gloria was overshadowed by that of Nassau or Las Vegas, and even more so on film. Fleming's hostile comments on Paris in 'A View To a Kill', a short story published in 1960 as part of *For Your Eyes Only* (1960), indicated that the continent was a somewhat alien sphere that he did not understand or sympathise with.

The same is true of the Third World. Africa plays only a minor role – Egypt in the film *The Spy Who Loved Me* (1977) and North Africa in *Never Say Never Again* (1983) and *The Living Daylights* (1987) – but again the local governments do not exist. Nor does that of Brazil in the film *Moonraker* (1979), or Thailand in the film *The Man With the Golden Gun* (1974), or India in *Octopussy* (1983). Non-alignment means non-existence for the local government. It is as if these countries are ungoverned, ripe for exploitation by international megalomaniacs, and waiting for the order (and purposeful glamour) brought by Western intervention in the shape of Bond. Furthermore, the books and films have imperial attitudes to the non-Western world, with the local population primarily presented in terms of native colour, for example crowded street scenes and festivals, as in the films *Thunderball, Live and Let Die, The Man With the Golden Gun, The Spy Who Loved Me, Never Say Never Again* and *Octopussy*. Thus, complexity is ignored.

This is a world away from the ambiguities seen, for example, in the detective novels of Ambler, Deighton and Le Carré, but the world of Bond is not characterised by ambiguity, neither in setting nor in ambience. Instead, there is good (including good rogues such as Draco, the head of the Union Corse, in the novel and film *On Her Majesty's Secret Service*) and bad. It is only in recent films that ambiguity has been offered, and the moral space of the film restructured, with traitors in the secret service, first with Alec Trevelyan, 006, in the film *GoldenEye* (1995), and most recently in *Die Another Day* (2002) with Miranda Frost, who added this new twist to the bad girl–good girl tension seen so often with the earlier Bond: as well as varying the ethnic/colour space as Miranda, the bad girl, is, unusually, the blonde.

In the films from *GoldenEye* on, the relationship between Bond and Judi Dench's M is far more edgy than that with Bernard Lee's earlier M. Thus, the intelligence world is shown as becoming more troubled and troubling. *GoldenEye* linked themes traditional to the series, not least megalomania and rogue space vessels, and offered a new site for much of the action – post-communist Russia; but the problematic portrayal of the Secret Service is novel. Trevelyan asks Bond 'Did you ever ask why. Why we toppled all these dictators?' and Bond's answer, that it was their job, is mocked. In another note of novelty, *Tomorrow Never Dies* (1997) shows inter-departmental rivalry, with Roebuck, the stiff, arrogant British admiral, accusing Judi Dench's M of having no balls, to receive the rejoinder that at least she does not think with them.

The cultural role can be taken further by contrasting Bond with spoofs, such as the epicene James Bond in *Carry On Spying* (1964), or *Austin Powers: International Man of Mystery* (1997), or *Johnny English* (2003), and other agents who in some way seek to emulate him (Arnold Schwarzenegger in *True Lies*) or very obviously differ (Michael Caine's Harry Palmer in the films of the more ambivalent Len Deighton stories).

The emphasis on the role of the individual in the Bond novels and films is a clear opportunity to provide the last-minute cliff-hanger, but also to comment on a cultural clash that helps to structure the works and the world. The villains believe in planning and, indeed, represent a conflation of plutocratic and bureaucratic man, the last understood by Fleming as a characteristic of communism. In Weberian terms, Bond was the persistence of charisma against the iron cage of rationalism and bureaucracy. Planning is necessary, not only for the villains' schemes, but also because they are control freaks, seeking order even as they pursue disorder. In the films, Stromberg and Drax are unhinged utopian planners. In *The Spy Who Loved Me* (1977), Stromberg claims that modern civilisation is corrupt and decadent, that it would inevitably destroy itself, and that he is merely accelerating the process when he plans a nuclear holocaust followed by the construction of a new civilisation under the sea. In the film *Moonraker*, Drax has similar hopes for a perfect space-based civilisation that will link eugenics and technology. In *Golden Eye* (1995), Bond is up against not only M's reliance on statistical analysis ('the evil Queen of numbers' is convinced that the Russians cannot have a GoldenEye project), but also against Trevelyan's belief in planning. Aside from the meticulous planning of his project, Trevelyan tells Bond when he breaks into his armoured train, 'Situation analysis hopeless. You have no backup.' When Bond triumphs in that film, it is an individualism of selfless dedication and loyalty that wins, not the selfishness of Trevelyan.

In another aspect of structuring, the mechanistic megalomania of many of the villains and the sadistic evil of their agents, is contrasted with Bond's sensuality. There is much male fantasy here, but it is central to the image of Bond's sexuality that he gives as well as receives pleasure, an ability and desire that can be imagined of few of the male villains, while Fleming's depiction of women who were not constrained or defined by the search for matrimony and motherhood contrasted with the women in the adventure stories of his childhood, many of whom were honorary chaps.

Class, place, gender, violence, sex, race: all are themes that can be scrutinised through the shifts in characterisation and plot. So also can be both popular culture, and the relationship between fiction and fact. The interview with Oleg Gordievsky (who, as head of the KGB station in London, and earlier, was an agent for the British, eventually defecting in 1985), was the item in the BBC Radio 4 programme 'The Politics of James Bond' (1 January 2001) that excited most press comment. Gordievsky claimed that the Central Committee of the Soviet Communist Party watched Bond films, that he was instructed to secure a copy as soon as one came out, and was also asked by the KGB to obtain the devices used by Bond, and, more significantly, suggested that the Bond stories contributed to the reputation of British intelligence; which ironically had been gravely compromised by Soviet penetration in the 1940s.

Such comments are a reminder that popular culture is not a distinct subject, widely separated from the real world of politics, but, instead, a factor that helps to shape the latter, just as it is shaped by it. If only for that reason, the politics of Bond rests in large part on the perceptions of those who read and/or watched the stories. At times, this can be risible. The 2003 conference 'The Cultural Politics of Ian Fleming and 007' at the University of Indiana (whose Lilly Library contains Fleming's papers) sponsored by its English Department, included unintentionally risible papers, as scholars offered readings of Bond focused on Lesbian[18] or anal-retentive[19] themes. Aside from misunderstanding the attitudes of Fleming – for example he did not present the SIS as a bureaucratic world akin to SPECTRE,[20] but offered, instead, a clear depiction of evil to provide a bedrock of value and values, there is the more general problem that some readings bore very little relationship to the text.[21] If this conference indicated the range of possible responses to Bond, generally the response is located in a popular culture that is readier to work with apparent meanings, rather than to pursue implausible and self-regarding approaches. Because these meanings are very much up-to-date in their political concerns, the stylish Bond works as a defender of the West in the here-and-now; and this topicality ensures that he is the key guide to the imaginative grasp of espionage in the modern world.

Notes

1 A. Christie, *The Big Four* (1927; London: Penguin, 1957), p. 21.
2 Christie, *Big Four* (1957 edn), p. 147.
3 S. Rohmer, *The Mystery of Dr. Fu-Manchu* (1913; London: Corgi, 1967 edn), p. 16.
4 Rohmer, *Fu-Manchu* (1967 edn), p. 65.
5 I. Fleming, *Thrilling Cities* (1963; London: Reprint Society, 1964), p. 33.
6 Works of a different kind include Oreste Del Buono and Umberto Eco (eds), *The Bond Affair* (London: Macdonald, 1966); James Chapman, *Licence to Thrill: A Cultural History of the James Bond Films* (London: I.B. Tauris, 1999); and Jeremy Black, *The Politics of James Bond: From Fleming's Novels to the Big Screen* (Westport, CT: Praeger, 2001).
7 D. Cannadine, 'Fantasy: Ian Fleming and the Realities of Escapism', in D. Cannadine, *In Churchill's Shadow* (London: Allen Lane, 2002), pp. 279–311.
8 Fleming, *Live and Let Die* (1954; London: Pan Books, 1957), p. 5.
9 Fleming, *Diamonds Are Forever* (1956; London: Pan Books, 1958), p. 19.
10 Fleming, *Live and Let Die* (1957 edn), p. 176.
11 Fleming, *Diamonds Are Forever* (1958 edn), p. 6.
12 Fleming, *Dr. No* (1958; London: Pan Books, 1960), p. 181.
13 Fleming, *Dr. No* (1960 edn), pp. 5–6.
14 Fleming, 'The Hildebrand Rarity', in Fleming, *For Your Eyes Only: Five Secret Occasions in the Life of James Bond* (1960; London: Pan Books, 1962), p. 179.
15 Fleming, *Thunderball* (1961; London: Pan Books, 1963), pp. 116, 197.
16 Fleming, *The Man With The Golden Gun* (1965; London: Pan Books, 1966), p. 136.
17 On which see a wide-ranging article by Klaus Dodds, 'Licensed to Stereotype: Popular Geopolitics, James Bond and the SPECTRE of Balkanism', *Geopolitics*, 8 (2003), pp. 125–56, esp. 138–40.
18 Judith Roof, 'Living the James Bond Lifestyle', Jaime Hovey, 'Lesbian Bondage'.
19 Edward Comentale in 'Fleming, Corporate England, and the Ruins of Modernism'.
20 For a sharp and accurate critique of the conference, A. Lycett, 'Lesbians and 007 – a licence to deconstruct', *Sunday Times*, 8 June 2003. Aside from the questionable nature of several of the papers, the publication plans for the conference reflect a woeful attempt to present an incomplete view that amounts to the censorship of different viewpoints. Thus, of the two keynote lectures, both by British historians, James Chapman, who criticised theoretical readings in his introductory lecture 'Why Take James Bond Seriously?' has, instead, been asked to write on 'Bond and Britishness', while my own concluding keynote paper has been dropped for the same reason.
21 As argued by Comentale.

10 Hunters not Gatherers

Intelligence in the twenty-first century

Charles Cogan

Three aspects of our security woes

In his Congressional testimony on 17 October 2002, a year after the devastating attacks on the World Trade Center and the Pentagon, George Tenet, the Director of Central Intelligence, stated that, 'The threat environment we find ourselves in today is as bad as it was...in the summer before 9/11.' This view was echoed by the report of a panel sponsored by the US Council of Foreign Relations (CFR), released a week later on 25 October 2002, the central conclusion of which was that, 'A year after 9/11, America remains dangerously unprepared to prevent and respond to a catastrophic terrorist attack on US soil.' This being so, we have to ask ourselves some urgent questions as to how we are organised and conditioned to conduct intelligence in the twenty-first century. This chapter highlights three aspects of the US security problem.

The first point is that the United States is not properly set up or, put another way, not properly centralised, to conduct the intelligence operations that are required to meet the security threats of the twenty-first century. Second, because of the built-in distrust of government that is central to US political culture and tradition, we are relatively weak in the domain of internal security. Third, intelligence is not a perfect world; indeed it is more imperfect than most other activities.

The threat we face is not that of a potential nuclear Armageddon, as during the Cold War. It is nevertheless a huge threat and from sources more varied and more unpredictable than our erstwhile enemies of the Cold War. It follows from this fact that the United States needs to restore on a permanent and continuing basis a culture of risk that hitherto it has had only in times of war. If we are not at war in the conventional sense, we are in a sort of para-war. We face the greatest threat to our homeland in US history, following on the greatest humiliation in our history: 3,000 people killed by 19 Arab terrorists with box cutters whose sponsors had repeatedly told the world over the previous years that they were going to carry out an attack. Yet our innate suspicion, from the birth of the Republic, of the Elizabethan model of a strong and even repressive government inhibits us, in some degree, in taking drastic measures to cope with this new problem of Islamist terrorism that seeks nothing from us except to do us damage.

The director of central intelligence: neither directing nor central

Let us begin with a discussion of why the United States is not organised to conduct integrated intelligence operations. The United States was created not in the model of a centralised and unitary Jacobin state, as in the French revolutionary tradition, but in that of a decentralised federal state with a rather loose authority at the centre, where power was split between the executive, the legislature and the judicial branches, in the manner of the checks and balances philosophy of Montesquieu. There was a conscious aversion to the Elizabethan model of a strong central authority, and indeed an aversion to government in general.[1]

The checks and balances built into the theory and practice of US political structures at every level is also reflected in the organisation of the intelligence community. When the CIA was created in 1947, there was considerable opposition from the military to the idea of a central (and civilian-led) intelligence service. As Anna K. Nelson observed, 'In 1946, the military services were opposed to a Central Intelligence Agency because they recognized the importance of military intelligence in wartime.'[2] In other words, if a war broke out, a civilian intelligence service would not be of much help to the military. Today, the opposition of the military to the CIA is still there, and the military and civilian intelligence cultures are still in the process of getting to know each other, but the military does not challenge the very existence of the CIA. Rather, it is a matter of the military calling into question the CIA's prerogatives, or more properly, its roles and missions. This questioning relates to the very issue of when we *are*, and when we are *not*, at war, because properly speaking, in a time of war – for example such as the Second World War – the CIA overseas comes under the orders of the military. But even now, without an official declaration of war, the military is already taking very substantial steps to create a CIA-like clandestine operational capability within the Department of Defense so it will not be required in the future to rely on the civilian-led CIA.

Today, more than a half-century after the passage of the National Security Act of 1947, the position of the military in US society has been incomparably strengthened. From having an army in the inter-war period that was about the same size as that of Bulgaria, the United States has transformed itself since the Second World War into what Kenneth Oye has described as 'a national security state'.[3] Under an aggressive Secretary of Defense, and spurred on by the shock of the events of September 11, the US military is in a phase of adaptation, some would say encroachment, both on the traditional intelligence terrain of the CIA and on the traditional policy role of the State Department.

In the operational domain, this change is evident in at least three areas. First, the Secretary of Defense moved to tighten his control over those organs of the intelligence community that are under his budgetary authority, by means of naming an Under Secretary of Defense for Intelligence, Stephen Cambone. Second, he created an intelligence analysis unit, the Office of Special Plans, headed by Douglas Feith, that undertook, among other things, to monitor CIA and Defense

Intelligence Agency (DIA) production to make sure that these traditional bureaucratic entities were not overlooking indications of proliferation of Weapons of Mass Destruction (WMD) in Iraq. And third, the Pentagon's Defense Science Board, an advisory body, envisaged in a study in the wake of September 11 a role for Special Forces in the war against terrorism that would move the military into terrain which has traditionally been that of the CIA. Though the study proposed that the CIA and the military jointly increase their paramilitary capability, the military apparently sees the giant part of such an increase as applying to them.

Initiatives such as those described above are part of a continuum in the jockeying for power between civilian and military intelligence that has been going on for some 50 years. However, they are also a recognition that, with the onset of *quasi in seriatim* wars – Bosnia, Kosovo, Afghanistan, Iraq – the demands of the military for intelligence support is crowding out other intelligence priorities. Finally, these moves reflect the fact that the boundary between peace and war has become blurred, with the effect that the military's Special Forces are being committed in overseas missions that heretofore were those of the CIA.

In the policy domain, the Secretary of Defense, by dint of press conferences held almost daily in the aftermath of September 11, began to make statements of a political nature that gave the impression of his being a maker of foreign policy at least on a par with Secretary of State Colin Powell. These included such indelicate references in the Arab–Israeli context to the 'so-called Occupied Territories', as well as an assertion that Kofi Annan does not represent the United Nations but rather that the Security Council does – the latter being true enough in the strict sense but surprising coming from the mouth of a Secretary of Defense.

Additionally, the Secretary of Defense appeared to be challenging the DCI's role as the chief intelligence adviser to the President, at least in the context of assessments regarding Iraq. Beyond the creation of an Office of Special Plans described above, the Pentagon began to question the CIA's own assessments, such as the one contained in a letter that DCI Tenet wrote to the chairman of the Senate Intelligence Committee on 7 October 2002: 'Baghdad for now appears to be drawing a line short of conducting terrorist attacks with conventional or chemical and biological weapons against the United States.' It was judgements such as these that seemed to raise hackles among the hawks in the Administration. According to the *New York Times*, '[Secretary] Rumsfeld and his senior advisers are laboring to strip away risk assessments that they say should be left to policy-makers.'[4] In other words, this role should not be performed by the analysts of the CIA. This, of course, would make a mockery of the intelligence process, which is supposed to provide objective analysis so that policy makers can be aided in coming to decisions which are theirs to make.

Alongside the mammoth US military machine lies the CIA, bereft of a domestic constituency and almost entirely dependent on the aleatoric nature of the relationship between a given Director of Central Intelligence (DCI) and a given President. This one-on-one relationship between the President and his chief intelligence adviser is crucial to whether the CIA is regarded as an effective and influential player in Washington. A few years ago, when a light plane accidentally crashed on the White House lawn, Washington wags had it that this must have been the then DCI, James Woolsey, trying to get an appointment with President Clinton. Fortunately for Woolsey's successor, George Tenet, Clinton's successor has reportedly said that he does not want Tenet very far from his side.

But let us come back to the founding act of the CIA, the National Security Act of 1947. The authors of this Act ensured that, in the spirit of checks and balances so central to the US political tradition, the Director of Central Intelligence would in fact be neither truly directing nor truly central. The DCI controls only about one-fifth of the Intelligence Community's budget. The technical collection agencies, the National Security Agency (NSA) for electronic intercepts, the National Reconnaissance Organisation (NRO) which puts the surveillance satellites into the sky, and the National Imagery and Mapping Agency (NIMA) which interprets the imagery that the NRO produces, plus the Defense Intelligence Agency and the intelligence branches of each of the military services, are all under the budget and management of the Pentagon. The DCI can establish collection priorities for these agencies, but in practical terms he has no direct control over these agencies: for quarters and rations, as they say in the military, these agencies are part of the Defense Department. Under the bureaucratic adage that 'where you stand is where you sit', one can be sure that the real master of these technical collection agencies is the Secretary of Defense.

In the spring of 2002, an outside panel of experts headed by General (Ret.) Brent Scowcroft recommended that a rationalisation of the Intelligence Community be effected which overall would draw a distinction between national and departmental intelligence. A Director of National Intelligence (DNI) would have complete control over all the 'national' agencies; that is, those that would be directly responsible to the President: NSA, NRO, NIMA and the CIA, the latter to be headed by a separate Director under the DNI. The Scowcroft panel's proposal was quickly countered by Donald Rumsfeld, a bureaucratic infighter at least on a par with Henry Kissinger, with whom he had had some jousts when they were both in the government back in the 1970s.

Mr Rumsfeld's counter-move was not only to reject Scowcroft's proposal openly but, as mentioned above, it was to create a post within the Pentagon for an Under Secretary who would control all the intelligence collection done by the Pentagon. Though Rumsfeld painted this change, which was subsequently approved by the Congress, as a way to assure better co-operation between the Pentagon and the CIA, it was clearly aimed at stopping Scowcroft's reform proposals. Despite the fact that Scowcroft remains an influential figure in Washington and is the chairman of the President's Foreign Intelligence Advisory Board (PFIAB), he is in the camp of former President George H.W. Bush and clearly out of step with the ascendant hawks of the current administration (Messrs Cheney, Rumsfeld, Wolfowitz, *et al.*).

The joint Congressional panel that spent nearly a year investigating the background to the September 11 attacks recommended, similar to the Scowcroft group, the creation of a cabinet-level post of Director of National Intelligence (DNI), who would be over the DCI.[5] But unless such a cabinet officer would be able to assume budgetary control over the national agencies (NSA, NRO, NIMA and the CIA), such a recommendation would fall far short of the Scowcroft proposals. Thus, assuming that the present system remains more or less intact, we are faced with the continuing prospect of jockeying between the Pentagon and the CIA, because the lines of authority between the Secretary of Defense and the Director of Central Intelligence are not clear; and concomitantly, the continuing accrual of power by the Pentagon at the expense of its weaker partner, the CIA.

The FBI: not the same as MI5 or the DST

The DCI has no control over the Federal Bureau of Investigation (FBI), which is in part, and in part only, an internal security agency. The function of overall control over those aspects of the FBI that have to do with foreign and national security matters should be the work of the National Security Council (NSC), which was also created by the National Security Act of 1947.[6] But the NSC, for historical reasons having to do in part with the fundamental US distrust of government, is reluctant to consider an amalgamated approach to foreign intelligence and counter-intelligence on the one hand, and internal security on the other. There is a so-called 'water's edge' separation between the CIA as an overseas agency and the FBI as a domestic agency that makes the process of overall control and co-ordination difficult.

Similarly, the recently created Office of Homeland Security, created as a result of the September 11 attacks, has control over neither the FBI nor the CIA – although there are some in Congress who would like to have the intelligence unit that is part of this Office centralise all information of a security nature coming in to the President. It is doubtful this will happen in the future, however, because it would negate a primary role of the DCI: that of the President's chief intelligence adviser.

So what we are faced with, given what Washington officials somewhat facetiously referred to as the first threat to our homeland since the War of 1812, is no interior ministry in the proper sense of the term – since our Interior Department concerns itself with national parks and monuments and the like – and no agency fully devoted to internal security. There is an MI5 in Britain and a *Direction de la Surveillance du Territoire* (DST) in France, but there is no full-fledged equivalent in the United States. To establish such a service would require, as one MI5 official has noted privately, an acceptance that the task of such a service would be to connect the external and internal security threats and as such would amount in some cases to spying on United States citizens. It will be recalled that Harry Truman disbanded the CIA's predecessor, the Office of Strategic Services (OSS) immediately after the Second World War, because he was concerned about it becoming an 'American Gestapo', that is, it might spy on American citizens. (He also did not like the cosy relationship General William Donovan, the Director of OSS, enjoyed with his predecessor, Franklin Roosevelt. Donovan's plan for a post-war centralised intelligence service outside of the military, which had been approved by Roosevelt, disappeared along with the OSS.)

As the authors of *The Age of Sacred Terror* put it, 'The FBI is not a domestic intelligence agency, like Britain's MI5, because the American people do not want to put their civil liberties at risk by permitting such an agency to entrench itself in this country.'[7] Hence the FBI is primarily a law-enforcement organisation, and some 80 per cent of its personnel at any one time are devoted to crime. There is, besides the Criminal Division, a National Security (counter-intelligence) Division and, since 1999, a Counter-terrorism Division. Officers rotate in and out between the latter two and the Criminal Division which is hardly conducive to building up a cadre of intelligence-oriented officers as distinct from crime-oriented officers.

Moreover, the FBI is a case-oriented organisation whose main focus has been to look back into the past in order to accumulate evidence aimed at bringing to justice those who have or are about to violate a statute. This is a different mindset from that of an intelligence officer, who must look into the future, seeking to identify threats *upstream* that may develop into an attack or an operation against the United States. As intelligence writer Thomas Powers has put it, 'The first task of any intelligence organization is to establish where the danger lies.'[8] What is deficient in the US system is the same kind of *upstream* intelligence look applied inside the United States, in the manner of MI5 and the DST. Also, there seems little doubt that the overseas–domestic symbiosis would work better between a proper internal security service and the foreign intelligence service (the CIA).

It is likely that, if the United States had had a full-fledged internal security service along the lines of MI5 or the DST, the report of 10 July 2001 prepared by FBI agent Kenneth Williams in Arizona would not have remained mired in an intray. This report concerned the possibility of al-Qaeda members taking flight training. Nor would the request from the Minneapolis office of the FBI for technical and other surveillance on Zacharias Mussaoui (who was under arrest at the time for a visa violation) have been refused on the quixotic ground that Mussaoui was not connected with a 'recognised foreign power' – especially given the fact that a query to the French (presumably the DST) had yielded the information that Mussaoui was connected with terrorists.

The surveillance request from the Minneapolis office to FBI Headquarters was dated 21 August 2000, well before September 11, and it stated that there was reason to believe that Mussaoui was acting with 'others yet unknown' to hijack an airliner and divert it to Washington. Mussaoui had reportedly told his flight instructor in Minnesota that he would 'love' to fly a simulated flight from Heathrow to JFK airport in New York. The Minneapolis office noted that if Mussaoui seized an aircraft flying from Heathrow to New York it would have the fuel to reach Washington. The CIA, learning of this report, sent a cabled advisory to its stations describing Mussaoui as a 'suspect airline suicide hijacker' who might be 'involved in a larger plot to target airlines travelling from Europe to the US'.[9]

All this came before September 11. In the ensuing investigation, not only was incriminating evidence found in Mussaoui's possession; it was established that Mussaoui received some 14,000 dollars from Germany prior to September 11. The fingerprints of Ramzi al-Shibh, the al-Qaeda leader arrested in Pakistan in 2002, are allegedly on the bank transfer draft that was sent from Frankfurt to Mussaoui. (Since the blunders revealed by the Mussaoui case, the system for obtaining a technical surveillance warrant under the Foreign Intelligence Surveillance Act (FISA) has been made less strict.)

Another example of blunders committed in the period prior to September 11, this time imputable to the CIA and not the FBI is the following: the CIA obtained information that two individuals suspected of al-Qaeda ties, who were known only as Khalid and Nazir, were going to attend a meeting in Kuala Lumpur in January 2000 with other terrorists. The Malaysian government was notified and photographed the meeting, enabling the identification of the two individuals, who were Khalid al-Midhar and Nazir al-Hazmi. Though the FBI was informed, the CIA failed to inform the State Department so that the latter could decide whether to put them on the watchlist. They were not put on the watchlist until the CIA recommended this be done in a memorandum dated 23 August 2001. By that time they were both in the United States. In fact, the CIA had received a report from overseas in March 2000 that al-Hazmi had already entered the United States at Los Angeles in January 2000 – but because the cable was marked 'Action: none; for information only', the report sat in the CIA. Furthermore, the FBI had an informant, whose identity I believe is still not disclosed publicly, who was al-Midhar's and al-Hazmi's landlord while they were living in southern California prior to September 11.

al-Midhar and al-Hazmi were among the hijackers on Flight 77 which struck the Pentagon. What was particularly unfortunate about this lapse in the notification process is that these were the only two of the 19 hijackers who were known prior to September 11 to have ties to al-Qaeda. The rest all had clean records. The point here is that if we had a fully functioning internal security service along the lines of MI5 or the DST, acting in seamless co-ordination with the CIA, it seems likely that this al-Qaeda pair would have been picked up on their arrival in the United States. This in turn would have had a major effect on the unfolding of Osama bin Laden's operation, perhaps even to the extent of wrapping it up before it could have taken place.

Intelligence: not a perfect world

The third point I would like to make is that intelligence is not a perfect game. It never will be. The military has a tendency to want perfect information on the situation on the ground before undertaking an operation. This is simply not possible. Since intelligence is not perfect, it requires political will and determination to drive an operation forward. A counter-example is that of the failure of US forces to rescue 53 American hostages in Tehran in April 1980.

Prior to the rescue operation, the military had been critical of the lack of intelligence on the exact location of the hostages. Even when they were finally pinpointed as still being kept in the embassy, according to a Pakistani cook who had escaped from the compound, the military were sceptical of the information because it did not come from American eyes. However, intelligence, sketchy as it was, was not the main problem in the rescue operation. Rather, it was an operational failure and also, it could be said, a failure of political will.

I am not going to go into the details of the operation which failed at the refuelling point inside Iran that was designated Desert One and which became the name commonly used for this unfortunate operation. The command relationships at Desert One were diffuse, and the chief of the overall Joint Task Force was back in Egypt. When the number of helicopters became unexpectedly reduced, due mainly to malfunctions, the question was whether to continue with the operation. An intelligence officer within the Task Force had this observation:

> Although it is easy to say in hindsight, the bottom line is that a daring commander in wartime could have and would have continued with five or even four helicopters. The Delta Force commander [at Desert One] was a fine Special Forces soldier, but his country was not at war...[In addition] the Joint Task Force Commander did not order the mission to go forward; and neither did the Chairman of the Joint Chiefs, the Secretary of Defense or the President.[10]

Desert One was an immense lesson and an immense turning point. We vowed that we would never again be found impotent in the face of a small group of individuals like the Iranian hostage-takers. The legislation that followed, in 1986, the Goldwater-Nichols Act, accompanied by the Cohen-Nunn Act, changed everything. Goldwater-Nichols spelled the end of the large independence that the various branches of service (Army, Navy and so on), had enjoyed, and also it strengthened the role of the Chairman of the Joint Chiefs of Staff. From then on, the emphasis was on joint operations; no more fractionalised command arrangements as in the Iranian hostage rescue operation. The accompanying Cohen-Nunn Act involved the reorganisation and the consolidation of all the Special Forces under a sole command called the United States Special Operations Command (USSOCOM) and located in Tampa, Florida.

Intelligence and political will

The Iranian hostage-takers had practised *soft* terrorism. By the time they were released, after negotiations, and at the moment Ronald Reagan became President, it turned out that none of them had been hurt. The hostage-takers had billed themselves as not beholden to a state but to a religious leader, Ayatollah Khomeini. Islamism had become a problem for the United States. It was to assume a much more diabolical and nihilist form in the 1990s in the person of Osama bin Laden.

During the 1990s, it gradually became apparent that Osama bin Laden had been involved in one way or another in a series of operations against US interests dating back to Mogadiscio in 1993, to the first World Trade Center attack in the same year, to the bombings of two US embassies in east Africa on 7 August 1998, and to the attack on the USS *Cole* in Aden harbor in October 2000. Then the culminating attack took place on September 11, 2001. During this period bin

Laden issued two fatwas, or supposed Islamic legal opinions. The first, in 1996, authorised attacks against Western military targets on the Arabian peninsula. The second, in 1998, just before the east Africa bombings, stated that Muslims have a religious obligation to attack US military and civilians world-wide.[11]

By 10 September 2001, and for several years before that, the CIA knew bin Laden's location almost every day – sometimes within 50 miles, sometimes within 50 feet. This was known from information provided by foreign governments, from CIA's own human sources and from technical sources like the 'Predator' unmanned aerial drone. The United States clearly had the capability to remove bin Laden, to take him out of Afghanistan, and/or to kill him. Special Forces capabilities had been developed over the previous 15 years following the legislative reforms that followed Desert One. The irony, and the tragedy, is that somewhere between 15 and 30 Special Operations personnel died or were injured during this period preparing for just that mission that would have removed bin Laden.

Through the late 1990s, policy makers repeatedly informed the CIA and the military that they lacked the necessary information to act against bin Laden. The instructions were to 'Go back and try again. Collect more information. We need to know well in advance exactly when bin Laden will be in such-and-such a house or on such-and-such a convoy trail.' But the fact is that intelligence alone will never deliver the kind of certainty which the policy makers say they require.

Instead, in a retaliatory gesture in response to the bombings in east Africa, on 20 August 1998 the United States launched cruise missile attacks on six bin Laden training camps in Afghanistan and on a pharmaceutical plant in Khartoum North formerly used by bin Laden and thought to be involved in producing precursor chemicals. 'We only missed him by a half and hour', ruefully – but also futilely – remarked a White House aide about bin Laden. The uproar over the Khartoum North target, whose validity was never clarified one way or another, was such that no further attacks were carried out by the United States until the shock of September 11. Thus the 75 cruise missiles that were launched on 20 August 1998, at a cost of 1 million dollars apiece, went for naught.

In the event, Washington went ahead and gradually applied sanctions against Afghanistan while at the same time negotiating secretly with the Taliban, in an attempt to get them to hand over bin Laden. This series of fruitless discussions continued right into the summer of 2001. The Saudis, in the person of former intelligence chief Turki bin Faysal (now the Saudi Ambassador to London) also tried in vain to pry loose from the Taliban his former protégé, bin Laden.[12]

On 17 October 2002, in testimony before the joint House and Senate select intelligence committee investigating the September 11 attacks, George Tenet judged that:

we should have taken down that [bin Laden] sanctuary [in Afghanistan] a lot sooner...there may have been lots of good reasons why in hindsight it couldn't have been done earlier...but we let them operate with impunity for a long time without putting the full force and muscle of the United States against them.[13]

In covert terms, what did Washington do in the wake of the August 1998 bombings of its embassies in Nairobi and Dar-es-Salaam? Following these attacks, President Clinton had signed a Presidential Finding, authorising a covert action to capture bin Laden, using lethal force if necessary. The President amended the finding three times, under a document known as a Memorandum of Notification. The first was to use lethal force without necessarily having to take bin Laden into custody. The second was to expand the targets of the covert action beyond bin Laden, to include a number of his lieutenants. The third was to shoot down an aircraft or helicopter that bin Laden might use to try to get out of Afghanistan.[14] But there were two red lines, or limitations, to this planned use of force. One was that US troops would only use weapons fired from a distance, in other words, not on the ground in Afghanistan. The second was that the enemy was defined as al-Qaeda and not also as the people protecting al-Qaeda – in other words the Taliban.[15] The upshot was that surrogate forces were used to try to capture bin Laden – Pakistanis, Uzbeks and Afghans. No Americans were used except for a few reconnaissance missions. These surrogate forces were unable to do the job.

In December 1998, in a memorandum to his deputies and to officials in the Intelligence Community, George Tenet stated that they should consider themselves at war with bin Laden. This message, however, seems not to have penetrated to the top echelons of the US government. The marriage between intelligence and political will was still not there.

Intelligence in the twenty-first century: the 'offensive hunt' strategy

It took the shock of September 11, 2001 to produce the political will to go over to the offensive. 'The National Security Strategy of the United States', published a year later, on 20 September 2002, advanced the doctrine of pre-emption. It evoked the case 'for taking anticipatory action to defend ourselves, even if uncertainty remains as to the time and place of the enemy's attack. To forestall or prevent such hostile attacks by our adversaries, the United States will, if necessary, act pre-emptively.'[16]

The sub-title of this conference is 'Understanding Intelligence in the Twenty-First Century'. I would submit that the hallmark of intelligence in this new century is going to be what I would term an 'offensive hunt' strategy. It will be outside the Westphalian mode; it will be markedly different from what went on in the twentieth century, which was essentially one of rivalries and conflicts among nation-states, the false cloak of ideologies notwithstanding. In the twenty-first century the clashes will be mostly between nation-states and what are called in social-science parlance non-state actors. The exception to this trend, which may not last long, is that of United States actions against so-called rogue states, in other words those seeking to acquire weapons of mass destruction.

The 'offensive hunt' strategy can be characterised as the intelligence and operational manifestation of the New Strategic Doctrine of the Bush administration. Such a strategy far outstrips the capability of an intelligence service, even such a large one as the CIA. It involves the hunting down of thousands of al-Qaeda and allied terrorists of the 'global reach' variety. It will be a combined intelligence and operational function, and it will have to involve, à la Afghanistan and Iraq, the CIA and Special Forces working together. In a peacetime situation, juridical underpinnings will have to be found, though not for the CIA, for whom a Presidential Finding and Congressional oversight system for covert action has been in place starting in 1970.[17]

The 'offensive hunt' strategy will also involve methods which were not the norm prior to September 11, 2001. The methods will involve not only hunting down and, if need be, killing terrorists but also, again where necessary, ignoring local sensitivities and the operating rules of local intelligence and security services.

What happened in the war in Afghanistan that followed the events of September 11 is instructive in understanding both the new 'offensive hunt' strategy and the symbiosis that is being imposed on the CIA and the US military. Within days after the attack, and according to a 'war plan' submitted by George Tenet to President Bush that included a new Presidential Finding authorising the outright elimination of bin Laden and his principal lieutenants, CIA elements arrived on the ground in Afghanistan, to renew contacts with the Northern Alliance and to forge contacts with Pushtun leaders in the south. In both the north and the south, saddlebags of CIA money played a key role.[18] In his Congressional testimony on 17 October 2002, and in an implied criticism of the policy that was previously in force, that is before September 11, George Tenet stated that, 'Nothing did more for our ability to combat terrorism than President [Bush's] decision to send us into the terrorist sanctuary. By going in massively, we were able to change the rules for the terrorists. Now they are the hunted.'

Put in another way, intelligence operatives in the twenty-first century will become *hunters* not *gatherers*. They will not simply sit back and gather information that comes in, analyse it and then decide what to do about it. Rather they will have to go and hunt out intelligence that will enable them to track down or kill terrorists. The 'offensive hunt' strategy involves sending operatives into countries with which we are not at war, indeed in some cases countries with whom we have correct relations. In some circumstances, obviously, we will hunt down terrorist leaders with the help of host country elements; in others we will not. The former was the case in Pakistan with the capture of the operational dispatcher of al-Qaeda, Abu Zubaydah. Together with the FBI and the CIA, the Pakistani authorities wounded and captured Abu Zubaydah after a chase. It was also the case in Yemen, referred to earlier, when a CIA drone with a Hellfire missile obliterated the al-Qaeda chief in the Gulf area, Abu Ali al-Harithi, and five of his followers, apparently done in co-ordination with the Yemeni authorities.

But the type of operation that would be envisaged in the new strategy – the hunting and capture of possibly thousands of terrorist leaders and technicians – is far above the scale of a law enforcement operation as practiced by the FBI and far above the limited paramilitary capability of the CIA. As it is carried out overseas, this will become primarily a military problem, involving the introduction of discreet military forces into a hostile environment, backed by a panoply of technical collection resources, and often without the agreement or knowledge of the country in question. It will be essentially a Special Forces mission aided by CIA elements.

The symbiosis on the ground between CIA officers, with contacts, money and intelligence collection capabilities, and Special Forces elements calling in artillery and air strikes, and participating in attacks, worked reasonably well in Afghanistan, albeit with some glitches. These CIA elements were instrumental in putting Special Forces personnel in contact with the Northern Alliance and other Afghan groups willing to fight the Taliban and al-Qaeda.[19] But in the aftermath, Secretary Rumsfeld was dissatisfied with some aspects of the campaign, and he ordered the Pentagon's Defense Science Board to study how things could be improved. Rumsfeld specifically posed the question, 'How is it that I have to have CIA elements on the ground first before I can put in my Special Forces?'

Here we arrive at the nub of the problem regarding the 'offensive hunt' strategy in the future. Hitherto, it is the CIA that has operated abroad clandestinely in peacetime, through covert action operations requiring approval by the President in a Presidential Finding.[20] This finding, in turn, must be briefed in near 'real-time' to the intelligence oversight committees of the Congress. Normally, uniformed US personnel are not sent to sovereign foreign countries unilaterally. They must be asked in, to work with the local forces. The intelligence oversight committees of the Congress are generally reluctant to have the military take part in or take over this kind of activity as, for one thing, this would escape their oversight, as they do not have jurisdiction over the armed forces.[21]

The military for some years have resisted this confinement or, to put it in another way, this privileged position of the CIA in peacetime. The military have maintained that, as a precursor to an operation abroad, it is necessary to send reconnaissance teams to collect intelligence on the area. In the past, this concept has been variously designated as a 'commander's reconnaissance' prerogative or, more recently, the necessity for 'preparation of the battlefield'. Now that we are in a situation of, if you will, 'war by another name' post-September 11, the Pentagon has pressed its case on an urgent basis.

The thinking of the Defense Department following the Afghan campaign was to find a juridical underpinning for the insertion of Special Forces abroad, whether with or without the knowledge of the host country, in Title 10 of the US Code. Title 10 deals with the employment of the armed forces. Specifically, Section 167 of Title 10 mandates a unified combatant command for special forces which may conduct certain missions not under the authority of the geographic combatant commands, if the President or the Secretary of Defense so directs; it excludes from Title 10 authorisation for any activity that would require giving notice to the intelligence oversight committees of the Congress; and it includes a broad range of operations as being within the writ of special operations, namely: direct action, strategic reconnaissance, unconventional warfare, foreign internal defence, civil affairs, psychological operations, counter-terrorism, humanitarian assistance, theatre search and rescue, and such other activities as may be specified by the President or the Secretary of Defense. The hunt for al-Qaeda operatives presumably would be carried out under the rubric of counter-terrorism.

Military analyst William M. Arkin has argued that fighting terrorism is the twenty-first century equivalent to the Cold War crusade against communism, and that the magnitude of the threat requires new, aggressive and unorthodox tactics.[22] As indicated by the Title 10 provisions cited above, the Pentagon is most interested first in freeing Special Forces operations from the authority of the geographic military commands; and, second, in freeing these operations from the oversight of the Congressional intelligence committees. With regard to the former, Defense Secretary Rumsfeld in the autumn of 2002 gave USSOCOM, which is not a geographic combatant command, the lead in the hunt for al-Qaeda operatives.[23] With regard to the latter, the problem arises of how to maintain the long-standing US principle of civilian control over the military. Modalities will have to be worked out between the Department of Defense and the CIA as to how such 'offensive hunt' operations are to be carried out. DCI Tenet is described as not opposed to a role for the military in this arena.[24] Clearly the assets of the military will have to be brought into play, as the threat is much too vast for an intelligence service to handle.

The Defense Science Board completed its post-September 11 study referred to above[25] in late October 2002. The 78-page classified document of the ten-member board, chaired by William Schneider, Jr., is entitled its '2002 Summer Study on Special Operations and Joint Forces in Support of Countering Terrorism'. The study recommended that new special operations of an offensive nature world-wide should be planned by the National Security Council through the aegis of a to-be-created 'Proactive, Preemptive Operations Group';[26] but the operations themselves would be executed by the military and/or the CIA, as the case may be.[27] At a level under the NSC there already exist joint inter-agency groups for the purpose of co-ordinating such special operations activities: at Fort Bragg, home of the Joint Special Operations Command; at Tampa, Florida, headquarters of the Central Command which is the geographical command for the southwest Asia and east Africa areas; and at Bagram airbase north of Kabul, Afghanistan.[28]

Conclusion

It seems as though we have been thrown back a century, to the beginning of the twentieth century, when the world was at peace, albeit an armed one, and the anarchist movement was the chief cause of unrest in the Western world, as evoked in Joseph Conrad's novel, *The Secret Sharer*. The anarchist movement did die out, however. The same cannot be forecast for the Islamist terrorist movement that reached a level of unprecedented ferocity with the attack on the Twin Towers on September 11.

The prospect now is that Islamist terrorism may last – with the United States as its chief enemy – for decades to come, indeed as long as Muslim aspirations remain far removed from cruel realities, and as terrorism, the weapon of the weak, continues to wreak unspeakable havoc among innocent people. In the face of this sombre prospect, 'offensive hunt' will have to become the strategy of choice for US intelligence. But unless the United States is willing to take radical steps to change its internal security structures, it will continue to remain vulnerable to further attacks against the homeland.

Notes

1 Author interview with Harvard historian Ernest May, Cambridge, MA, 21 June 2001.
2 *Miller Center Newsletter*, 18, 3 (Summer 2002), p. 22.
3 From a talk at Harvard University entitled 'The End of the Postwar World: Some Causes and consequences', 24 November 1991.
4 *New York Times*, 24 October 2002, p. A14.
5 *New York Times*, 8 December 2002, p. 1.
6 In the view of Ernest May, the NSC was created in part to get the military involved in foreign policy. (Author interview with Ernest May, Cambridge, MA, 21 June 2001.)
7 Dan Benjamin and Steven Simon, *The Age of Sacred Terror* (New York: Random House, 2002), p. 395. The authors are two former counter-terrorism officials in the Clinton White House.
8 Thomas Powers, 'The Secret Intelligence Wars', *New York Review of Books*, 26 (September 2002), p. 32.
9 *New York Times*, 18 October 2002, p. A13.
10 Interview with Robert Mattingly.
11 Testimony of Cofer Black, former Director of the CIA's Counter-terrorism Center, before the Joint September 11 inquiry of the Intelligence Committees of the Congress, 27 September 2002.
12 Benjamin and Simon, *The Age of Secret Terror*, pp. 271–2.
13 *New York Times*, 18 October 2002, p. A12.
14 *Washington Post*, 19 December 2001.
15 Ibid.
16 *New York Review of Books*, 7 November 2002, p. 4.
17 This system is in the form of successive amendments to the National Security Act of 1947. The Act itself and these amendments are incorporated into the United States Code Title 50, called Defense and National Security, in Chapter 15, Section 413b entitled, 'Presidential Approval and Reporting of Covert Action'.
18 *Washington Post*, 17 November 2002. N.B. It is this finding, apparently, that provides the juridical basis for actions such as the 'Predator' attack in Yemen and which seems to render the 1981 Executive Order 12333 banning assassinations in effect caduc. Although the Executive Order states explicitly that 'no person employed by or acting on behalf of the United States Government shall engage in, or conspire to engage in, assassination', it appears to be obviated by the subsequent finding and by the fact that the President has stated that we are at war with al-Qaeda.
19 www.truthout.org/docs_02/08.14C.rums.nu.covert.htm, p. 2.
20 In a wartime situation in the normal sense, as in the Second World War, there is no question where the authority lies: the military takes command over all activities of war, including intelligence, just as the military exerted control over the OSS during the Second World War. From the military's point of view, it is imperative that it has control over intelligence in wartime.
21 The military have a responsibility to the armed forces committees of the Congress and not to the intelligence committees and have nothing to do, in terms of budget or oversight, with the latter. Furthermore, the intelligence committees have evolved into exercising a close monitoring role of CIA covert actions. This is not the same case with the military, whose actions are subject to broad review under the War Powers

Act, which is still a contested piece of legislation between the Congress and the President, but this kind of review does not resemble the close oversight exercised by the intelligence committees over the covert actions of the CIA.

22 William M. Arkin, 'The Secret War', *Los Angeles Times*, 27 October 2002.
23 Greg Miller, 'Wider Pentagon Spy Role is Urged', *Los Angeles Times*, 26 October 2002.
24 www.truthout.org/docs_02/08.14C.rums.nu.covert.htm, p. 2.
25 See ibid., pp. 2–3.
26 Arkin, 'The Secret War'.
27 Miller, 'Wider Pentagon Spy Role'.
28 Arkin, 'The Secret War'. N.B. In the Iraq war of March–April 2003, US Special Forces were active inside Iraq before the war started. The spearhead of this activity was Task Force 20, drawn largely from Delta Force. Its mission was to locate Weapons of Mass Destruction (it found none); to attack sensitive targets (it secured the Haditha dam above Baghdad); to capture high-ranking Iraqi leaders (which it did with some success) and take them to Baghdad airport for joint interrogation with the CIA; and to rescue US prisoners (which it did in the case of Pfc. Jessica Lynch). According to Barton Gellman, 'Task Force 20 employs the best-trained combat forces in the US military. It can launch a mission with less than an hour's notice and communicate securely from anywhere in Iraq . . . It has full-time access to stealthy helicopters . . . that enable it to move covertly and defend itself.' (Barton Gellman, 'Covert Unit Hunted for Iraqi Arms', *Washington Post*, 13 June 2003, p. 1.)

11 Secret Intelligence, Covert Action and Clandestine Diplomacy

Len Scott

'The essential skill of a secret service is to get things done secretly and deniably.'
(John Bruce Lockhart, former Deputy Chief of SIS)[1]

Much contemporary study of intelligence concerns how knowledge is acquired, generated and used. This chapter provides a different focus that treats secrecy, rather than knowledge, as an organising theme. Instead of scrutinising the process of gathering, analysing and exploiting intelligence, it examines other activities of secret intelligence services, often termed covert action. This broader framework draws upon both pre-modern 'Secret Service' activities that predated modern intelligence organisations,[2] as well as many Cold War studies. It resonates with the perspective of Richard Aldrich that secret service activity includes 'operations to influence the world by unseen means – the hidden hand'.[3] Exploration of secret intervention illuminates important themes and issues in the study of intelligence, and identifies challenges and opportunities for enquiry, particularly in the context of the British experience. One further aspect is examined and developed – the role of secret intelligence services in conducting clandestine diplomacy, a neglected yet intriguing dimension that also provides insights into the study of intelligence.

Many intelligence services perform tasks other than gathering secret intelligence. Conversely, intelligence activities are conducted by organisations other than secret intelligence services. The relationship between organisation and function varies over time and place. In wartime Britain, for example, the Secret Intelligence Service (SIS) conducted espionage and the Special Operations Executive (SOE) was responsible for special operations.[4] While the CIA conducted much US Cold War propaganda, in Britain the Information Research Department was part of the Foreign Office.[5] In the United States, covert paramilitary action has long been undertaken by the Department of Defense,[6] while there is a veritable plethora of US government agencies with intelligence gathering capabilities. And in the wake of September 11 the CIA has expanded its paramilitary capabilities (evident in Afghanistan) while the Pentagon appears committed to developing Special Forces able to conduct their own intelligence gathering. Notwithstanding the fact that different tasks are performed by different organisations, since 1945 Western intelligence services have nevertheless used the same organisations and the same groups of people to perform different tasks.

For many observers, and especially for many critics, secret intervention is synonymous with intelligence and loomed large in Cold War debates about the legitimacy and morality of intelligence organisations and their activities. Since September 11, Washington's agenda for taking the offensive to the United States' enemies has rekindled such arguments. To exclude such activities from discussion about intelligence and intelligence services raises questions about the political agendas of those seeking to delineate and circumscribe the focus of enquiry. For many writers, for example, on British intelligence, special operations are integral to the study of the subject.[7] But for others they are not.[8] So, do those who marginalise or downplay covert action do so as part of an agenda to legitimise intelligence gathering? Do those who focus on covert action do so to undermine the legitimacy of intelligence (or the state in general or in particular)? Or are these unintended consequences reflecting unconscious biases? Or legitimate choices of emphasis and focus?

Among the obvious and critical questions about secret interventions are: how do we know about them? And how do we interpret and evaluate them? Many of the terms used – 'covert action', 'special operation', 'special activities' and 'disruptive action' are used interchangeably though there are also important terminological differences. The Soviet term 'active measures' (*activinyye meropriatia*) embraced overt and covert actions to exercise influence in foreign countries, whereas most other terms focus exclusively on the covert.[9] Critics and sceptics often use the more generic description of 'dirty tricks'.

The more prominent definitions of covert action are American, dating back to the celebrated 1948 National Security directive 10/2 which authorised the CIA to engage in:

> propaganda; economic warfare; preventive direct action, including sabotage, anti-sabotage, demolition and evacuation measures; subversion against hostile states, including assistance to underground resistance movements, guerrillas and refugee liberation groups, and support of indigenous anti-Communist elements in threatened countries of the free world.[10]

More recent US government statements cover most of these activities though some of the language has altered (notably the demise of 'subversion'). In US law covert action became defined as:

> an activity or activities of the United States Government to influence political, economic, or military conditions abroad, where it is intended that the role of the [government] will not be apparent or acknowledged publicly, but does not include...traditional counter-intelligence...diplomatic...military...[or] law enforcement activities.[11]

Whether phrases such as 'regime change' that have emerged in public debate over Iraq will enter the covert lexicon remains to be seen.

One commonly accepted aspect of these definitions is that they refer to actions abroad. In the United States this reflects the legal status of the US intelligence services. Elsewhere, the distinction between home and abroad may be less clear. Some governments practice at home what they undertake abroad. Oleg Kalugin has recounted how the KGB conducted active measures against one of its leading dissidents, Alexander Solzhenitsin, culminating in attempts to poison him.[12] Various British government activities in Northern Ireland, for example, appear to fall within otherwise accepted definitions of covert action.[13]

British terminology has moved from 'special operations' to 'special political action' to 'disruptive action'.[14] These semantic changes reflect broader shifts in policy. The 'special political action' of the 1950s, for example, was synonymous with intervention aimed at overthrowing governments and in some cases assassinating leaders.[15] Since then, changes in the scope and nature of operations have reflected the priorities and perspectives of governments and of SIS itself. Although the Intelligence Services Act 1994 makes clear that SIS's mandate is to engage in 'other tasks' beside espionage, the scope and nature of these other tasks is unclear.[16] 'Disruptive action' is nowhere officially defined, though there are some official references to the term.[17] What is involved is unclear from official references. It may be unwise to infer that disruptive activity is exclusively clandestine. Some activities might involve passing information to other states and agencies to enable them to act against arms dealers or terrorists, and would fall within the ambit of intelligence liaison. How far, and in what ways, actions are undertaken without knowledge or permission of the host nations or organisations are the more controversial questions. David Shayler, the former MI5 officer, has revealed or alleged that SIS supported groups seeking to overthrow and assassinate the Libyan leader, Colonel Ghaddafi, in 1995/96, and what appears to be SIS documentation has been posted on the internet providing apparent corroboration.[18] The SIS 'whistleblower', Richard Tomlinson, has indicated that SIS is required to 'maintain a capability to plan and mount "Special Operations" of a quasi-military nature' which are 'executed by specially trained officers and men from the three branches of the armed forces'.[19] He also provides examples of disruptive action, discussed below. Lack of clarity about the term disruptive action reflects the determination of the British government to avoid disclosure of the activities involved.

Elizabeth Anderson has argued that 'the specific subject of covert action as an element of intelligence has suffered a deficiency of serious study'; she notes a failure to generate the theoretical concepts to explain other instruments of foreign policy such as trade, force and diplomacy.[20] Nevertheless, the American literature provides typologies that distinguish between political action, economic action, propaganda and paramilitary activities.[21] The nature and scope of these activities differs across time, place and context. How far these categories reflect the distillation of American experience and reflection is one question to ask. Yet whatever the theory and practice in other states, American debates about whether covert action should be viewed as a routine instrument of statecraft, a weapon of last resort or the subversion of democratic values will presumably be familiar to many of those contemplating such options.

Knowledge and trust

This leads to the second general consideration: the problem of knowledge. For scholars and citizens alike, knowledge of secret intervention is crucial to understanding and evaluation. How far this is a problem is a matter of debate. Stephen Dorril, for example, has argued that in the British context there is far more in the public domain than anyone has realised and that 'the reality [is] that secrets are increasingly difficult to protect, and it would not be a great exaggeration to suggest that there are no real secrets any more'.[22] In contrast, Roy Godson argued in 1995 that our knowledge of covert action (and counter-intelligence) is 'sketchy at best',[23] and this in a book that drew heavily upon both US and pre-Cold War historiography. Since Godson published that view there have been significant developments in the declassification of US archival records on Cold War covert actions.[24] And since September 11 we have learned of specific covert actions including those planned and authorised by the Clinton administration.[25] How far this information was provided to protect Clinton administration officials and/or CIA officers against accusations that they were supine in the face of the terrorist threat is one question. Such revelations also reflect a Washington culture where the willingness of individuals and agencies to provide information to journalists presents incentives for others to preserve or enhance their individual and organisational reputations.

We know about covert action in the same ways that we learn about other intelligence activities – through authorised and unauthorised disclosure: memoirs, journalism, defectors, archives, whistle-blowers and judicial investigation. The veracity and integrity of these sources may differ, though there are generic questions to be posed about the agendas and intentions of those who provide us with information about covert action, as about intelligence in general. How we assess what we are told reflects our values and assumptions. Our understanding of KGB active measures, for example, has been greatly informed by the revelations of defectors whose accounts have been sanctioned by the intelligence services with whom they worked. For critical commentators who believe official sources are by definition tainted sources, any public disclosure of an adversary's activities is synonymous with disinformation and the manipulation of public opinion. Accounts written by retired Soviet intelligence officials raise different, though no less intriguing, questions about the veracity of the material disclosed. Pavel Sudoplatov's memoir of his work for Stalin's NKVD generated much controversy with its strongly disputed claims that leading atomic scientists on the Manhattan Project provided crucial intelligence to the Soviets.[26] Yet the book contains material about active measures and assassinations conducted by Soviet intelligence during the Stalin era that has not been denounced.

The study of intelligence (as with the practice of intelligence) requires consideration of the motives and agendas of sources and how far they can be dissociated from the substance of what they provide. In some ways this goes to the heart of the study of the subject. On what basis, for example, do we believe or not believe Richard Tomlinson when he recounts that SIS engaged in assassination planning against the Serbian President, Slobodan Milosevic, that it endeavoured to disrupt the Iranian chemical warfare programme, and that it acted as an instrument of the CIA in defaming the UN Secretary-General, Dr Bhoutros Bhoutros Ghali?[27] For some, the account of the whistleblower or the defector is inherently reliable. For others, the motives of betrayal and exposure cast doubt on reliability or judgement. Does Pavel Sudoplatov's role in Stalin's assassination policy, and the fact that he remained 'a Stalinist with few regrets',[28] lend credence to his testimony or does it render his concern for the truth as incredible as his claims about Oppenheimer, Bohr, Fermi and Szilard? How far pre-existing assumptions inform how we assess individuals and their motives is important to consider. 'If we trust the motive, we trust the man. Then we trust his material', opines a British intelligence officer in John Le Carré's *The Russia House*.[29] Trust and judgement are as essential to the academic enterprise as they are to the professional intelligence officer. And like the professional intelligence officer judgements on veracity require corroboration and evaluation of all available sources.

One interesting response to this problem has been collaboration between insiders and outsiders. Joint endeavours between journalists and former intelligence officers have provided a variety of intriguing texts and valuable accounts. Western academics have also helped pioneer exploitation of Soviet intelligence archives, most notably Fursenko and Naftali's work (see below). In Britain the pattern of these collaborations ranges across various kinds of relationship. Gordon Brook-Shepherd was allowed access to SIS archival records for his study of Western intelligence and the Bolshevik revolution where *inter alia* he traced SIS involvement in the plot to overthrow and assassinate Lenin.[30] Tom Bower completed a biography of Sir Dick White, begun by Andrew Boyle, which drew upon extensive recollections and testimony of the man who led both the Security Service and the Secret Intelligence Service, and which contains much material not only on Cold War but on colonial and post-colonial operations.[31] Other writers have enjoyed more opaque relationships with officialdom while some have clearly been used by individuals to disseminate particular perspectives or grievances. More recently SIS enabled Christopher Andrew to collaborate with the KGB defectors Oleg Gordievsky and Vassili Mitrokhin in a new form of relationship, which yielded new public insights into KGB practices both in peacetime and in preparation for war.

One question is whether we know more about covert action than intelligence gathering and analysis. A second is whether we know more about certain kinds of covert actions than others – especially the more dramatic. Some covert operations have been easier to discover because they fail. We know about the targeting in 1985 of the Greenpeace protest ship, *Rainbow Warrior*, because the operation went wrong, and because officers of the French foreign intelligence service, the *Direction Generale de la Securite Exterieure*, were caught and tried by the

New Zealand authorities. It can also be argued that by definition the most successful covert actions are those that no-one knows has ever been conducted: the analogy with the perfect crime. A different definition of success is that while knowledge of them may leak out (or may be impossible to conceal), the identity of those engaging in them remains secret. For many governments the concept of plausible deniability has been integral to the activity. So among the obvious questions: do we learn more about unsuccessful operations than successful ones? Among the more perplexing questions: when we think we are learning of secret intervention are we in fact the target of covert action and the recipient of disinformation or propaganda?

Understanding the limits of knowledge is important. If we know more about secret intervention than intelligence gathering we may draw distorted conclusions about the priorities of the organisations involved. Moreover, if our knowledge of the phenomenon is drawn from a particular period of history and politics and from particular states in that period, then how useful a guide is our knowledge for understanding the world we now inhabit? Much of our understanding of the phenomenon is drawn from particular phases of the Cold War. So do we make assumptions about how states behave on the basis of generalisations drawn from atypical examples? Most specifically do our examples and our categories of analysis reflect US assumptions and experiences? Notwithstanding the observations of Roy Godson, the study of covert action in the United States has generated a considerable and sophisticated literature based on extensive US experience, and a body of scholarship that notably extends to ethical debate about covert actions.[32] Public and political accountability of covert action has also made a significant contribution to that knowledge and understanding, though it underlines a distinctive (and hitherto frequently unique) US approach to public knowledge of the secret world.

One reason for exploring these questions is that these activities loom large in public perceptions of intelligence services, both nationally and internationally. The image of the CIA, for example, has been coloured at home and especially abroad by what has been learned of its activities in places like Cuba, Guatemala, Iran and Chile.[33] Whether these activities buttressed democracy in the Cold War or undermined the moral authority of the United States in the 'Third World' are essential questions for scholars interested in the role of intelligence in world politics.[34]

Interpretation

The interpretation and evaluation of covert action should extend beyond utility into ethics and legality. Many of the ethical, legal and political debates on overt intervention do not give consideration to covert action. Such debates are clearly hampered by secrecy. Yet concepts of 'ethical statecraft' and debates about Britain's 'ethical foreign policy' have largely ignored covert action, and indeed intelligence in general. Since the end of the Cold War and since September 11 significant changes in world politics have been apparent. In the last decade, for example, the belief that humanitarian intervention in other states was legally and ethically synonymous with aggression has altered. Ideas of humanitarian intervention, though contested, have underpinned military action in Kosovo. American embrace of pre-emptive (or rather preventive) action to forestall attacks on the United States and its allies, portends radical changes in world order. Predicting future trends is inherently problematic, but it is reasonable to speculate that public and academic debate will engage with the normative questions about covert action in the 'war against terror' in more robust and systematic fashion.

Locating secret intervention within broader debates in international politics should not obscure critical questions about whether they work. Assessing their effectiveness and their consequences are crucial. As with diplomacy and military action such assessments cannot be fully evaluated by examining only the actions of the state that undertakes them. Understanding foreign policy making is a necessary but not sufficient part of understanding international politics. This has been apparent in recent historiography of the Cold War that has drawn from the archives and from the scholarship of former adversaries, and provided new insights and perspectives. The international history of secret intervention is surely part of this enterprise and of how mutual perceptions and misperceptions informed the Cold War struggle. This is an area that parallels the nuclear history of the Cold War where Soviet archival disclosures raise fascinating and disturbing questions about Soviet threat perceptions.

Until recently, these aspects have been under-explored. While John Gaddis' acclaimed 1997 study of the new historiography of the Cold War provides evidence of how Soviet covert action impacted on Western approaches, there is little on how Soviet leaders interpreted Western secret intervention.[35] Other accounts drawn from Soviet archival sources have begun to emphasise the importance of Soviet perceptions and misperceptions. Vojtech Mastny has explored how Western covert action in eastern Europe and the Soviet Union exerted a significant and undue influence on Stalin's paranoia.[36] Richard Aldrich has raised the controversial question of whether Western covert action in eastern Europe was specifically designed to provoke Soviet repression in order to destabilise and weaken Soviet hegemony.[37] Recent interpretations of the nature and role of US covert action have indeed provoked radical revisions of the Cold War itself.[38]

Such perspectives should not obscure the fact that although the Cold War provided context and pretext for many secret interventions since 1945, it is misleading to view all such action in these terms. There is a risk that the literature repeats the mistakes of Western decision makers in viewing post-colonial struggles through the lens of East–West conflict. As Ludo de Witte argues persuasively in his study of the Belgian intelligence service's involvement in the assassination of the Congolese leader, Patrice Lumumba, the events of 1960–61 should be viewed primarily as a struggle against colonialism.[39] Other studies and critiques have focused on secret interventions in post-colonial contexts.[40] Yet while the end of the Cold War generated new opportunities to study Cold War intelligence conflicts, post-colonial politics provide very differing contexts and challenges to understanding.

In 1995 Roy Godson observed that 'for many Americans, covert action, in the absence of clear and present danger, is a controversial proposition at best'.[41] Perceptions of the immediacy and presence of danger have changed since September 11. The impact on long-term attitudes, both in the United States and Europe, is difficult to assess and will in part be informed by other events and revelations, not least war on Iraq. It is a reasonable assumption that American use of particular kinds of covert activity will be more robust and intrusive, through which organs of the US government will be intruding and where remains to be seen (assuming it can be seen). How these actions are viewed in Europe and elsewhere also remains to be seen. At the height of the Cold War covert action was justified as a quiet option, to be used where diplomacy was insufficient and force was inappropriate. If the United States and its allies consider themselves in semi-perpetual war against 'terrorism', and preventive action in counter-proliferation and counter-terrorism (in overt and covert policy) becomes increasingly prevalent, the implications for covert action will be profound.

Clandestine diplomacy

Diplomacy has been defined as the 'process of dialogue and negotiation by which states in a system conduct their relations and pursue their purposes by means short of war'.[42] It is also a policy option that can be used as an alternative to, or in support of, other approaches, such as military force. The use of secret services to conduct diplomacy was characteristic of pre-modern inter-state relations, when diplomacy, covert action and intelligence gathering were often conducted by the same people. The creation of modern intelligence bureaucracies led to a greater separation of functions, though not as clearly as might seem. Although clandestine diplomacy is a neglected area of enquiry, there are a number of examples of where intelligence services are used to engage in secret and deniable discussions with adversaries. One question is whether clandestine diplomacy can be conceived as a form of covert action intended to influence an adversary or whether it is distinct from covert action because it involves conscious co-operation with the adversary and potential disclosure of the officers involved.

Conceptually, there may be an overlap between diplomacy and liaison where relations between the actors are in part antagonistic – as in information exchanges between political adversaries in the 'war against terror' (for example, between the Americans and Syrians[43]). There may also be overlap between conducting clandestine diplomacy and gathering intelligence. In 1945 the American Office of Strategic Service (OSS) identification of Japanese 'peace feelers' assisted its analysis that war against Japan could be terminated by negotiation.[44] And there may also be overlap with secret intervention: in 1983 the CIA apparently co-operated with the Iranian secret service by providing details of Soviet agents in the Tudeh party in Iran.[45] One further and important distinction needs to be drawn, between intelligence services acting as diplomatic conduits, and intelligence services acting as quasi-independent foreign policy makers. While it may be difficult to distinguish between the two, the use of intelligence services by governments to conduct negotiations is distinct from where intelligence services have their own agendas and priorities. Various accounts of CIA and SIS activity in the Middle East in the 1950s, for example, suggest that both organisations were pursuing their own foreign policies at variance with their foreign ministry colleagues.[46]

Examples of the clandestine diplomatic role of secret intelligence services that have emerged in recent years include the role of British intelligence in the Northern Ireland peace process,[47] the role of Israeli intelligence services, including Mossad, in Middle East diplomacy and peace building,[48] the CIA's relations with the Palestine Liberation Organisation and SIS's relations with Hamas.[49] These examples illustrate that the activity concerns not just relations between states, but between states and non-state actors, in particular between states and insurgent or 'terrorist' groups.[50] The value of clandestine diplomacy is that it is more readily deniable, and this is particularly significant where the adversary is engaged in armed attacks and/or terrorist activities. One difference between dialogue with states and with a paramilitary group is the greater potential of physical risk to the participants. Professionally, using intelligence officers to facilitate and conduct inter-state diplomacy risks blowing their cover. Paramilitary groups may harbour factions opposed to negotiation, and exposure of the intelligence officer may risk their safety. The paramilitary negotiator may well have parallel concerns.

The role of intelligence services can be to promote the cause of dialogue and reconciliation, both national and international. Depending upon our political assumptions and values, many would conclude that this role is intrinsically worthwhile, although of course, the intelligence service is but an instrument of a political will to engage in dialogue. For those who seek to justify the world of intelligence to the political world, clandestine diplomacy provides some fertile material. For those who wish to explore the ethical dimension of intelligence this is an interesting and neglected dimension. For those who seek to study intelligence, clandestine diplomacy is not only intrinsically interesting, but also a useful way of further exploring problems and challenges in studying the subject.

From the perspective of the study of intelligence, clandestine diplomacy illustrates one of the basic questions and basic problems. How do we know about things? Who is telling us? For what reason? Clandestine diplomacy involves often highly sensitive contacts and exchanges whose disclosure may be intended as foreclosure on dialogue, and where the provenance of our knowledge is a calculation of a protagonist. Secret contacts may be scuppered by public awareness. After disclosure in a Lebanese newspaper of clandestine US negotiations to secure the release of US hostages in the Lebanon in the 1980s that dialogue came to an end as the Iran-Contra fiasco unravelled. Two examples of clandestine diplomacy are discussed below which illustrate the activity and issues in studying the subject. One involves diplomacy between states informed by archival disclosure as well as personal recollection. The other is between a state and a non-state actor based on testimony from the protagonists.

The Cuban missile crisis

In studying clandestine diplomacy it is rare to have details from both sides, and even rarer to have that in documentary form. The study of the Cuban missile crisis provides several examples of intelligence officers being used to undertake clandestine diplomacy. It provides material for exploring the problems of understanding the role of intelligence services, and moreover it provides opportunities to study how clandestine diplomacy was integrated into foreign policy making and crisis management.

Three examples have emerged of intelligence officers acting in diplomatic roles between adversaries in 1962: Georgi Bolshakov (GRU) and Aleksandr Feklisov (KGB) in Washington, and Yevgeny Ivanov (GRU) in London. There are also examples of intelligence officers working in co-operative political relationships: Aleksandr Alekseev (KGB) in Havana, Chet Cooper (CIA) in London, Sherman Kent (CIA) in Paris, William Tidwell (CIA) in Ottawa and Jack Smith (CIA) in Bonn.[51] Alekseev enjoyed the confidence of the Cuban leadership as well as that of Nikita Khrushchev, who recalled him to Moscow to consult on the missile deployment, and promoted him to ambassador. Chester Cooper conveyed the photographic evidence of the Soviet missile deployments to London, and helped brief Prime Minister Macmillan. Sherman Kent accompanied Dean Acheson in briefing General De Gaulle and the North Atlantic Council; William Tidwell briefed Prime Minister Diefenbaker and Jack Smith briefed Konrad Adenauer.

The role of Bolshakov and Feklisov in Washington has generated a particularly fascinating literature. Most significantly, this draws upon Soviet sources and in particular Soviet archival sources, and illustrates the role of secret intelligence in the conduct of Soviet–US diplomacy, as well as problems of both conducting and studying that role.[52] In the case of Ivanov, although we have British Foreign Office documentation and Lord Denning's report into the Profumo Affair, the only Soviet source is Ivanov's memoir, written in retirement, unaided by access to or corroboration from archives.[53] With both Feklisov and Bolshakov, however, we have US and Soviet archival sources, as well as memoirs and personal testimony.

Before access was gained to Soviet sources, it was known that Bolshakov, working under cover as a TASS correspondent, formed a secret back-channel of communication between Kennedy and Khrushchev.[54] This was routed through the Attorney General, Robert Kennedy, with whom he held over 50 meetings in 1961 and 1962. Part of the historical interest of this was that Bolshakov was used by Khrushchev to reassure Kennedy about Soviet intentions in Cuba, and to deceive the US President about the secret deployment of Soviet nuclear missiles. Fursenko and Naftali have now provided evidence of the role of Bolshakov both before and during the missiles crisis.[55] They argue that Bolshakov 'shaped the Kremlin's understanding of the US government'.[56]

Contrary to previous understanding, Bolshakov was not immediately 'discontinued' when Kennedy learned of the missiles, but played an intriguing part in crisis diplomacy. Yet, once the missiles were discovered in Cuba his role in Soviet deception was apparent. Like other Soviet officials, including Ambassador Dobrynin in Washington, he was unaware of the truth. Another probable example of deception concerns Yevgeny Ivanov, a fellow GRU officer, who later in the week admitted to the British that the Soviets had missile deployments in Cuba, but insisted that they only had the range to strike Florida but not Washington.[57] The nature and provenance of this disinformation (or misinformation) remains unclear. Indeed the provenance of Ivanov's mission is not yet fully clear. Ivanov approached the British government to encourage Macmillan to pursue an international summit. Whether this was done on the instructions of Moscow rather than as an initiative of the London *Residentura* has yet to be confirmed.

Perhaps the most intriguing episode during the crisis involved the role of Aleksandr Feklisov (identified at the time and in the early literature as Aleksandr Fomin). Feklisov was the KGB *Rezident* in Washington. At the height of the crisis he contacted a US journalist, John Scali, who then conveyed to the State Department an outline deal to facilitate the withdrawal of the Soviet missiles from Cuba. The missiles were to be withdrawn under verifiable conditions in return for assurances that the United States would not invade Cuba. This outline deal was followed by the arrival of a personal letter from Khrushchev to Kennedy, which was seen within the White House to signal a willingness to find a negotiated solution. When Khrushchev then publicly communicated a different proposal involving 'analogous' US weapons in Turkey this greatly exercised the US government.[58]

The revelations from the Soviet side provide fascinating vignettes into the workings of the KGB. It is clear that Feklisov was not acting under instruction from Moscow when he met Scali, and that the initiative was his. Second, when the Americans responded and Feklisov reported back to Moscow, Fursenko and Naftali show how communications in Moscow worked – or rather failed to work. Feklisov's crucial report remained on the desk of the Chairman of the KGB while events passed by.[59] So the Americans were mistaken in believing they were communicating with Khrushchev. The general point this underlines is that the mechanics and procedures of channels of communication are crucial. Without understanding how communication and decision-making processes work, neither the participant nor the student of clandestine diplomacy can properly understand events.

A second aspect concerns archival records. Both Scali's and Feklisov's contemporaneous records have now emerged, and both men have openly debated the episode. According to Feklisov it was the American who proposed the deal. According to Scali it was the Soviet official. So who to believe? The question assumes an additional interest given that the missile crisis provides examples of contending accounts of Americans and Soviets where the latter have proved reliable and the former deliberately misleading.[60] Yet, Scali had no reason at the time to misrepresent what he had been told. While there may have been confusion about what was said, Feklisov had good reason not to tell Moscow Centre that he had taken an initiative in Soviet foreign policy at a crucial moment in world history. In his memoir Feklisov admits that he did overreach his authority in threatening retaliation against Berlin in the event of an American attack on Cuba.[61] Yet, he maintains that the initiative for the outline of the deal came from Scali.

It may be that further clarification will eventually become possible. The FBI encouraged Scali to meet Feklisov and it is conceivable that records exist of FBI surveillance of their meetings. In the meantime the episode is a reminder of the potential fallibility of archives as well as memory, and indeed provides what appears a good example of an intelligence document written for a purpose that hides part of the truth. And of course what this shows the intelligence historian, as indeed any historian, is that an archival record is a not a simple statement of truth – it is what someone wrote down at a particular time for a particular purpose.

The Scali–Feklisov back-channel now turns out not to have been a back-channel, and was not significant in the resolution of the crisis. When the US government needed to communicate urgently with Khrushchev to offer a secret assurance to withdraw the missiles from Turkey, it did not choose Soviet intelligence officers, but Ambassador Dobrynin. This is a further reminder that evaluating the importance of secret intelligence channels needs to be done within a broader framework of decision making and diplomacy. And it is also a reminder that that which is secret is not *a priori* more significant.

British intelligence and Northern Ireland

Just as the Reagan administration vowed never to negotiate with hostage takers, the Thatcher government made clear it would not talk to terrorists. Yet since the early 1970s the British intelligence services established and maintained lines of communication with the Provisional Irish Republican Army (PIRA) which eventually involved government ministers, and played a role in the political process in the 1970s and the 1990s, culminating in the Good Friday agreement.[62] There were clear historical precedents in the 1920s for this kind of activity.[63] In 1971, after Prime Minister Edward Heath involved SIS in Northern Ireland, lines of communication were opened with Sinn Fein/PIRA, leading to ministerial level dialogue with the PIRA in 1972. Contacts continued at a lower level and in the 1990s were reactivated following intelligence on potential reassessments within Sinn Fein/PIRA of political and military strategies.

Some details of the role of SIS (and later MI5) in the secret negotiations between the PIRA and the British government became known though disclosure and testimony, most interestingly on the British side. The role of two SIS officers, Frank Steele and Michael Oatley, has been described. Both Steele and Oatley have provided testimony of their activities and Michael Oatley has indeed appeared on camera speaking of his experience.[64] This is of note as it was only in 1993 that a former senior SIS officer, Daphne Park, appeared on television with unprecedented authorisation from the Foreign Secretary (and when it was made clear that SIS engaged in disruptive activity).[65] It is a reasonable assumption that Michael Oatley had similar dispensation. Moreover the former SIS officer wrote an article in the *Sunday Times* in 1999 in which he argued forcefully in support of the Republican leadership in the face of Unionist attacks on the PIRA's failure to decommission its weapons.[66]

Why Frank Steele and Michael Oatley chose to make their views and their roles known, and how far this was sanctioned by SIS or by ministers are interesting questions. Frank Steele's assertion that he 'wanted to set the record straight', while no doubt sincere, is hardly a sufficient explanation.[67] Certainly Oatley appears to have been motivated by his personal view that the Sinn Fein leadership, in particular Gerry Adams and Martin McGuinness, were genuinely committed to political solutions and political processes. The fact that former SIS officers have provided such testimony without appearing to provoke official disapproval (or indeed prosecution), suggests that SIS and/or the government do not see the disclosure of such information in the same way as other disclosures by security and intelligence officers. The revelation that British intelligence 'talked to terrorists' is potentially embarrassing and politically problematic in dealing with Unionist opinion. A more considered response is that the British government understood that while it could thwart the PIRA's objectives it could not defeat them by military means. Many in the military (and the Unionist community) believed that military victory was possible and that negotiating with the terrorists was counter-productive. Whichever is true, the role of SIS certainly provides contrast with the role of other security and intelligence agencies. As the Stevens Enquiry has concluded, elements of the RUC and the Army colluded with loyalist paramilitaries in murder and other crimes – findings that damage the credibility and legitimacy of the British security forces and indeed the British state in Northern Ireland.[68]

The role of SIS also raises aspects of broader interest in the study of intelligence, concerning the role of the individual and the nature of accountability. The essence of clandestine diplomacy is that the participants can deny that they are engaging in talks or negotiations. Michael Oatley operated under strict regulations governing contacts with the paramilitaries. Yet he and Frank Steele engaged creatively with these, and both appear to have enjoyed some latitude to pursue their own initiatives. The people who constitute the secret channel may be more than just a conduit, and their own initiative may be an important element. Just as Aleksandr Feklisov initiated what US officials took to be a back-channel of communication to Nikita Khrushchev, Michael Oatley appears to have developed contacts on his own initiative. His success in winning the trust of his adversaries reflected his skills and his understanding of those he dealt with.[69] This raises intriguing questions about where plausible deniability ends and personal initiative begins.

Clandestine diplomacy is an activity undertaken by secret intelligence services where deniable communication between adversaries may be helpful, especially where the adversary is a paramilitary group with whom open political dialogue may be anathema for one or both sides. As an activity, clandestine diplomacy may overlap with gathering intelligence and/or conducting deception. One purpose may be to influence the behaviour of the adversary toward political as against military action, as appears the case in the actions of Aleksandr Feklisov and Michael Oatley. Yet clandestine diplomacy is distinct from secret intervention inasmuch as those involved may need to reveal their identity and risk exposure as intelligence officers.

Critics of clandestine diplomacy (or specific cases of clandestine diplomacy) would argue that it undermines other approaches such as counter-insurgency or conventional diplomacy. Other examples of back-channel diplomacy such as in Soviet–US arms negotiations certainly afford examples of where circumvention of professional diplomatic expertise risked major policy errors. And Bolshakov's role as a personal emissary of Khrushchev illustrates the risk of deception. Whether the risks of making mistakes or being deceived are greater where an intelligence service is involved than where diplomats are used is an interesting question.

Conclusion

Clandestine diplomacy presupposes a willingness to talk to an adversary, even if talking may not lead to negotiation. There are clearly many political contexts in which the prospect of negotiation or agreement is illusory. To suggest that there might come a time when the US government could engage in clandestine diplomacy with al-Qaeda would seem beyond credulity and acceptability, although negotiations with allies or sponsors of the group or its associates may be another matter. And there are, of course, other states friendly to the United States who would have less political qualms about such contacts. Such reflections should be placed firmly in the context of the intelligence-led 'war against terror', where gathering and analysing secret intelligence is the overriding priority, and where covert action is given a new relevance and (arguably) a new legitimacy.

For critics, Western covert action undermined the legitimacy of Western (especially US) intelligence if not indeed Western (especially US) foreign policy during the Cold War. For their supporters they represented (usually) discreet forms of intervention that obviated more violent methods. The United States' current mood shows little aversion to using force, and overt action is less constrained by domestic opposition or international restraint. US political and bureaucratic debates about covert action will for some time occur within a different context to much of the Cold War.

Cold War critics of covert action saw secret intervention not as instruments of statecraft but tools of political and economic self-interest designed to serve hegemonic, if not imperialist, aims. How far the events of September 11 and the search for Iraqi Weapons of Mass Destruction have strengthened the legitimacy of secret intelligence remains to be seen. Covert action may rest on a more secure domestic US consensus. Yet international support for a policy of pre-emptive or preventive attack is a different matter. Whether the war on Iraq reflects a sea change in the norms of intervention or the high tide of US belligerence remains to be seen. Covert action promises to deliver much of what it promised to deliver in the Cold War. As US action against Iraq demonstrated, the US government has limited interest in the views of others, even its allies. Yet is it conceivable that specific forms of covert action might be sanctioned in specific contexts, if not by the United Nations itself then by regional security alliances? Most probably not. Legitimising covert action risks weakening the legitimacy of the institutions of international society.

Such discussion reflects how far covert action can be viewed as an American phenomenon. Many questions – from the operational to the ethical – apply equally to other states. One consequence of September 11 is that much more has become known of intelligence activities and operations. Either the sophistication with which covert action is kept secret will need to increase. Or we may learn more about the phenomenon. The problems of learning about covert action (and clandestine diplomacy) will nevertheless persist, as the need to evaluate and judge them will undoubtedly grow.

Notes

1 John Bruce Lockhart, 'Intelligence: A British View', in K.G. Robertson (ed.), *British and American Approaches to Intelligence* (Basingstoke: Macmillan, 1987), p. 46.
2 Christopher Andrew, *Secret Service: The Making of the British Intelligence Community* (London: Sceptre, 1986), pp. 21–9.
3 Richard Aldrich, *The Hidden Hand: Britain, America and Cold War Secret Intelligence* (London: John Murray, 2001), p. 5.
4 See M.R.D. Foot, *SOE: An Outline History of the Special Operations Executive 1940–6* (London: British Broadcasting Corporation, 1984).
5 Aldrich, *The Hidden Hand*, pp. 128–34, 443–63.
6 See John Prados, *Presidents' Secret Wars: CIA and Pentagon Covert Operations from World War II through Iranscam* (New York: Quill, 1985).
7 See, for example, Stephen Dorril, *MI6: Fifty Years of Special Operations* (London: Fourth Estate, 2000) and Aldrich, *Hidden Hand*.
8 For example, Michael Herman, *Intelligence Power in Peace and War* (Cambridge: Cambridge University Press, 1996) and *Intelligence Services in the Information Age: Theory and Practice* (London: Frank Cass, 2001).
9 For detailed accounts of Soviet practice see Christopher Andrew and Oleg Gordievsky, *KGB: The Inside Story* (London: Hodder & Stoughton, 1990) and Christopher Andrew and Vasili Mitrokhin, *The Mitrokhin Archive: The KGB in Europe and the West* (London: Allen Lane/Penguin Press, 1999).
10 NSC 10/2 18 June 1948, quoted in Christopher Andrew, *For the President's Eyes Only: Secret Intelligence and the American Presidency from Washington to Bush* (London: HarperCollins, 1995), p. 173.
11 Intelligence Authorization Act, Fiscal Year 1991, P.L. 102–88, 14 August 1991, quoted in Abram Shulsky, *Silent Warfare – Understanding the World of Intelligence* (London: Brassey's, 1993), p. 84. The CIA's definition is 'An operation designed to influence governments, events, organizations, or persons in support of foreign policy in a manner that is not necessarily attributable to the sponsoring power; it may include political, economic, propaganda, or paramilitary activities.' CIA, *Consumer's Guide to Intelligence* (Washington DC: CIA, 1995), p. 38, quoted in David Rudgers, 'The Origins of Covert Action', *Journal of Contemporary History*, 35, 2 (2000), p. 249.
12 Oleg Kalugin with Fen Montaigne, *The First Directorate: My 32 Years in Intelligence and Espionage against the West* (London: Smith Gryphon, 1994), p. 180.
13 See Mark Urban, *Big Boys' Rules: The SAS and the Secret Struggle against the IRA* (London: Faber & Faber, 1992).
14 See Philip H.J. Davies, 'From Special Operations to Special Political Action: The "Rump SOE" and SIS Post-War Covert Action Capability 1945–1977', *Intelligence*

and National Security, 15, 3 (2000). For accounts of operations see Aldrich, *Hidden Hand*, Mark Urban, *UK Eyes Alpha* (London: Faber & Faber, 1996) and Dorril, *MI6*.

15 For accounts of operations and planning in the Middle East see Tom Bower, *The Perfect English Spy: Sir Dick White and the Secret War 1935–90* (London: Heinemann, 1995), pp. 185–224; Aldrich, *Hidden Hand*, pp. 464–93, 581–606; Dorril, *MI6*, pp. 531–699.

16 *The Intelligence Services Act 1994*, Chapter 13, section 7.1 states that the functions of SIS are: '(a) to obtain and provide information relating to the actions or intentions of persons outside the British Islands; and (b) to perform other tasks relating to the actions or intentions of such persons'. The legal formula is similar to the US legislation that created the CIA in 1947 that speaks of 'other functions and duties'. Rudgers, 'The Origins of Covert Action', p. 249.

17 The *1998–1999 Intelligence and Security Committee Annual Report* (Cm 4532) makes reference to the fact that British agencies 'may be required to undertake disruptive action in response to specific tasking' on the proliferation of weapons of mass destruction, Cm 4532 para 58. I am grateful to Marc Davies for drawing my attention to this.

18 The document can be found at: www.cryptome.org/qadahfi-plot.htm.

19 Richard Tomlinson, *The Big Breach: From Top Secret to Maximum Security* (Edinburgh: Cutting Edge Press, 2001), p. 73.

20 Elizabeth Anderson, 'The Security Dilemma and Covert Action: The Truman Years', *International Journal of Intelligence and CounterIntelligence*, 11, 4 (1998/99), pp. 403–4.

21 See Roy Godson, *Dirty Tricks or Trump Cards: US Covert Action and Counterintelligence* (London: Brassey's, 1995); Shulsky, *Silent Warfare*; Loch Johnson, *Secret Agencies: US Intelligence in a Hostile World* (London: Yale University Press, 1996).

22 Dorril, *MI6*, p. xiv.

23 Godson, *Dirty Tricks*, p. xii.

24 The pattern of declassification is not entirely uniform. Documents detailing CIA operations against Iran in the early 1950s have apparently been systematically destroyed. Craig Eisendrath (ed.), *National Insecurity: US Intelligence after the Cold War* (Washington: Center for International Policy, 1999), p. 3.

25 Bob Woodward, *Bush at War* (London: Simon & Schuster, 2002), pp. 5–6.

26 Pavel and Anatoli Sudoplatov (with Jerrold L. and Leona P. Schecter), *Special Tasks: The Memoirs of an Unwanted Witness – a Soviet Spymaster* (London: Little, Brown, 1994).

27 Tomlinson, *The Big Breach*, pp. 106–7, 140, 179–96.

28 Jerrold L. Schecter and Leona P. Schecter, 'The Sudoplatov Controversy', *Cold War International History Project Bulletin*, 5 (Spring 1995), p. 155.

29 In Le Carré's novel it is Walter who says this, whereas in the film of the same name, it is Ned. Walter and Ned are SIS officers. John Le Carré, *The Russia House* (London: Hodder & Stoughton, 1989) p. 110; *The Russia House* (Pathe Entertainment, 1990).

30 Gordon Brook-Shepherd, *Iron Maze: The Western Secret Services and the Bolsheviks* (Basingstoke: Macmillan, 1998).

31 Bower, *Perfect English Spy*.

32 See for example, John Barry, 'Covert Action can be Just', *Orbis* (Summer 1993) pp. 375–90; Charles Beitz, 'Covert Intervention as a Moral Problem', *Ethics and International Affairs*, 3 (1989), pp. 45–60; William Colby, 'Public Policy, Secret Action,' *Ethics and International Affairs*, 3 (1989), pp. 61–71; Gregory Treverton, 'Covert Action and Open Society', *Foreign Affairs*, 65, 5 (1987), pp. 995–1014, idem, *Covert Action: The Limits of Intervention in the Postwar World* (New York: Basic Books 1987), idem, 'Imposing a Standard: Covert Action and American Democracy', *Ethics and International Affairs*, 3 (1989), pp. 27–43; and Johnson, *Secret Agencies*, pp. 60–88.

33 For documentary sources of CIA covert action and accounts based on these see the National Security Archive website: www.gwu.edu/~nsarchiv/.

34 For recent criticisms of CIA covert action see Eisendrath, *National Insecurity*. For an excoriating attack on US policy see the views of former CIA analyst Melvin Goodman, 'Espionage and Covert Action', ibid., pp. 23–43. For a more general caustic critique of the CIA, see Rhodri Jeffrey-Jones, *Cloak and Dollar: A History of American Secret Intelligence* (London: Yale University Press, 2002).

35 John L. Gaddis, *What We Now Know: Rethinking the Cold War* (Oxford: Oxford University Press, 1997).

36 Vojtech Mastny, *The Cold War and Soviet Insecurity* (Oxford: Oxford University Press, 1996).

37 Aldrich, *The Hidden Hand*, pp. 160–79.

38 See Sara-Jane Corkem, 'History, Historians and the Naming of Foreign Policy: A Post-modern Reflection on American Strategic Thinking during the Truman Administration', *Intelligence and National Security*, 16, 3 (2001), pp. 146–63.

39 Ludo de Witte, *The Assassination of Lumumba* (London: Verso, 2002).

40 Bower, *Perfect Spy*; Dorril, *MI6*; Jonathan Bloch and Patrick Fitzgerald, *British Intelligence and Covert Action* (Dingle, Ireland: Brandon Books, 1983).

41 Godson, *Dirty Tricks*, p. 120.

42 Adam Watson, *Diplomacy: The Dialogue Between States* (London: Routledge, 1991), p. 11.

43 Jim Risen and Tim Weiner, 'CIA Sought Syrian Aid', *New York Times*, 31 October 2001. The article also suggests a similar approach may have been made to Libyan intelligence.

44 Gar Alperovitz, *The Decision to use the Atomic Bomb* (London: HarperCollins, 1995), pp. 25–7, 292–301.

45 Shulsky, *Silent Warfare*, pp. 90–1. Apparently 200 agents were killed as a result of this operation. A senior KGB officer who defected to the British supplied the information to the CIA.

46 See for example, Bower, *Perfect Spy*, pp. 185–254; Aldrich, *Hidden Hand*, pp. 464–93.

47 Peter Taylor, *The Provos: The IRA and Sinn Fein* (London: Bloomsbury, 1997) and *Brits: The War Against the IRA* (London: Bloomsbury, 2001); Michael Smith, *New Cloak, Old Dagger: How Britain's Spies Came In From The Cold* (London: Victor Gollancz, 1996), pp. 211–30; Urban, *UK Eyes Alpha* and *Big Boys' Rules*.

48 Hesi Carmel (ed.), *Intelligence for Peace* (London: Frank Cass 1999).

49 'Keeping a link to Hamas', *The Guardian*, 29 September 2003, p. 19.

50 Michael Smith uses the term 'parallel diplomacy' to describe this activity. *New Cloak*, p. 211.

51 On Alekseev see Aleksandr Fursenko and Timothy Naftali, *'One Hell of a Gamble'*: *Khrushchev, Castro, Kennedy the Cuban Missile Crisis 1958–1964* (London; John Murray, 1997). On Cooper, Kent, Tidwell and Smith see Sherman Kent, 'The Cuban Missile Crisis of 1962: Presenting the Photographic Evidence Abroad', *Studies in Intelligence*, 10, 2 (1972).

52 See in particular, Fursenko and Naftali, *'One Hell of a Gamble'*.

53 Yevgeny Ivanov (with Gennady Sokolov), *The Naked Spy* (London: Blake, 1992). For discussion, see L.V. Scott, *Macmillan, Kennedy and the Cuban Missile Crisis: Political, Military and Intelligence Aspects* (Basingstoke: Macmillan Palgrave, 1999), pp. 102–12.

54 See Michael Beschloss, *Kennedy v. Khrushchev: The Crisis Years 1960–63* (London: Faber & Faber, 1991), pp. 152ff.

55 Fursenko and Naftali, *'One Hell of a Gamble'*, pp. 109ff.

56 Ibid., p. x.

57 Scott, *Macmillan, Kennedy*, p. 109. The medium-range ballistic missiles in Cuba had a range of 1,100 miles enabling them to strike Washington.

58 For details of the various exchanges on 26–27 October see Ernest May and Philip Zelikow (eds), *The Kennedy Tapes* (London: Belknap, 1998), pp. 439–629.

59 Aleksandr Fursenko and Timothy Naftali, 'Using KGB Documents: The Scali–Feklisov Channel in the Cuban Missile Crisis', *Cold War International History Project Bulletin*, 5 (Spring 1995), pp. 58–62.

60 The testimony of Ambassador Dobrynin on the US offer to remove NATO nuclear missiles from Turkey proved truthful, in contrast to contemporary public testimony of Kennedy administration officials, and Robert Kennedy's posthumously published account, as edited by Theodore Sorensen, *Thirteen Days* (Basingstoke: Macmillan, 1969).

61 For Feklisov's account see Alexander Feklisov and Sergei Kostin, *The Man Behind the Rosenbergs: by the KGB Spymaster who was the Case Officer of Julius Rosenberg, and helped resolve the Cuban Missile Crisis* (New York: Enigma Books, 2001), pp. 362–402.

62 Taylor, *The Provos*, pp. 129–47 and *Brits*, pp. 80ff.; Smith, *New Cloak*, pp. 220–30.

63 Smith, *New Cloak*, pp. 211–19.

64 See remarks by Oatley in transcript of BBC TV, 'The Secret War', BBC News, www.news.bbc.co.uk/hi/english/static/in-depth.ireland/2000/brits/.

65 BBC TV Panorama, 'On Her Majesty's Secret Service', 22 November 1993.

66 Michael Oatley, 'Forget the Weapons and Learn to Trust Sinn Fein', *Sunday Times*, 31 October 1999; BBC Panorama, 'The Secret War'.

67 Taylor, *Provos*, p. 129.

68 Stevens Enquiry, *Overview and Recommendations*, 17 April 2003, www.met.police.uk/index/index.htm.

69 Oatley, transcript of 'The Secret War'.

12 Ethics and Intelligence after September 2001

Michael Herman

Perhaps there is no need to mix intelligence and ethics. The *Times* took a strictly realist view some years ago that 'Cold War or no Cold War, nations routinely spy on each other', and the British Security Service's official handout takes the view that 'spying has been going on for centuries and as nations emerged they began spying on each other and will probably always do so'.[1] Some would say that that is all that need be said. Intelligence is information and information gathering, not *doing* things to people; no-one gets hurt by it, at least not directly. Some agencies do indeed carry out covert action, which confuses the ethical issues, but this is a separable and subsidiary function; thus the British Joint Intelligence Committee is emphatically not a covert action committee.

Yet, even as information gathering, intelligence carries an ethical baggage with it, or – to be more accurate – a baggage of unworthiness. This dates back at least two centuries, when Kant condemned espionage as 'intrinsically despicable' since it 'exploits only the dishonesty of others',[2] and its modern version was illustrated in the judgement of two respected British academics in the 1990s that it was all 'positively immoral', apart 'from certain extreme cases'.[3] This baggage owes a lot to the visceral dislike of espionage, and to intelligence's role of internal surveillance, but the distaste ranges wider. David Kahn, the doyen of the history of codebreaking, concluded that as an activity it is 'surreptitious, snooping, sneaking...the very opposite of all that is best in mankind'. It was justified in defence, but 'when a nation is not threatened, it is wrong for it to violate another's dignity by clandestine prying into its messages'. Views are further confused by the media's penchant for describing all intelligence collection as 'spying', producing a kind of guilt by association. Thus GCHQ, the British SIGINT centre, is always described as 'the Cheltenham spy centre', which it certainly is not.

Recent events have given intelligence a more favourable image, but there is still a world-wide distrust of it, from liberal, anti-American, anti-authoritarian and other standpoints. There is still some feeling that its activities are internationally improper, unbefitting for example the ethical dimension of foreign policy announced by the new British Labour Foreign Secretary in 1997. To at least a swathe of liberal opinion, there still is a much bigger question mark against it than for the general run of government service.

So there is a real issue. Intelligence exists as a government institution and cannot be disinvented. But is it to be encouraged internationally, in the way governments accept the value of statistics, meteorology, epidemiology and other knowledge specialities as important inputs to national and collective policy making? Are its practitioners members of a valued profession? Or is it like nuclear weapons, which most people dislike and seek to limit, even if they disagree about what else to do about them? It may be part of the international game, but is it a necessary evil to be discarded eventually for an intelligence-free world; or should it remain, perhaps with its rules improved?

This paper outlines these issues as they seemed in the decade after the end of the Cold War, and discusses how far the events of the new century have changed them. It limits itself to three of intelligence's aspects. First, it bases itself on its roles and rationales: what is expected of it, not its historical record of successes and failures. Second, it treats it as the essentially national activity that it will remain as far as can be foreseen; it does not consider the scope for developing it as an international institution, building on precedents such as the blue-helmeted tactical intelligence units that have featured in some UN operations, and the U-2s and UAVs under UN control for UNSCOM and UNMOVIC. Third, it concentrates on the familiar English-speaking, to some extent 'Western' system, and does not discuss others, such as Russian, Chinese and Arabic intelligence; this is an ethno-centric treatment, but is all that can be done in the present state of intelligence studies. For intelligence within these parameters, then, what ethics can be held to apply?

What ethics?

Ethics fuse ideas of personal morality and social utility; on the one hand the dictates of good conscience, and on the other accepted standards (or ideals) of human intercourse and the social consequences if they are flouted. Cheating at cricket is condemned at one level because it is intrinsically dishonest, and at another because the game has no point if players do not play to common rules.[4] States' international activities are judged by similarly complex morality. The second element – the societal *consequences* – often predominates; thus the Argentine invasion of the Falklands was condemned internationally for trying to settle a dispute by force, as anti-social behaviour in the modern society of states, even though not deeply offensive in purely humanitarian terms. Yet states' actions are also regularly judged by a morality deeper than rules of a game. In an extreme case, the bombing of Dresden is criticised (rightly or wrongly) for its inhumanity, irrespective of law, custom and precedent. At a more prosaic level, states' inter-national reputations include ethical-like judgements of reliability and consistency, or duplicity and untrustworthiness.

International law draws on both these elements, though often partially and imperfectly. It legalises some things, prohibits others and says nothing about others. Nothing is prohibited for intelligence by the laws of war, except the torture of prisoners. A similar lacuna applies over most peacetime information gathering;

states have no inherent rights of privacy against other states. Some peacetime collection has been palpably illegal, such as the violations of Soviet airspace and territorial waters in some Western operations, but the illegality was in the collectors' presence and not their intelligence purpose.

Nevertheless, there are some traces of a legal recognition of information gathering as an activity. The Law of the Sea excludes information gathering as a purpose covered by legal rights of innocent passage through territorial waters.[5] The International Telecommunications Union Convention of 1973 provided for the secrecy of international communications, though the small print left governments with escape clauses.[6] The 1961 Vienna Convention specified diplomacy's purpose of collecting information by *lawful* means, but left these tantalisingly unexplained. The US–Soviet SALT and ABM agreements of the 1970s and a succession of more recent and wider agreements, notably the Comprehensive Test Ban Treaty, recognised National Technical Means (the euphemism for technical intelligence collection) for verifying arms control, provided that the (undefined) 'recognised principles of international law' applied to their operation. And its customary element – 'that informal, unwritten body of rules derived from the practice and opinions of States'[7] – is developed aspirational and normative directions.

This paper does not seek to unpick these various constituents of international legitimacy.[8] Its main emphasis is on intelligence's observable international effects; in crude terms, whether it is good or bad for international society, using the commonsense yardsticks whether it promotes or discourages responsible government behaviour, good inter-state relationships, the minimisation of tension, co-operation for internationally valuable purposes, and the avoidance of war.[9] But this 'consequentialist' approach does not exclude the more absolute views of Kant and his successors. 'Moral conduct means acting within a constraining framework of principles that are independent of consequential considerations.'[10] Legitimacy with any real force 'embodies, rules, values, and shared purposes that create some sense of felt obligation'.[11] Nor can the hints of international law be ignored altogether. The three elements make up the elements of the ethical balance sheet attempted here.

The twentieth-century position

Intelligence up to the end of the twentieth century was then, as it still is, a dyad of two overlapping functions: collecting and producing information by special means; and acting as government's expert on its own particular subjects, drawing on overt as well as covert sources. In both functions it has been characterised as 'telling truth to power'. The idea of 'truth' in any absolute sense is open to argument, but crediting intelligence with a professional ethos of *truthfulness* – or at least attempting it – is less controversial.

On that basis I argued some years ago that intelligence did not raise first-order ethical questions akin to those of war and peace; but that it did raise some. At that time I put forward three propositions that bore on them.[12] First, governments drawing on a professional standard of intelligence knowledge tended to behave as more responsible members of international society than those that had to manage without it, or chose to do so – less ignorant, less insensitive and (I would now add of democratic states) less impetuous.[13] This was a general effect, though specific cases could also be adduced in which intelligence had been deliberately used to underpin specific stability producing, conflict reduction arrangements, as in arms control, or some of the US mediation efforts in the Middle East and south Asia. There was indeed a contrary line or argument that criticised intelligence as an institutionally distorting prism, with vested interests in 'worst case' views of the world or in reinforcing governments' preconceptions; but it seemed that the historical record of Western intelligence did not bear this out in any consistent way. Intelligence is liable to be wrong, but underestimates threats as often as exaggerates them.

Second, much of intelligence's information gathering still followed the well-established pattern of targeting other states. By and large this caused no observable problems for inter-state relations. Just occasionally, indeed, the United States and the Soviet Union had accepted and co-operated with the other's intelligence collection against them as a means of verifying arms control.[14] But some of intelligence collection was particularly intrusive and could be perceived as a mark of hostility, reinforcing its target's perceptions of threat or tension. Examples from the Cold War were Western overflights of the Soviet Union, the position of diplomats and embassies in providing cover for covert collection (and also as the targets of intelligence operations directed against them), and above all the sheer scale of Russian espionage. Even outside a context of threats, intrusive collection of these kinds implied a disrespect for the target governments, an international equivalent of a two-fingered gesture.

None of this had ceased with the end of the Cold War. Russia and the West moved towards better relationships, yet more espionage cases between them seemed to hit the headlines than before. It was difficult not to believe that intrusive collection when detected or suspected was an obstacle to close relations and collaboration between states, even if it was not one of the major ones.

Third, however, a newer category of collection had expanded after the end of the Cold War, directed not at what the nineteenth century would have called other 'civilised' states, but at an increasing number of different targets: non-state and quasi-state entities of many kinds, including terrorist organisations; the varied actors involved in situations of breakdown and suffering, typically wars within states rather than between them; and the so-called rogue states, outside the pale as far as the main club of states was concerned. Targeting of this kind did nothing to produce friction among the civilised state community, and indeed usually supported international collaboration between them in good causes.

So intelligence knowledge got good ethical marks, but the effects of its collection were variable. Some of it against other states could still be seen as producing its own version of the security dilemma. What intelligence was produced, reduced irresponsible and ignorant national behaviour and on balance made the world better; but some of the activities producing it made the world marginally worse. So before September 2001 there already seemed scope for developing an intelligence variant of medieval Just War doctrine for such activities. By extension, the criteria of restraint, necessity and proportionality might be applicable to intrusive inter-state collection rather as it applies to the violence of war.[15]

At the same time, however, the extension to the newer, post-Cold War non-state and pariah-type targets pointed in a different direction. Absolutists might still have reservations about some of the methods used, but consequentialists judging observable effects could feel that there need be no inhibitions about their effects on international society; indeed quite the reverse, where considerations of inter-national security and humanitarianism were among the motives. The present writer's sympathy was with the view that, on such targets and in such circumstances, *almost* any methods of collection were justified, short of gross violations of human rights.[16] The scope for 'Just Intelligence' seemed quite wide.

Of course this was a simplification. The newer, post-Cold War targets were only new in scale and not in kind; collection against terrorism dated back at least 30 years. As for the purposes served by targeting them, no causes are unambiguously good or have universal international support. International society is itself not just a well-defined club of respectable states, with clear divisions between them and other targets outside it. The difference between intrusive and non-intrusive collection is equally a matter of degree; the seriousness of intrusion is anyway in the eye of those intruded upon, as in the way the French and European Parliaments worried greatly before September 2001 about the English-speaking countries' Echelon system for collecting international communications, despite the fact that its big dishes pointed into the heavens and were not pointed at any particular group of states. There were no general criteria of acceptability and unacceptability.[17]

Nevertheless, distinctions could reasonably be drawn between the three effects: those of intelligence knowledge, intrusive collection on respectable states (in the extreme case, 'spying on friends'), and collection against the other, newer targets, including support of counter-terrorism and other international good causes. How far have they now been modified by the events of 2001 and 2002?

Changed status

The main change has been the dramatic increase in intelligence's own importance after September 11, 2001. A trend in that direction had begun earlier; after intelligence budgets had been reduced as part of the peace dividend at the end of the Cold War, they were already being restored to cope not only with terrorism but also with the requirements of the 1990s for support of multi-lateral and international peace enforcement and humanitarian operations, and for intelligence on WMD proliferation, sanctions evasion, drug trafficking and the other emerging targets of the decade. Governments were already adapting themselves to what seemed an increasingly unstable world, and to the information revolution within it both in the information available and in governments' ability to collect and process it. Intelligence as a whole was growing again and was no longer quite such a deniable activity.

Nevertheless, before September 11, it was still not seen as a defence against an overarching and common threat. The Western military interventions of the 1990s had been interventions by choice, and international terrorism and other threats were still seen as peripheral ones, slightly remote. Terrorists struck at US citizens overseas but not at home. I could argue that intelligence would become increasingly variegated, flexible and opportunistic. In terms of Britain's survival it is now less vital than during the Cold War, but probably more useful... British intelligence's national importance therefore needs to be judged mainly in rather general contexts: public assumptions about foreign policy and defence; long-standing expectations of intelligence as a strong card in government's hand; the links between intelligence and the transatlantic political relationship.[18]

The events of September 11 and what followed radically altered this position. As in the Cold War, intelligence's main target has become once again a major and widely shared threat – except that it is now actual, and not potential. In the Cold War, intelligence was helping governments to avoid war; now it is actively involved in fighting one, seeking to save lives and defend national security in the most literal sense, in an asymmetrical contest whose nature gives it a special importance. Whatever reservations were expressed about the US declaration of a 'war on terrorism', the wartime metaphor fits intelligence's current status rather well. Apparently reliable reports in January 2003 that since September 11, 2001, 100 terrorist attacks have been thwarted world-wide and 3,000 suspects detained in 100 countries (including Britain) leave little doubt about its seriousness.[19] The current prominence of Iraq and North Korea has reinforced the effect. Major decisions now seem to turn particularly on what intelligence is able to discover on the intentions and capabilities of highly secretive targets.

So its budgets are increasing everywhere, and hardly a day passes without its appearance in the news. President Bush mentioned it 18 times in his National Security Strategy of 20 September 2002, almost as frequently as military power and over twice as often as diplomacy.[20] Prime Minister Blair waxed eloquently about intelligence in January 2003; it was 'Britain's first line of defence against terrorism'.[21] Most Western countries have amended existing legislation to give it greater scope and reduced restrictions. Intelligence is confirmed as a major attribute of national soft (or semi-soft) power.[22] All nations except the smallest in the world's near-200 states will soon develop its institutions if they do not have them already. The Security Council's Resolution 1373 on terrorism mandated exchanges on it; the first mandate of this kind.[23] All this has given intelligence some new legitimacy, though this by no means unambiguous. The UN mandate is still for 'information exchanges', and not intelligence.

Events have also had two other related effects. One is to re-emphasise the importance of covert collection and the secrecy needed to protect it. In the years after the Cold War ended commentators could argue that in an increasingly open world intelligence's emphasis would shift away from collection and towards analysis: there would be more emphasis on 'intelligence-as-information', drawing on more open source material, and less on 'intelligence-as-secrets'.[24] On this view a liberal could expect that intelligence would become rather less mysterious and 'special', and eventually rather more like a normal information service such as government statistics; more open and unspectacular, and attracting less media curiosity and hype.

This now seems very dated. Already by the end of the 1990s the pendulum was swinging back some way towards the older view. Operations in the former Yugoslavia had demonstrated the importance of secret collection, even in situations with media coverage. Now, as in the Cold War, intelligence's main obstacle is the secrecy of intensely difficult targets. Analysis remains important everywhere. But counter-terrorism puts a renewed emphasis on intrusive collection – particularly the human agent, but also eavesdropping on national and international communications – accompanied by rapid investigation and operational use. Dame Stella Rimington's claim in 1994 that the security forces in Northern Ireland were by then frustrating four out of every five attempted terrorist attacks had earlier illustrated the cumulative but unspectacular significance of successful pre-emptive warning.[25] As in any war, intelligence's value in a counter-terrorist campaign is sometimes less to high-level decision taking than in nitty-gritty tactical use. Intelligence as a whole is again 'special', secret, an object of great public curiosity: all characteristics that a few years earlier could be felt to be on the wane.

The other, apparently contradictory effect has been to make it at the same time more international. In itself this was also nothing new. Even before September 11, the CIA already had liaisons with some 400 foreign intelligence, security and police organisations.[26] By comparison, the Russian FSB (the internal security part of the old KGB) was similarly claiming to have 'around 80 missions representing the special services of 56 countries' working permanently in Moscow, and formal agreements with '40 foreign partners in 33 countries'.[27] Up to UNSCOM's withdrawal in 1998, up to 20 nations are said to have passed information to it on Iraqi sanctions busting and weapons development.

But September 11 brought a great boost to this 'internationalisation'. Despite being an intelligence superpower, the United States cannot meet all its counter-terrorist requirements itself. Almost every nation is able to supply some unique intelligence on global terrorism, from its local records and local human and technical sources. The United States accordingly developed a set of new or deeper counter-terrorist relationships, and Britain followed suit. The Blair–Putin statement after their meeting of 20–21 December 2001 confirmed that 'co-operation on intelligence matters has been unprecedentedly close' and announced an Anglo-Russian agreement to set up a new 'joint group to share intelligence'. The Security Service, necessarily the most domestically oriented of the British agencies, had over 100 links with foreign intelligence and security services in 2002.[28] In the United States the Presidential message of September 2002 formally confirmed the objective of co-ordinating closely with allies for common assessment of the most dangerous threats.

This internationalization has not been completely centred on the US hub or the English-speaking communities. The European Union for its part developed its 'anti-terrorist roadmap' for European action, including common measures for improving databases on individuals, making more information available from public electronic communications, and the establishment of a new group of heads of security and intelligence agencies to meet regularly.[29] There have been similar regional agreements elsewhere. Thus in southeast Asia the Philippines, Cambodia, Indonesia, Malaysia and Thailand have signed anti-terrorist agreements, most recently under the influence of the Bali atrocity.[30] In the United Nations, the new British-chaired Counter-Terrorism Committee initially declared one of its aims to be 'to establish a network of information-sharing and cooperative action'.[31]

Of course US influence predominates, and its intelligence community is no doubt influenced by the conflicting tugs in all US policy making between unilateralism and multi-lateralism. But intelligence is one subject on which the United States needs some foreign help, and this will tend to underpin the world-wide trend, which seems to be towards increased intelligence collaboration, sometimes between unlikely allies including the former Cold War antagonists. Equally striking have been the public demands of the chief of UNMOVIC in the winter of 2002–03 for more national intelligence inputs to the Commission's investigation of Saddam Hussein's WMD programme: demands on behalf of the United Nations which earlier would have been put very discreetly or not at all.

This is all a considerable shift. Despite all its bilateral and multi-lateral foreign liaisons, intelligence was previously regarded as still an essentially separate, eremitic national activity. It is now becoming an increasingly important international network in its own right, in the world of ever-growing inter-governmental co-operation. The effect on its ethical balance sheet is twofold. It narrows the area to which the security dilemma applies; yet simultaneously sharpens the dilemma where it does.

Anything goes?

The last two years have increased the credit balance for intelligence knowledge. Its recent importance is obvious enough in the general run of world events, particularly over Iraq; and above all there is its wartime-like importance in counter-terrorism. Events are also emphasising the importance of professional qualities throughout its whole process of collection, evaluation, assessment and distribution. At a national level, both the CIA and British agencies seem to have acted as governments' consciences over Iraq. The CIA has kept a low profile in the divisions between hawks and doves in the US Administration, but there have been some press reports of its protests over exaggerations at policy level over the evidence of Iraqi contacts with al-Qaeda.[32] In Britain, whatever misjudgements intelligence may have made, even those most opposed to action against Saddam Hussein have not suggested that it has wilfully tailored its product to fit government policy.

This importance of standards spreads well beyond the English-speaking communities and applies to intelligence's internationalisation. The era of increased inter-government co-operation increases the need not only for intelligence exchanges, government but also for professionalism in handling it. Exchanges of information for international action are of only limited value without some corresponding international growth of depoliticisation and the pursuit of truthfulness in producing and interpreting them.

This importance of knowledge and standards might seem to increase the dilemma of results versus collection methods, yet in one way its scale is reducing. More intelligence is now targeted for objectives shared by the 'civilised' international community, and not on the community itself. On international terrorism alone, the British SIGINT organisation – by far the largest of the national agencies – was officially stated to be devoting 30–40 per cent of its total effort to the post-September 11 crisis, and it would be surprising if this has subsequently decreased greatly; and to this should be added all the (relatively) newer targets discussed earlier, such as counter-proliferation and the pariah states, outside the 'respectable' parts of the international system.

To conclude that literally 'anything goes' on such targets may still be an exaggeration. As Sir Michael Quinlan pointed out some years ago, covert collection carries some moral debits even in good causes. Secrecy fits awkwardly into the accountability of open democracies; and intelligence has now become more secret again. More international co-operation on terrorism means consorting with politically dubious foreign bedfellows. Espionage may involve normally reprehensible activities or associations (though its agents may equally be motivated by high principles). Nevertheless on collection against this class of target the events of the last two years have tipped the balance further against substantial ethical restraints, such as those on whose account the US Executive, Congress and media are said to have knocked the stuffing out of CIA's HUMINT in the 1990s. If the wartime metaphor fits counter-terrorism, it implies relatively few moral restrictions on information gathering on its targets. To repeat the opening of this paper: information gathering is not action to which separate ethical criteria must be applied.

Spying on friends?

Yet on some other targets the last two years have at the same time sharpened the ethical dilemma. If intrusive 'spying on friends' formerly increased the problems of inter-state friction in a rather general way, now it also poses particular difficulties for the increased international collaboration now developing. Even if terrorism took up 30–40 per cent of GCHQ's effort after September 11 and the other 'newer' targeting was substantial, sizable resources were still presumably devoted to the older-style coverage of other states, excluding the pariahs; and probably still are. Relatively few of these states are actually 'friends'; most inter-state relationships are somewhere on a long scale between the extremes of friendship and enmity, and have conflicting elements anyway. But the likelihood remains that, despite the growth of international consultation and collaboration on common causes, significant intelligence is still collected to defend or advance purely national interests; for example, helping governments to get the best deal they can in the welter of trade, economic, financial and other negotiations that make up international society's daily substance. Some of this intelligence – perhaps not a large part – is produced by means which the targets would consider to be intrusive. Can this targeting really be squared with the governments' simultaneously seeking closer intelligence collaboration in common causes?

Governments' increasing transparency gives additional force to this old dilemma. Covert collection does not upset anyone if it remains truly covert, but it is now harder than it used to be for governments anywhere to keep secrets for long; most of them leak out sooner or later. And democratic foreign policies are now more influenced than formerly by mass opinion formers who react strongly to finding spies under the national bed; more strongly than the worldly wise diplomats who previously accepted intrusive intelligence as part of the game, provided as little was said about it as possible. Modern democracies are easily insulted, even if not significantly threatened, and do not take easily to hushing up the detection of foreign spies. They have correspondingly tender consciences about their own methods, and demand a corresponding Caesar's wife-like standard over their own governments' clean hands and international legality.

It still cannot be proved that revelations of 'spying' (in its extended popular sense) really matter. The cases in Moscow and Washington in the 1990s and the related expulsions of diplomats did not prevent a gradual development of US–Russian understanding; no-one can judge whether they delayed it. It has recently been claimed that CIA used its Russian opposition numbers to plant devices to detect emissions from the North Korean nuclear weapons programme sometime in the 1990s,[33] so it may be that intelligence co-operation can continue to co-exist with spying on each other. But this is to be doubted in the long term. It is difficult to believe that the extended Anglo-Russian intelligence exchanges announced in December 2001 would survive a cause célèbre connected with a large undeclared Russian intelligence presence in the London embassy; or vice versa.

So intelligence as a booming world institution still has a doubtful reputation. If it were a multi-national corporation it might ask 'do we need to clean up our act?' But it would be too much to ask any state to engage again in the kind of unilateral disarmament that the US Secretary of State undertook to close the American codebreaking 'Black Chamber' in 1929 with the feeling that 'gentlemen don't read each others' mail'.[34] Neither is the United Nations likely to endorse any covert collection methods, even for the information whose exchanges on terrorism it mandates. The ethical dilemma over intelligence of this kind can only be reduced by inter-governmental reciprocity.

Customs and understandings

This would not be breaking completely new ground. Collection has not been conducted against other states in peacetime in a spirit of short-term realism; there has often been some restraint. This has been neither strong nor widespread enough to be a recognised international norm, assuming that a norm is rather stronger and more widely shared than an attitude.[35] But intelligence's networks of liaisons and alliances have had the result that some countries do not conduct operations of any kind against each other. The Britain–United States–Old Commonwealth community is the normally quoted example, but there may be other areas of tacit abstention; some or all of the Scandinavian countries, for example. Israeli intelligence was reputed not to collect against the US government until the disastrous Pollard case in the 1980s. Close intelligence liaisons do not necessarily rule out all mutual targeting, but probably limit the use of the most potentially embarrassing methods. But understandings about restraint are tacit or tightly held. The only recent public declaration was the agreement between Russia and the new Confederation of Independent States around it to foreswear operations against each other, shortly after the break-up of the Soviet Union. There must be doubts whether its effect was ever more than cosmetic.

Some restraint has also been exercised against adversaries. The British overflights of the Soviet Union were conducted in the first half of the 1950s because President Eisenhower was not prepared to authorise the US Air Force to mount them. Subsequently the position was reversed when Anthony Eden refused authorisation for such operations, including American U-2 flights from British bases. British peripheral flights around the Soviet Union, though entirely legal, remained subject to ministerial approval throughout the Cold War, as were more genuinely covert collection operations. All depended on the circumstances of particular cases, including the risk of being found out. But at least in the West there was some recognition of intelligence's provocative quality, perhaps entwined with considerations of governments' international and national images and older ideas of national 'honour'. It would be interesting to know whether the authors of the new British government's 1997 foreign policy statement had intelligence in mind when including 'respect for other states' as a principle, returning full circle to Kant's principles of international morality.[36]

In the decade after the end of the Cold War there were some indications of tentative moves towards restraint, perhaps in reaction to the spy cases of the period. Russia was reported to have pressed the UN Secretary-General in 1998 for an international treaty banning information warfare.[37] A Russian spokesman had denied in 1996 that there were any agreements with the United States about high-level penetration agents,[38] but the possibility of mutual US and Russian reductions was raised, apparently from the US side, in July 1999 in Washington discussions between the US Vice President and the Russian Prime Minister of the day, and remitted for further examination.[39] Reducing the scale of Russian espionage in Britain was said similarly to have been raised by Blair with Putin at a one-to-one meeting in March 2001.[40] The idea of 'intelligence arms control' had had some slight airing before September 11, 2001.

Now it has additional relevance. Not only is there the increased need for closer intelligence collaboration, but there are also the practical resource issues raised by the scale of counter-terrorism and the other newer requirements. Ever since the end of the Cold War 'intelligence arms control' would have been of mutual benefit to Russia and the United States, both intensely concerned at the threat of foreign espionage; it would also have benefited Britain, though London has in practice seemed rather less anxious about foreign espionage threats. Now the benefit would be even greater, freeing intelligence resources for deployment on counter-terrorism, instead of mutual espionage and all the defensive counter-intelligence and counter-espionage it necessitates. Smaller intelligence powers might also be influenced by the example of restraint in inter-state targeting by larger ones.

The only actual pointer in this direction has been Putin's announcement in late 2001 of his intention to close the large Russian interception station on Cuba, long a source of Congressional opposition to closer US–Russian relations, as well as the similar station at Cam Rahn in Vietnam. The announcement was welcomed by President Bush at the time as 'taking down relics of the Cold War and building a new, cooperative and transparent relationship for the twenty-first century',[41] though there has been no obvious reciprocity.[42] It might be significant that in December 2001 the annual Russian end-of-year summary of detected espionage cases pointed less than on previous occasions to US and British complicity.[43] On the other hand a British media article in late 2002 claimed that 'Russia was engaged in a massive expansion of espionage in Europe and North America', and that the Russian intelligence presence in the London embassy had increased from one in 1991 to 33.[44] So intelligence restraint may not yet be on the international agenda; though it is unlikely to be publicised even if it ever is.

A new intelligence paradigm?

Perhaps what is needed is a new paradigm. Intelligence's place has been determined historically by ideas of national sovereignty, threats and inter-state competition. Despite alliances and exchanges, one state's gain in knowledge has been seen basically as another's defeat in information protection. Yet September 11 and the counter-terrorist campaign link with other events of recent years to produce a mood for new ideas. Intelligence could be seen no longer as primarily an element in states' competition with others, but as a means of co-operation for shared objectives against common targets: a legitimised activity, with some recognised international standards similar to those of other professions, such as law enforcement. Michael MccGwire has written of the possibility of a 'paradigm shift' in the concept of national security, taking a paradigm to be 'the mixture of beliefs, theory, pre-conceptions and prejudices that shapes ideas of how the international system works, generates expectations and prescribes appropriate behaviour', and argues for an international rather than a national view of security.[45] A revision of the mental framework for intelligence might be part of some much larger process of that kind.[46]

This may seem pie-in-the-sky, yet states can change their working assumptions radically. In the nineteenth century the Red Cross owed its development to a private initiative which caught on and moved governments;[47] and the Hague Conference of 1899 and its contributions to the laws of war originated in an unexpected initiative from the Tsar, possibly from reading a book on future war.[48] Sir Michael Howard reminded us before 2001 that, until the eighteenth-century enlightenment, war between states 'remained an almost automatic activity, part of the natural order of things'.[49] 'If anyone could be said to have invented peace as more than a mere pious aspiration, it was Kant.'[50] The changing view of military power provides another analogy. Armies are still national, but John Keegan argued in 1998 that democracy's professional soldiers are now also international society's check upon violence; 'those honourable warriors who administer force in the cause of peace'.[51] *Mutatis mutandis*, the twenty-first century may bring us to see intelligence in that light.

So intelligence's ethics are at least worth consideration. They are not international society's greatest problem. The ethical issues they pose are Second Division and not First Division ones. Yet events have confirmed intelligence everywhere as a major national attribute, and an increasingly significant factor in international relations amid the Information Revolution of which it is part. It cannot now be handled entirely in a mood of old-fashioned realism; and indeed never has been. The idea of ethical foreign policy got a bad press when given political salience in Britain in 1997, but was in reality a statement of the obvious. Intelligence has to fit into the ethics of an increasingly co-operative system of states, perhaps with bigger changes in thinking than have previously seemed possible. I hope that there will be opportunities for practitioners and academics to join together to explore a concept of 'ethical intelligence', and where its implications point.

Notes

I am grateful to Sir Michael Quinlan and Toni Erskine for their comments on earlier drafts of this paper.

1 *MI5: The Security Service* 4th edn (London: The Stationery Office, 2002), p. 15. It shows 14.4 per cent of the service's resources as allocated to counter-espionage.
2 H. Reiss (tr. H.B. Nisbet), *Kant: Political Writings* (Cambridge: Cambridge University Press, 1991), pp. 96–7.
3 L. Lustgarten and I. Leigh, *In from the Cold: National Security and Parliamentary Democracy* (Oxford: Clarendon Press, 1994), p. 225. This work concentrates on intelligence's domestic aspects, but incidentally provides ethical criticism of foreign intelligence.
4 Cricket in fact has 'laws', which interestingly have traditionally included observing the 'spirit of the game', and in recent years have attempted to codify it.
5 The relevant law on maritime collection is *United Nations Convention on the Law of the Sea 1982*, articles 19 and 29. 'Innocent passage' excludes 'collecting information to the prejudice of the defence or security of the coastal state' (19.2 (c)).
6 Details in the author's *Intelligence Power in Peace and War* (Cambridge: Cambridge University Press, 1996), p. 89.
7 Michael Byers, 'Terrorism, the Use of Force and International Law after 11 September', *International Relations*, 16, 2 (August 2002).
8 For modern legitimacy, see Andrew Hurrell, '"There Are No Rules" (George W. Bush): International Order after September 11', *International Relations*, 16 (August 2002).
9 For the idea of international society I draw on David Armstrong, 'Globalization and the Social State', *Review of International Studies*, 24, 4 (October 1998).
10 Terry Nardin, 'International Pluralism and the Rule of Law', *Review of International Studies*, 26, Special Issue (December 2000), p. 100.
11 Hurrell, 'There Are No Rules', p. 189.
12 Set out in M. Herman, *Intelligence Services in the Information Age: Theory and Practice* (London: Frank Cass, 2001), Ch. 13.
13 It has recently been argued that decision takers have varied attitudes to risks that produce different but equally 'rational' decisions over possible gains and losses; in situations of equal uncertainty, some are risk-averse and others risk-acceptant (Barry O'Neill, 'Risk Aversion in International Relations Theory', *International Studies*

Quarterly, 45, 4 (December 2001)). But intelligence's role is to provide both classes with accurate calibrations of uncertainty and risk.

14 This has continued. 'On 24 August 2001 the last 450 US Minuteman missile silos earmarked for destruction under SALT I were destroyed. The detonation of explosives turns the silos into 90-foot craters, which are then filled with rubble, capped and left for 90 days to allow Russian satellites to verify their elimination.'(Vertic *Trust and Verify*, 100 (January–February 2002).)

15 For the idea of 'Just Intelligence', see Michael Quinlan, 'The Future of Covert Intelligence' and M. Herman, 'Modern Intelligence Services: Have They a Place in Ethical Foreign Policies?', both in Harold Shukman (ed.), *Agents for Change: Intelligence Services in the 21st Century* (London: St Ermin's Press, 2000), pp. 68, 307–8. But note that Just War theory starts from the premise that war is quite special in the ethical problems its raises.

16 Set out, for example, in Herman, *Intelligence Services in the Information Age*, pp. 211–12.

17 But there are sometimes tacit yardsticks of what is acceptable and unacceptable even between antagonists. During the Cold War the Russian Commander of the Soviet Forces in East Germany protested that the British Military Mission had gone too far; one collection operation had gone beyond recognised '*razvedka*' (reconnaissance) to an unacceptable degree of '*shpionazh*' (espionage). I am grateful to Colonel Roy Giles for this example.

18 M. Herman, *British Intelligence towards the Millennium* (London: Centre for Defence Studies, 1997), pp. 64–5.

19 Richard A. Serrano and Greg Miller, '100 Terrorist Attacks Thwarted, U.S. Says', *Los Angeles Times*, 11 January 2003.

20 There were 23 references to military forces, and seven to diplomacy.

21 Address to House of Commons Liaison Committee, 21 January 2003.

22 Compare Nye's definition of soft power as the ability 'to get others to want what you want' (Joseph Nye, 'The New Rome Meets the New Barbarians', *The Economist*, 23 March 2002).

23 The Security Council in that Resolution decided that 'all states shall...take the necessary steps to prevent the commission of terrorist acts, including by provision of early warning to other States by exchange of information' (2(b)). Various parts of item 3 'called upon' states to exchange terrorist information to prevent the commission of terrorist acts.

24 Gregory F. Treverton, *Reshaping National Intelligence for an Age of Information* (Cambridge: Cambridge University Press, 2001), *passim*.

25 S. Rimington, Richard Dimbleby Lecture, *Security and Democracy* (London: BBC Educational Developments, 1994), p. 9.

26 Treverton, *Reshaping National Intelligence*, p. 137.

27 Article by FSB Director N. Patrushev, Russian National Information Service, 20 December 2001.

28 *MI5: The Security Service*, p. 26.

29 Summary in *Statewatch*, 11, 5 (August–October 2001).

30 Details from *Straits Times*, 16 January 2003.

31 Sir Jeremy Greenstock (Chairman), press conference 19 October 2001 (http://www.un.org/Docs/sc/committees/1373).

32 *The Guardian*, 10 October 2002.

33 James Risen, *New York Times*, 20 January 2003. This was however denied by a spokesman for the Russian SVR the following day.

34 Note however that the actual words were the speaker's rationalisation 17 years later: see correspondence in *Intelligence and National Security*, 2, 4 (October 1987).

35 But norms do not have to be universally accepted. For discussion see Vaughn P. Shannon, 'Norms Are What States Make of Them: The Political Psychology of Norm Violation', *International Studies Quarterly*, 44, 2 (June 2000), especially pp. 294–6.

36 Nardin, 'International Pluralism and the Rule of Law', p. 97 n.

37 *Sunday Times*, 25 July 1999, p. 21.
38 *Nezavisimaya Gazeta*, 22 November 1996.
39 Russian accounts of the press conference refer to 'total mutual understanding' having been reached on 'one sensitive topic', and existing agreements 'to work in a fairly correct sort of way' (FBIS and BBC translations of 28 and 29 July 1999 items).
40 *Sunday Times*, 25 March 2001.
41 Details from the Association of Former Intelligence Officers Weekly Notes October 2001 (www.afio.com/sections/wins).
42 The Russian Foreign Ministry suggested that the United States should close down 'the radar station in Vardoe (Norway)'. (Gordon Bennett, *Vladimir Putin and Russia's Special Services* (Sandhurst: Conflict Studies Research Centre, 2002)), p. 69.
43 Ibid., p. 24.
44 *Jane's Intelligence Review*, 3 December 2002.
45 Michael MccGwire, 'The Paradigm that Lost its Way' and 'Shifting the Paradigm', *International Affairs*, 77, 4 (2001), and 78, 1 (2002). The quotation is from the first, p. 649.
46 A changed framework for intelligence would involve changes for covert action, on similar lines.
47 Pam Brown, *Henry Dunant: The Founder of the Red Cross* (Watford: Exley, 1988).
48 Geoffrey Best, 'Peace Conferences and the Century of Total War: The 1899 Hague Conference and What Came After', *International Affairs*, 75, 3 (July 1999), p. 622.
49 M. Howard, *The Invention of Peace: Reflections on War and International Order* (London: Profile Books, 2000), p. 13.
50 Ibid., p. 31.
51 Concluding words in J. Keegan, *War and Our World* (London: Hutchinson, 1998), p. 74.

13 'As Rays of Light to the Human Soul'? Moral Agents and Intelligence Gathering

Toni Erskine

Writing more than 300 years ago, Thomas Hobbes likens intelligence agents both to spiders' webs and to rays of light.[1] Spiders' webs consist of 'incredibly fine threads spread out in all directions' that 'convey outside movements to the spiders sitting in their little cavities inside'.[2] The image is effective and revealing. The spider is, of course, meant to represent those who exercise sovereign power – those who, for Hobbes, are burdened with the task of protecting the citizens of the state. The threads, or intelligence agents, together form an intricate web with which these rulers surround themselves and upon which they depend: 'Without *intelligence agents*', Hobbes observes, 'sovereigns can have no more idea what orders need to be given for the defence of their subjects than spiders can know when to emerge and where to make for without the threads of their webs'.[3] Lest one take from this metaphor that Hobbes views intelligence agents or the activity of gathering intelligence as in any way lacking in virtue, it should be read alongside his other chosen image. 'Reliable intelligence agents', Hobbes asserts unequivocally, 'are to those who exercise sovereign power like rays of light to the human soul.'[4] Elaborating on his position, Hobbes makes it clear that intelligence gathering is not only beyond reproach, but suggests that for the sovereign to fail to engage in it would be morally reprehensible.

Hobbes's assessment is not lacking in relevance today. Intelligence gathering, and the roles and responsibilities of those engaged in this pursuit, are currently subjects of much discussion. In the wake of both the September 11, 2001 terrorist attacks on the Pentagon and the World Trade Center, and the 'anticipatory' war against Iraq, the topic of intelligence evokes complex questions concerning how the activities involved in its collection might be variously condoned or condemned with regard to notions of, *inter alia*, national interest, self-defence, international obligation and appropriate conduct. Responding to these questions involves ethically evaluating the practices of intelligence.

Making judgements about the ethics of intelligence gathering – whether or not one is ultimately to agree with Hobbes – is, however, an arduous task. To assume otherwise would be to underestimate the complexity either of intelligence or of moral judgement. One must first establish that intelligence gathering is something that is open to ethical evaluation. It is then necessary to set out the criteria by which it might be deemed morally prohibited, permissible or, indeed, as Hobbes advises, required.

In what follows, I will address each issue in turn. Establishing intelligence gathering as accessible to ethical evaluation is relatively straightforward (although not uncontentious). It entails recognising the collection of intelligence as being defined by particular actions, and identifying those who perform them as possessing certain capacities. The matter of then determining criteria by which these actions might be evaluated is not at all straightforward. In addressing this more challenging problem, I will survey a number of ethical frameworks that have been variously, and sometimes problematically, employed in assessing actions involved in intelligence collection. These often-competing approaches will be labelled 'realist', 'consequentialist' and 'deontological', respectively. In reviewing these approaches, and the ways that they have been applied to intelligence gathering, I will be concerned with the degree to which each serves to challenge – or justify – existing practices.

Intelligence practitioners as moral agents

Michael Herman defines intelligence in terms of 'information and information gathering';[5] Abram Shulsky and Gary Schmitt make a similar distinction between 'information' and 'activities' as two categories of phenomena to which the label intelligence is applied.[6] Intelligence as information is open to many different types of assessment. We might be concerned with its accuracy, its relevance, the nature of its sources, or its possible significance in terms of policy making. However, it would seem odd to ask whether intelligence, as information, were 'ethical', 'just' or 'morally acceptable'. As has been evident in debates in the United Kingdom and the United States surrounding intelligence dossiers made public prior to the Second Gulf War, such judgements are made of the ways that this information is collected, analysed and employed. It is with this first enterprise, intelligence gathering, that this article will be primarily concerned. Significantly, intelligence thus understood as an *activity* – indeed, as many different activities associated with the gathering of information, from espionage and communications interception to aerial photography – is what is open to specifically ethical evaluation.

Fundamental to this account is the assumption that intelligence gathering involves performing actions. This is not a particularly controversial basis upon which to build an argument. Nevertheless, the idea that intelligence gathering does not involve actions – or at least does not involve actions that are subject to ethical evaluation – is one that has been proposed and, therefore, warrants a brief response.

Herman boldly asserts that intelligence is 'not *doing* things to people'.[7] This statement raises two points of concern. First, it seems to rely on some blurring as to what constitutes action – especially when it is taken together with Herman's earlier statement that 'the essential difference should be recognized between the morality of information-gathering and action'.[8] If, by his own definition, intelligence involves gathering information, then there would appear to be little doubt that it involves 'doing' something. This might seem like a rather banal semantic point, but the fact that intelligence involves acting is significant if one is to contemplate moral guidelines by which one can both prescribe and judge appropriate conduct in the way that it is carried out. It is possible that the emphasis in Herman's statement is misplaced. Perhaps what he wants to claim is that intelligence is 'not doing things *to people*'.[9] Indeed, he elaborates that 'no one gets hurt by it, at least not directly'.[10] The argument here seems to be that intelligence gathering does not involve the types of action that we need to be concerned with from an ethical perspective. Yet, this assertion itself raises important and difficult issues about the ways in which concepts of harm, intention and consequence affect our evaluation of actions. If simply 'monitoring' someone leads to his or her being injured in some way, does it matter that this result is 'indirect'? How can harmful effects of human intelligence collection, for example, be measured? Can such activities be considered wrong independently of the harm they may cause? Does the fact that one does not intend to adversely affect others when engaged in an aspect of intelligence gathering offer an effective ethical get-out clause when this is, in fact, the consequence? I will address these issues below.

Herman's statement should also elicit some discussion both of how one characterises those actions involved in the collection of intelligence, and of the moral distinctions that one can make – and coherently defend – between, for example, intelligence 'hunting' and 'gathering',[11] intelligence 'attack' and 'defence',[12] 'messy' and 'clean',[13] or more or less 'intrusive' forms of collecting information,[14] and 'direct' and 'indirect' resulting harm. I will, for the purpose of this article, accept Herman's account of intelligence gathering as belonging to a category separate from 'covert action'. I will not, however, automatically accept that intelligence gathering is, even by this account, a generally innocuous (and somehow passive) endeavour. Nor will I concur with the implication that intelligence gathering thus understood could be removed from ethical scrutiny.

It is important to acknowledge that even if an activity were deemed not to harm others, including in ways that were indirect and unintended (a tall order when referring to policy and practice in international relations), it would not, on these grounds, be exempt from ethical scrutiny. Instead, the judgement that a means of gathering intelligence is beyond moral reproach (perhaps on the basis that it is, indeed, harmless) can only be the *result* of such evaluation.[15] This ethical evaluation is viable simply because the actions involved in intelligence collection are performed by moral agents.

The concept of a 'moral agent' refers to those actors whose possession of certain capacities for deliberation and action mean that we can expect them to respond to moral guidelines, and, by extension, hold them accountable for their conduct. We can quite confidently assume that the individuals who occupy intelligence roles at MI5 and MI6, for example, possess capacities that allow them to deliberate over possible courses of action and their consequences and to act on the basis of this deliberation. In other words, these individuals, whether we commend or criticise their particular actions, are moral agents. As such, we can coherently talk about them behaving 'morally' or 'immorally', 'justly' or 'unjustly', 'ethically' or 'unethically'. It is on this point that Hobbes' metaphors are flawed. Those involved in obtaining intelligence are not simply conduits of information, either as rays of light or intricate threads of a web that convey movement to the spider (or 'truth to power'). Their function may be, in part, one of communication, but they are not simply instruments. They are purposive actors and active participants in the practices of intelligence.[16]

Individual intelligence professionals – however they are portrayed – are not the only moral agents involved in intelligence activities. Although we often think of bearers of moral responsibilities in terms of individual human actors, formal organisations, whether state governments or intelligence agencies, can also be considered moral agents.[17] These organisations can be expected to respond to ethical guidelines, and to promote adherence to these guidelines among their constituents (by, for example, establishing formal codes of conduct, creating a culture within which the prescriptions and constraints embedded in these codes are followed, and ensuring that policies are commensurate with such codes). Moreover, these bodies can also be held accountable for what are deemed to be transgressions of ethical guidelines – although determining who is morally responsible for either 'intelligence failures' or 'inappropriate conduct' is never going to be easy when dealing with multiple, multifarious actors that include complex organisations.

Importantly, if we accept that moral reasoning can and should guide actions and shape practices, then there is nothing *sui generis* about the human activity of intelligence gathering that would render it exempt from such reasoning. Actually evaluating the actions of moral agents involved in the practices of intelligence – whether individuals or organisations – is, however, considerably more difficult than maintaining that such an endeavour is viable. Taking this next step requires an understanding of the various approaches that one might take to the ethics of intelligence.

Competing approaches to the ethics of intelligence

The ethical frameworks that we invoke affect how we variously champion or challenge, justify or rationalise, accept or excuse, a wide range of practices and policies. In what follows, I will not provide an exhaustive list of the possible ethical arguments that could be made regarding the collection of intelligence. Rather, I will offer a survey of some very diverse moral positions that have been embraced with reference to intelligence gathering. In order to discuss both their strengths and weaknesses, and make comparisons between them, I will arrange these positions according to a simple typology – one that will also serve to highlight links between approaches to the ethics of intelligence and to International Relations (IR) theory more broadly.[18]

A realist approach: raison d'état, pre-emption and reciprocity

One might easily be forgiven for thinking that a 'realist' approach to intelligence would be devoid of moral considerations. Indeed, a realist approach to international politics is often taken to be the antithesis of an ethical approach. There are two problems with this assumption. First, it fails to recognise the diversity of approaches placed in the category of 'political realism'. Classical theorists such as Thucydides, Hobbes and Niccolo Machiavelli are retrospectively – and somewhat haphazardly – assigned this label. Twentieth-century scholars of international relations such as Hans Morgenthau adopt it as a term of self-description, and proponents of a more 'scientific' approach to international politics, such as Kenneth Waltz, redefine it for their own use. Each of these unlikely bedfellows has a very different understanding of the role of ethics in international politics. Some lend legitimacy to the caricature of realism as committed to an amoral international realm. Very many do not.

The second shortcoming of equating realism with moral scepticism is that doing so neglects an important and distinctive ethical approach to international politics – one that sees moral reasoning as compatible with, even if not exclusively defined by, self-interest, prudence and *raison d'état*. This is an understanding of moral reasoning that differs markedly from the approaches that will be surveyed below, as it allows one to justify courses of action with reference to the good of the political community, rather than by aspiring to a more cosmopolitan stance that would grant equal moral weight to all actors, whether friend or foe, ally or adversary. It is also an understanding of moral reasoning that warrants attention, particularly as it seems to fit remarkably well with some common assumptions about intelligence gathering.

The realist approach that I will discuss briefly here does not hold that morality is inapplicable to international politics – and to the practices of intelligence – but, rather, maintains that acting in the national interest is itself complying with a moral principle. (Again, not all so-called realists share this view. Some understand foreign policy as necessarily guided by the interests of the state, but present this as a strictly prudential, and in no way moral, position.) Hobbes is one political theorist, frequently portrayed within IR as exemplifying realism, who presents the defence of the national interest as a moral duty. This understanding of moral obligation informs Hobbes' position on intelligence.

As alluded to above, according to Hobbes, discussion of the morality of intelligence gathering does not involve contemplation of the limits and prohibitions that one must apply to this practice, but focuses on the imperative to take certain actions:

> [F]or the citizens' safety, sovereigns need to get intelligence of enemy plans...and since princes are obliged by the law of nature to make every effort to secure the citizens' safety; it follows not only that they are permitted to send out spies, maintain troops, build fortifications and to exact money for the purpose, but also that they may not do otherwise.[19]

Despite the lack of restraint that this position allows vis-à-vis action directed at those beyond the borders of the state, the sovereign's relations with the external world *are*, nevertheless, morally grounded: these relations arise from the sovereign's moral obligations to his subjects.

Significantly, Hobbes takes the sovereign's duty to protect the citizens of the state beyond mere defence from existing or imminent threats. Implicitly endorsing Francis Bacon's assertion that 'as long as reason is reason, a just fear will be a just cause of a preventive war',[20] and prefiguring President Bush's recent policy of 'pre-emptive' and 'anticipatory' action,[21] Hobbes maintains that sovereigns

> may also do anything that seems likely to subvert, by force or by craft, the power of foreigners whom they fear; for the rulers of commonwealths are obliged to do all they can to ensure that the calamities they fear do not happen.[22]

This not only supports more aggressive forms of intelligence collection – 'hunting not gathering' to use Charles Cogan's useful phrase – but also provides a moral justification for covert action (however high up on Loch Johnson's ladder of escalation specific operations might be situated).[23] Although this ethical realist position may lend legitimacy to any means of conducting external intelligence activities (that serve the interest of the state), it is also, at least contingently, compatible with policies that would advocate restraint in these activities.

Somewhat counter-intuitively, the ethical realist framework that I have outlined could support reciprocal agreements to place limits on intelligence collection (of the type to which Herman refers, for example).[24] Agreements on mutual restraint in intelligence collection would be compatible with this ethical realist position if they were motivated by the desire to protect the members of one's own political community from intrusive methods of collection.[25] There is an important caveat that must be offered here, however: the same position would justify such agreements being quickly and unilaterally rescinded. This is simply because a state's commitment to such agreements must be determined according to the degree to which it serves the well-being of the citizens of the state at any one point in time. As Hobbes states, 'agreements are invalid in the natural state [of hostility], whenever justified fear is a factor'.[26] Moral arguments in favour of reciprocal constraints on the practices of intelligence can be made by the ethical realist, but adherence to such constraints would necessarily remain dependent upon subjective and fluid interpretations of the national interest.

Many aspects of this realist approach to intelligence collection seem very near to common positions about intelligence policy and practice.[27] Moreover, such a stance is associated with often compelling claims to the value of the political community, the legitimacy of preventive self-defence, and the importance of patriotic sentiments. Without assigning it the label 'realist' – or acknowledging it as exemplifying a specifically ethical perspective – Johnson identifies an approach to intelligence activities based on 'an acceptance of the pre-eminence of the nation-state and the correctness of its defense'. This is an approach that Hobbes would no doubt endorse. This is also an approach that Johnson maintains is 'accepted by most contemporary scholars, government officials, and citizens'.[28] Yet, despite its apparent broad acceptance, an ethical stance that places national self-interest before broader international obligations would be deemed 'immoral' from the approaches to which I will now turn.

A consequentialist approach: calculating an 'ethical balance sheet'

A 'consequentialist' judges actions by the value of their consequences. The most common version of this position, and the one that will be addressed here, is known as 'act-consequentialism', according to which the right course of action is necessarily the one that produces the most good.[29] Indeed, a consequentialist aspires to a world in which good enjoys the greatest balance over bad. This approach has been championed with respect to the ethics of intelligence by Herman who makes the bold claim that '[i]ntelligence has to be judged in the first instance on its manifest consequences'.[30] In order to make such judgements, he relies on the distinction cited above between intelligence collection and intelligence as knowledge. 'Knowledge and activities can be examined separately', he argues, 'but then have to be integrated into an ethical balance sheet.'[31] This moral accounting allows him to balance what he maintains are the overall good effects of intelligence knowledge against what he acknowledges can be the less acceptable means by which it is collected. At the bottom of the ledger, the benefits of intelligence knowledge are found to be in credit: the means employed to gather intelligence can be morally justified by the positive impact of the knowledge acquired.

Positive effects of intelligence knowledge can, of course, be variously conceived. These benefits might be defined in terms of international peace or national security, reduced 'enemy' civilian casualties in war or none of *our* soldiers coming home in body bags. In other words, one might envisage positive effects of intelligence collection from a global perspective or from the point of view of a particular state. Indeed, the ethical realist approach addressed above can be seen to be structurally parallel to consequentialism in the sense that the morally right action is the one that maximises the good. However, while the realist position advocates maximising the good of a particular political community, the consequentialist position outlined here is based on impartial consideration of the interests of others – including those beyond one's own political community. The position to which Herman aspires very clearly embodies this feature of a consequentialist approach. In exploring whether the gathering of intelligence is an ethical activity, he is centrally concerned with whether 'it make[s] for a better world or a worse one'.[32] This provides a stringent test for determining the moral acceptability of intelligence gathering. It also makes Herman's own claim that there exists a credit balance of intelligence results over collection – a particularly difficult one to sustain.

Before turning to an explanation of why a consequentialist approach to intelligence collection establishes a stringent criterion for judging particular actions, it is important to note how such an approach can also, in some respects, be seen as excessively – and perhaps unacceptably – permissive. Act-consequentialism does not require recognition of some activities – such as torture or killing the 'innocent' – as intrinsically wrong. Rather, these activities can be deemed morally acceptable if they maximise the good. In other words, if one adopts a consequentialist approach, a good end can justify even extreme means. Herman exemplifies this line of argument when he maintains that the overall good of intelligence knowledge not only provides strong moral backing for intelligence gathering, but also means that, in some circumstances, 'almost anything goes' in terms of methods of collection. 'Should one torture terrorists to forestall imminent operations?', Herman asks. Presumably taking this as an example of the positive impact of knowledge outweighing the less appealing means by which it is collected, he suggests that, '[p]erhaps one should'.[33] Although a consequentialist approach might seem by this (albeit tentative) conclusion to be as permissive as the ethical realist approach to intelligence collection, it is not. For a consequentialist, the acceptability of any means of intelligence collection is necessarily contingent upon the benefits of knowledge outweighing the costs of collection on a global scale. Such a calculation is onerous, and many accounts of the resulting balance would be highly critical of methods of intelligence collection much less extreme than torture.

There are (at least) three problems with relying on a consequentialist approach to lend moral legitimacy to intelligence collection. First, balancing the good outcomes made possible by intelligence knowledge against the detriment of certain activities involved in acquiring it requires one to define both that which is good and that which is detrimental, and to assign relative moral weight to each point along a spectrum between the two categories. This is a challenging – and some might argue impossible – endeavour. One might infer that in order for Herman's ethical balance sheet to yield such a strong moral backing for even controversial means of intelligence collection, he must place a great deal of weight on the positive, cosmopolitan outcomes of intelligence knowledge. Such gains, he suggests, include a reduction in 'irresponsible and ignorant national behaviour'.[34] What remains problematic is that there is likely to be debate about whether – and when – these outcomes are achieved. Did intelligence knowledge pertaining to Iraq's weapons of mass destruction ensure that the United Kingdom behaved in a more informed and responsible manner? This is an issue on which reasonable people might disagree. Moreover, even if one could establish when such criteria were met, there remains the prior problem of identifying which outcomes would have to be realised to contribute to 'a better world'. Tensions between notions of the 'global good' championed by capitalism and communism, 'the West' and 'fundamentalist Islam', and multi-national corporations and anti-globalisation movements demonstrate the difficulty of doing so.

Of course, similar issues necessarily arise when we attempt to define, and assign value to, those activities that would, in Herman's words, make the world 'marginally worse'.[35] Although Herman suggests that, when faced with certain adversaries, torture may be condoned as a means of acquiring information, he asserts that 'the more intrusive methods of peacetime collection – espionage, some bugging, and perhaps diplomatic targeting' might not be similarly justified 'when used against legitimate states'.[36] He thereby considers the ethical debit attached to the practice of torture conceivably to be outweighed by its positive effects in a way that the ethical debits arising from other forms of intelligence collection (against other types of actors) could not be. Many would challenge this calculation. Some, of course, would deny that such moral considerations could be 'calculated' at all and would consider certain acts to be intrinsically wrong. (I will address this position below.) Yet others might condemn torture on the consequentialist grounds by which Herman would, somewhat hesitantly, allow it. In addition to the point that torture might not be the most effective way of gathering information, one could argue that granting any legitimacy to the practice would produce more 'harm' than bugging the embassies of allies – in terms of overall suffering, or by allowing an initial step down a slippery slope that would see the erosion of fundamental standards of human dignity. In short, it is fine to claim that the overall good achieved as a result of intelligence knowledge outweighs the possible detriment of the way that it was collected, but if we cannot agree on what constitutes that which is good or that which is detrimental, then this cannot take us very far.

Second, even if we could agree on what constitutes both the good outcomes that intelligence knowledge can achieve and the harmful activities that these outcomes would have to outweigh, a consequentialist analysis allows one to assign moral significance to indirect, unintended and even unforeseen outcomes of actions. Herman's defence of intelligence gathering as 'at least not directly' hurting anyone therefore encounters obstacles according to the consequentialist position that he claims to advocate. The observation that some means of obtaining information produce harm – to persons with regard to torture, and to relations between states with regard to the bugging of embassies – would seem difficult to dispute (even if there is disagreement regarding the relative weight that such harms should be given when added to an 'ethical balance sheet'). However, even activities that have less obvious effects on others cannot necessarily be dismissed as being harmless. The mere experience of being observed can conceivably affect an actor's behaviour and trigger a response of aggression or, indeed, paranoia.[37] James A. Barry refers to 'psychological injury to innocent people' as a byproduct of covert action that is to be avoided.[38] This seems equally applicable to some forms of intelligence collection. A plethora of indirect harms might not be so easily outweighed by a claim to a (contested) global good. If an ethical balance sheet is to satisfy a careful consequentialist audit, it must register such harms as debits.

Finally, if one attempts to employ Herman's global ethical balance sheet, one must rely on *projections* of whether intelligence information would outweigh in utility the harm of the means by which it was gathered. As Michael Quinlan cautions with regard to applying consequentialist reasoning to covert intelligence collection,

> it is ... hard even with hindsight – and policy, alas, has anyway to be made looking forward, not back – to measure the reality and scale of the possible benefits in any concrete way and to bring them into common calculus with the costs. Much intelligence effort is directed towards insurance against events whose probability, importance and cost cannot themselves be measured.[39]

Simply put, ascertaining whether a positive outcome will result from bugging the embassy of an ally or torturing a suspected member of a paramilitary organisation is extremely difficult. (Declaring that positive outcomes have *already* been achieved and, therefore, lend legitimacy to certain collection activities retrospectively might be a convenient form of rationalisation, but does little to guide actions.) Moreover, any attempt to make accurate projections about the international benefits of intelligence knowledge is further impeded by the reality that the impact of intelligence knowledge ultimately depends on how the knowledge is analysed, disseminated and employed – and by whom. Indeed, the actors facing particular ethical decisions regarding acceptable means of collecting intelligence are often not those who then decide how intelligence knowledge will be used. Intelligence knowledge helps to shape policy; policy outcomes cannot be used to justify how this information is collected before the fact.

There is an important addendum to this final point that also follows on from the concern noted above regarding the significance of indirect consequences of actions. When different activities associated with intelligence are carried out by different moral agents, there can be a sense of 'fragmentation of responsibility'.[40] This occurs when one focuses only on the immediate consequences of one's own actions – even if one recognises that one's actions play a vital role in a chain of activities that ultimately result in harm. For example, the act of gathering information might be seen as divorced from any harmful consequences of the way that the resulting knowledge is exploited. This might allow one to disclaim responsibility for the harm. A student member of the Palestinian Security Services whose job it was to observe fellow students involved in political parties within Al-Azhar University was quoted as saying, '[w]e don't try to harm. We just monitor.' In addition to the point made above about the possible psychological impact of 'just monitoring' people, it is interesting to note that the student then acknowledges that if his monitoring demonstrates that a particular party is gaining in strength, 'there is interference' by the security department.[41] Important to him, however, is that his own monitoring does not itself involve interference or harm. Intelligence collection and the exploitation of the resulting knowledge – including covert action that relies on this knowledge – might represent discrete activities. The consequences of these activities cannot, however, be so neatly disaggregated. Consequentialist reasoning allows for much more complex and extended causal links.[42] From this perspective, the harm caused by forms of covert action that rely on intelligence knowledge, for example, cannot be as easily discounted by the moral agents responsible for mere 'monitoring' as this Palestinian security guard – or Herman – might assume.

A deontological approach: duties and intentions

Radically opposed to an act-consequentialist approach to intelligence collection are positions according to which some acts are wrong in themselves, *regardless of their consequences*. Such positions are referred to as 'deontological', a label derived from the Greek word *deon*, meaning 'duty'.[43] For the deontologist, an ethical balance sheet cannot guide our moral deliberations; ethical evaluations must be made with reference to the 'goodness' or 'badness' of the actions themselves. As some actions associated with intelligence gathering are morally unacceptable means to the pursuit of *any* end (regardless of how noble), the deontologist cannot condone methods of intelligence collection with reference to the knowledge that they produce. Torturing a paramilitary leader to extract information about the location of a bomb that will kill hundreds of people, or engaging in deception to infiltrate a foreign intelligence agency, not only cannot be justified from a deontological perspective, but such actions are morally prohibited. As Charles Fried maintains, such constraints

> are not mere negatives that enter into a calculus to be outweighed by the good you might do or the greater harm you might avoid. Thus the deontological judgments...may be said to be absolute. They do not say: 'Avoid lying, other things being equal', but 'Do not lie, period'.[44]

Principle, according to this approach, is more important than calculation.

One example of a deontological ethical approach can be found in the work of Immanuel Kant, whose defence of absolute constraints on certain actions leads him to articulate an unsparing moral indictment of intelligence activities.[45] Kant's view of both the state that engages in covert intelligence and the individuals that it puts to use for this purpose could not be more radically opposed to Hobbes's glowing account. Far from acting out of duty by employing spies, Kant maintains in *The Metaphysics of Morals* that a state is prohibited – even in self-defence – from 'using its own subjects as spies' and 'for using them or even foreigners... for spreading false reports'.[46] While he notes that such acts 'would destroy the trust requisite to establishing a lasting peace in the future', this damaging consequence of employing spies and engaging in counter-intelligence is an ancillary factor in his indictment. In stark contrast to Hobbes' portrayal of the virtuous intelligence agent, Kant asserts that such activities render those who perform them 'unfit to be citizens'.[47] Indeed, in *Perpetual Peace*, Kant claims that 'the employment of spies' is included within those 'diabolical acts' that are 'intrinsically despicable'.[48]

To understand Kant's unconditional condemnation – and how his approach to ethically evaluating intelligence differs from the realist and consequentialist approaches already addressed – one must refer his 'Categorical Imperative', by which he endeavours to identify fundamental principles of action by following rational procedures.[49] According to two related formulations of the Categorical Imperative, one must act only in such a way that the principle guiding one's action might coherently become universal law (and thereby be valid for all other agents); and, one must treat other rational actors as having value as ends in themselves, rather than solely as means to an end. Many activities presently associated with the gathering of intelligence – particularly human intelligence collection – simply fail to meet either criterion.

With respect to the first formulation of the Categorical Imperative, the gathering of intelligence is associated with acts that are morally unacceptable because they are not universalisable. Both coercion and deception are examples of actions that are, on these grounds, categorically prohibited. Coercion might be more associated with covert action than with intelligence gathering narrowly defined (although the procurement of 'controlled' sources, or sources that feel themselves somehow bound to fill the role of informant, routinely involves some form of coercion).[50]

Deception, however, is a fundamental aspect of intelligence. This conception might run contrary to some articulations of the role of intelligence. As E. Drexel Godfrey, Jr. asserts, 'at heart intelligence is rooted in the severest of all ethical principles: truth telling'.[51] Yet, even if the goal of intelligence collection is (ideally) to provide the policy maker with as accurate a picture of a situation as possible, exacting 'the truth' from those with no interest in sharing it often and unavoidably involves deception. There's the rub. Not only is deception intrinsic to clandestine collection, but it is also central to counter-intelligence activities such as the deployment of 'double agents' and the sending of false messages when it is we who would rather keep our secrets to ourselves. Onora O'Neill provides a clear explication of why, for Kant, attempting to universalise a maxim of deception involves a 'contradiction in conception':

> A maxim of deceiving others as convenient has as its universalized counterpart the maxim that everyone will deceive others as convenient. But if everyone were to deceive others as convenient, then there would be no trust or reliance on others' acts of communication; hence nobody would be deceived; hence nobody could deceive others as convenient.[52]

The universalised version of deceiving others is that everyone deceives. In such a world, both truth and deception lose all meaning. Importantly, Kant does not assume coercion or deception to be morally wrong simply because of their alleged harmful affects (as a consequentialist might), but primarily because they cannot form principles that could be universalised. Actions that fail this latter test are morally prohibited.

As noted above, the second formulation of Kant's Categorical Imperative demands that human beings be treated as ends in themselves, rather than exclusively as means to any end. Any attempt to deceive another in order to obtain intelligence would involve treating this other as a tool, thereby contravening Kant's demand that the person be respected. Not only would torturing an individual to derive information – regardless of how many lives might be saved by obtaining this information – be absolutely prohibited, but less extreme actions would also be deemed immoral. Human intelligence collection, defined by Godfrey as 'extracting from others information or national assets that they *would not willingly part with* under normal circumstances', is, then, highly problematic.[53] One might envisage acts of clandestine collection in which information would not, under normal circumstances, be so tightly guarded and might even have been obtained openly. This does not, however, mitigate the 'wrongness' of obtaining it in such a way that the human source is not aware of, and therefore cannot consent to, this transfer of knowledge. As O'Neill explains, '[o]n Kant's account to use another is not merely a matter of doing something the other does not actually want or consent to, but of doing something to which the other *cannot* consent. For example, deceivers make it *impossible* for their victims to consent to the deceiver's project.'[54] Deception, even in defence of the state (as Hobbes would advocate), or in pursuit of morally admirable goals (as Herman condones), is, for

Kant, and other deontologists, absolutely prohibited. For Kant, this prohibition has its roots in the non-universalisability of deception and its concomitant disregard of human dignity.

One final question might be raised regarding the moral acceptability of human intelligence collection according to Kant's imperative that persons be respected. What are the implications of making use of the intelligence provided by an informant who, for example, arrives unexpectedly in a foreign embassy and (avoiding being inadvertently turned away) provides this information willingly? Importantly, this 'walk in' source is not being treated solely as a means to an end, but is acting autonomously. The intelligence officer who accepts information from this person would not seem to be contravening Kant's imperative. His or her hands remain clean. The informant might, however, have contravened Kant's prohibition against deception in obtaining the information (and thereby have acted 'immorally'),[55] but this need not be the concern of the second party receiving it, assuming, of course, that this officer neither incited nor coerced the informant to engage in this deception. (The stark contrast with a 'controlled' source here is clear. Extracting information from such a source involves both coercion *and* treating the source simply as a means to an end.)

To turn from the particular example of Kant's condemnation of intelligence and back to the deontological approach to ethics more generally, it is important to emphasise that some acts deemed immoral from a consequentialist perspective might actually be considered *permissible* from a deontological stance. This is an important point, as deontological approaches have been associated with restricting activities involved in intelligence gathering, whereas consequentialist arguments have been presented as being more permissive.[56] This observation is also highly relevant to Herman's defence of intelligence collection that it 'does not hurt anyone – at least not directly'.

Although the deontologist categorically condemns many intelligence activities that are at least contingently acceptable from a consequentialist perspective, the deontologist's focus on his or her actions (rather than on their consequences) means that constraints on other methods of intelligence collection are *less* onerous and far-reaching than those constraints facing the consequentialist. This is particularly apparent with regard to the example of 'mere monitoring' addressed above. A moral agent deliberating over which actions are acceptable from within a consequentialist framework must account for both the 'indirect harm' of the targets' psychological response to being observed, and the harm caused by other agents engaging in more overtly intrusive and harmful activities which draw on the intelligence knowledge gained through the initial monitoring. Invoking a deontological framework, however, affords the luxury of focusing much more narrowly on 'keeping one's hands clean' with respect to one's immediate actions. From this perspective, one might, indeed, argue that one's actions are acceptable because they do not 'directly' harm anyone. In short, when faced with overt surveillance activities, the deontologist might find means of intelligence collection ethically unproblematic that the consequentialist would have to enter as a debit on an ethical balance sheet.

Although not universally accepted by those who adopt a deontological approach to ethics, some contemporary adherents, such as Thomas Nagel, explain this apparently permissive aspect of deontological reasoning with reference to a distinction between what we do intentionally and the consequences of our actions that we foresee (and allow), but which are not fundamental to our aims. As Nagel argues, 'to violate deontological constraints one must maltreat someone else *intentionally*'.[57] By this view, even projected harmful consequences do not constrain actions – as long as they are unintended. Although this feature of a deontological moral framework might relieve moral agents involved in intelligence gathering from being constrained by some 'unintended' effects of their actions, the same perspective is unyielding in its condemnation of employing deception or coercion in the collection of intelligence.

Conclusion

The title of this article poses the problem of how intelligence practitioners – as *moral* agents – are best depicted. This is not merely an incredibly difficult question to answer, but it is, perhaps, an impossible one. At least, it is impossible to answer in general terms. Making moral judgements about the actors and practices involved in intelligence collection requires careful consideration of some fundamental issues. First, it is necessary to acknowledge that 'intelligence collection' encompasses a multitude of diverse activities. None is exempt from moral evaluation. However, asking whether the (archetypal) intelligence practitioner, or intelligence gathering *as such*, is moral or immoral threatens to overlook the myriad distinctions that can be made between different methods of collection. Indeed, those activities that have been associated with intelligence gathering (with far from unanimous agreement as to its defining parameters) range widely from open source collection to espionage. Making a blanket pronouncement on the moral acceptability (or otherwise) of all such activities would be neither coherent nor helpful.

A second crucial point that must be taken into account before accepting or rejecting Hobbes' portrayal of those engaged in intelligence collection 'as rays of light to the human soul' is that different ethical approaches to intelligence gathering yield distinct guidelines for acting (and judging action). Respective approaches also disagree on the moral relevance that should be assigned to the various ways of distinguishing between different types of activities. For one approach, the degree to which activities have overall harmful consequences establishes a morally relevant way of distinguishing between them; for another, whether or not activities involve deceiving others is of primary concern. Judging the conduct of an individual intelligence practitioner (or an intelligence organisation if we are to refer to collective moral agents) requires one to explore the degree to which the actor in question conforms to the evaluative criteria of a particular ethical framework. The realist, consequentialist and deontological approaches addressed above provide radically different ways of thinking about the ethical boundaries within which moral agents engaged in intelligence collection might deliberate, act, and, indeed, be judged.

The realist position inspired by Hobbes can manifest itself in powerful arguments for the justice of actions that are deemed necessary to preserve national security – or, more boldly, to prevent other actors from achieving the capacity to threaten it. Even the intelligence practitioner who engages in aggressive, intrusive and overtly harmful means of collection as part of the state's external affairs need not, from this position, be guilty of a moral transgression. Significantly, this does not mean that such an approach is an amoral one. To the contrary, realism thus understood is an important – and arguably prominent – moral position. It is a position that establishes strict criteria for appropriate action rather than offering carte blanche approval of any policy or practice. Methods of intelligence collection are morally justified if they serve the well-being of the state; intelligence practitioners who contribute to this objective are the objects of praise (as long as, following Hobbes, they are 'reliable' in their roles). This approach lends legitimacy to intelligence collection as it is currently conceived and practiced. Such a conclusion is not meant to imply that intelligence gathering is devoid of either rigorous codes of conduct or practitioners that deliberate and act in light of these codes. Rather, it is meant to suggest that limits to the practices of intelligence are presently understood and applied in ethical realist terms.

Herman's consequentialist position makes a valuable contribution to thinking about the ethics of intelligence – one that is, however, more conducive to setting very high standards of conduct to which one might aspire than to legitimating existing practices. The moral agent who invokes Herman's ethical balance sheet as a guide to appropriate conduct in the gathering of intelligence is burdened with the task of taking into account a multitude of possible harms that might result from his or her actions – regardless of whether they are indirect or unintended. As the same moral agent is committed to weighing these harms against necessarily indeterminate global benefits, this perspective is restrictive of many actions associated with intelligence gathering – perhaps more restrictive than Herman would care to acknowledge. Yet, despite the prohibitions on performing intelligence gathering activities that can be argued from this perspective – with regard to practices from torture to overt surveillance – it is important to note that such prohibitions must always remain provisional and open to alternative understandings of the consequences of certain actions, alternative articulations of the 'global good', and alternative conceptions of harm. The provisional nature of these consequentialist restrictions is most apparent when the moral agent is faced with a claim to 'supreme emergency', variously articulated in terms of circumstances (or adversaries) that 'shock the conscience of humankind', 'threaten our free world', or 'embody a universal evil'.[58] When it is argued that the 'global good' (however defined) faces such a threat, Herman's ethical balance sheet might appear deceptively straightforward and a policy of 'anything goes' in intelligence collection might seem well within moral reach.

A policy that 'anything goes' in the means of intelligence collection could never be justified from a deontological perspective. Deontological approaches, such as Kant's, defend maxims that absolutely prohibit certain actions. Some interpretations of a deontological approach allow what critics might call an ethical loophole by condemning only those prohibited actions that are intended. Foreseen but unintended psychological damage done to individuals who are the objects of overt monitoring, for example, can then be excused as a mere side effect of intelligence collection, or as unfortunate but acceptable 'collateral damage'. Nevertheless, many forms of intelligence collection involve doing things that are categorically prohibited from a deontological perspective and could not be convincingly presented as unintended effects of other (intended) actions. (Deception, for example, when employed as a means of acquiring intelligence, simply cannot be presented as a side-effect of some other aim.) Deontological approaches might support a radical revamping of intelligence collection, but they cannot condone many of the activities that it is generally understood to encompass.

After surveying these three approaches, one might reasonably ask whether any one of them can be applied in a critical capacity without condemning altogether activities that are presently seen as fundamental to effective intelligence collection. One might argue that, individually, the frameworks outlined above are either too accepting of the intelligence status quo, or too demanding in light of current political realities, to provide viable guides for action. Significantly, some theorists, borrowing principles from the Just War tradition, have alluded to a fourth approach that might demand restraint in certain activities without condemning them outright. Such an approach, variously labelled 'Just Espionage' and 'Just Intelligence', has been proposed but not pursued in detail in the context of intelligence collection.[59] Interestingly, and not unproblematically, it draws selectively on each of the three approaches addressed above.[60] Although the disanalogy between intelligence collection and war needs to be addressed by potential proponents of such an approach – particularly in relation to the notion of 'Just Cause' – a 'Just Intelligence' perspective warrants further attention and elaboration.

Indeed, further investigation into ethics and intelligence is essential. At the beginning of the twenty-first century, the moral dilemmas and competing demands facing intelligence practitioners and organisations have arguably become more challenging than ever before. Understanding the different moral arguments that can be invoked to confront these difficult circumstances, and critically engaging with the assumptions that underlie them – whether embedded in realist, consequentialist, deontological, or 'Just Intelligence' frameworks – are vitally important endeavours.

Notes

This article began as a set of discussant's comments presented at 'Journeys in Shadows: Understanding Intelligence in the Twenty-first Century', the University of Wales Conference Centre, Gregynog, 9–11 November 2002. I am indebted to Michael Herman for presenting such a stimulating paper – and set of issues – to which I had the opportunity to respond. I am also very grateful to Jeroen Gunning, Michael Herman, Peter Jackson, Andrew Linklater, Len Scott and Howard Williams for valuable written comments on earlier versions of this article.

1 Thomas Hobbes, *De Cive [On the Citizen]*, ed. and trans. by Richard Tuck and Michael Silverthorne (Cambridge: Cambridge University Press, 1998). *De Cive* was

written in the 1630s and first published in 1647. Hobbes's discussion of intelligence is presented in chapter 13, 'On the Duties of those who Exercise Sovereign Power', pp. 145–6. I am very grateful to Howard Williams for directing me towards these passages.

2 Hobbes, *De Cive*, p. 145.

3 Ibid. Emphasis in the original.

4 Ibid.

5 Michael Herman, 'Ethics and Intelligence after September 2001', this volume, p. 180.

6 Abram N. Shulsky and Gary J. Schmitt, *Silent Warfare: Understanding the World of Intelligence* (Dulles, VA: Brassey's, 3rd edn, 2002), p. 1. Shulsky and Schmitt also refer to a third category of 'organisations'. These three categories were first suggested by Sherman Kent in *Strategic Intelligence for American World Policy* [1949] (Princeton, NJ: Princeton University Press, 1966).

7 Herman, 'Ethics and Intelligence', p. 180. Emphasis in the original.

8 M. Herman, 'Modern Intelligence Services: Have They a Place in Ethical Foreign Policies?', in H. Shukman (ed.), *Agents for Change: Intelligence Services in the 21st Century* (London: St Ermin's Press, 2000), p. 308. It might be that Herman is attempting to highlight a distinction between intelligence gathering and covert action in this passage. However, defining intelligence gathering negatively as not involving action is problematic.

9 Although elsewhere Herman states that '[c]ollection is necessarily *against* someone . . .'. See his 'Modern Intelligence Services', p. 304.

10 In his *Intelligence Services in the Information Age* (London: Frank Cass, 2001), p. 211, Herman argues in a similar vein that, '[u]nlike armed force, intelligence does not kill or cause suffering'.

11 Charles Cogan, 'Hunters not Gatherers: Intelligence in the Twenty-first Century', this volume, pp. 147–61.

12 Herman, 'Modern Intelligence Services', p. 298.

13 Shulsky and Schmitt, *Silent Warfare*, p. 168.

14 Herman suggests that there is an inverse correlation between ethical acceptability and the degree of intrusion in the way that intelligence is collected in 'Modern Intelligence Services', p. 299. Loch Johnson's 'ladder of escalation' for covert operations – the aim of which is to distinguish between acceptable and unacceptable intelligence operations – is based on 'a rising level of intrusion'. See his *Secret Agencies: US Intelligence in a Hostile World* (New Haven, CT: Yale University Press, 1996), p. 60. It is interesting to note that Johnson provides examples of 'intelligence collection' on each of the four rungs of his ladder.

15 As I will address below, some ethical approaches require that we judge actions on criteria other than their harmful consequences.

16 For Hobbes, however, who would not accept the voluntarist conception of agency that I am assuming, these metaphors are unproblematic. Indeed, Hobbes presents the motion of individual human beings as reducible to the effects of a machine. See, for example, his introduction to *Leviathan* [1651] (London: Penguin, 1968).

17 For a further discussion of the possibility of treating formal organisations as moral agents, see T. Erskine, 'Assigning Responsibilities to Institutional Moral Agents: The Case of States and Quasi-States', *Ethics and International Affairs*, 15, 2 (October 2001), pp. 67–85 and T. Erskine (ed.), *Can Institutions Have Responsibilities? Collective Moral Agency and International Relations* (New York and Basingstoke: Palgrave Macmillan, 2003).

18 This typology makes connections particularly with what is called 'normative IR theory', or the area of IR that deals explicitly with the study of norms and values in international politics. The ethical realist framework with which I begin touches on IR theory generally, but also overlaps with some aspects of the 'communitarian' position in normative IR theory (although, importantly, not with regard to the specific example of Hobbes). The subsequent two frameworks, consequentialism and deontology, constitute

two streams of the 'cosmopolitan' approach to normative IR theory. For what remains the most thorough and accessible account of cosmopolitanism and communitarianism in normative IR theory, see Chris Brown, *International Relations Theory: New Normative Approaches* (New York: Columbia University Press, 1993), especially pp. 23–81.

19 Hobbes, *De Cive*, p. 146.

20 Francis Bacon, *The Letters and the Life*, VII, ed. by James Spedding (London, 1874), p. 477. Cited by Richard Tuck in *The Rights of War and Peace: Political Thought and the International Order from Grotius to Kant* (Oxford: Oxford University Press, 1999), p. 19.

21 George W. Bush, speech to the graduating class at the US Military Academy at West Point, New York, 1 June 2002, www.whitehouse.gov/news/releases/2002/06/20020601-3.html and 'The National Security Strategy of the United States of America', 17 September 2002, www.whitehouse.gov/nsc/nss.pdf.

22 Hobbes, *De Cive*, p. 146.

23 Cogan, 'Hunters not Gatherers'; Johnson, *Secret Agencies*, pp. 60–88.

24 Herman, 'Ethics and Intelligence After September 2001', pp. 189–91.

25 I elaborate on this line of argument in the context of what I call a 'communitarian realist' approach to restraint in war in 'Embedded Cosmopolitanism and the Case of War: Restraint, Discrimination and Overlapping Communities', *Global Society*, 14, 4 (2000), pp. 569–90 (p. 580).

26 Hobbes, *De Cive*, p. 145.

27 Another so-called 'realist' position appropriated by IR scholars, but that is less dependent on the notion that national self-defence itself constitutes a moral principle, also appears to fit well with some articulations of 'the' intelligence ethos. E. Drexel Godfrey, Jr's explication, in 'Ethics and Intelligence', *Foreign Affairs* (April 1978), pp. 624–42 (p. 629), of 'the grim ethos of clandestine collection' as rooted in the concept that 'the weak or the vulnerable can be manipulated by the strong or the shrewd', is a very close rendering of the principle found in Thucydides' *History of the Peloponnesian War* (Harmondsworth: Penguin, 1954), p. 402, that 'the strong do what they have the power to do and the weak accept what they have to accept'.

28 Johnson, *Secret Agencies*, p. 73. If Johnson's statement were qualified to maintain that the defence of the nation-state cannot eclipse duties that we owe to our adversaries, then it would also be compatible with the 'Just Intelligence' approach that I will touch on below.

29 Another form of consequentialism is referred to as 'rule-consequentialism'. According to the rule-consequentialist, an action is right if it complies with a set of rules or principles that would best promote the good if generally followed. 'Utilitarianism' is one type of consequentialist position (with both act- and rule-variations), according to which good and bad consequences are understood in terms of happiness and suffering.

30 Herman, *Intelligence Services in the Information Age*, p. 202. Throughout his work, Herman provides a thoughtful and nuanced analysis of the ethics of intelligence collection, and it would be inaccurate to say that he champions a consequentialist approach to the disregard of other positions and influences. Indeed, Herman acknowledges the significance not only of Kantian imperatives, but also of international law and notions of custom and legitimacy in addressing the ethics of intelligence gathering. In fact, Herman's two most recent articles on ethics and intelligence, his contribution to this volume and his '11 September: Legitimizing Intelligence', *International Relations*, 16 (August 2002), pp. 227–41, reveal the influence of what might be called an 'international society' approach to intelligence, according to which (following the 'English School' in IR) the legitimacy of certain actions is rooted in the shared values, rules and customs of the 'society of states'. (I am grateful to Andrew Linklater for emphasising this strand of thought in Herman's recent work.) Despite these other influences, the most prominent ethical approach in Herman's work remains the consequentialist one presented here. In his contribution to the present collection, Herman reasserts that his

'main emphasis is on intelligence's observable effects', and refers explicitly to his '"consequentialist" approach' to the ethics of intelligence gathering.

31 Herman, 'Modern Intelligence Services', p. 290.

32 Ibid., p. 289. In his most recent work, Herman defines this global good in terms of what is 'good or bad for international society'. See his 'Ethics and Intelligence', p. 182.

33 Herman, 'Modern Intelligence Services', p. 306. Somewhat incompatibly, however, Herman's more recent characterisation of this position allows '*almost* any methods of collection...short of gross violations of human rights'. See his 'Ethics and Intelligence', p. 184.

34 Herman, 'Ethics and Intelligence', p. 183.

35 Ibid.

36 Herman, 'Modern Intelligence Services', p. 306.

37 I am grateful to Len Scott for this example. See also Herman's acknowledgement of what one might call 'indirect harm' in 'Ethics and Intelligence', p. 183. Herman observes that some 'particularly intrusive' intelligence collection 'could be perceived as a mark of hostility, reinforcing its target's perceptions of threat or tension'.

38 James A. Barry, 'Covert Action Can Be Just', *Orbis* (Summer 1993), pp. 375–90 (p. 378).

39 Sir Michael Quinlan, 'The Future of Covert Intelligence', in Shukman (ed.), *Agents for Change*, p. 69.

40 The phrase 'fragmentation of responsibility' is employed by, *inter alia*, Jonathan Glover in *Humanity: A Moral History of the Twentieth Century* (London: Pimlico, 2001). He uses this phrase in a number of related ways. Most relevant to the argument here is the notion that when many people have a role in generating a harm a '[d]ivision of labour [makes] evasion of personal responsibility easier' (p. 350).

41 'Academic Freedom at the Palestinian Universities', *Palestinian Human Rights Monitor*, 3, 4 (August 1999). See www.phrmg.org/monitor1999/aug99-disruptions.htm. I am grateful to Jeroen Gunning for drawing my attention to this example.

42 Bernard Williams makes a similar point in 'A Critique of Utilitarianism', in J.J.C. Smart and Bernard Williams, *Utilitarianism: For and Against* (Cambridge: Cambridge University Press, 1973), pp. 93–4: 'Consequentialism is basically indifferent to whether a state of affairs consists in what I do, or is produced by what I do, where the notion is itself wide enough to include, for instance, situations in which other people do things which I have made them do, or allowed them to do, or encouraged them to do, or given them a chance to do . . . [F]or consequentialism, all causal connections are on the same level, and it makes no difference, so far as it goes, whether the causation of a given state of affairs lies through another agent or not.'

43 Nancy Ann Davis, 'Contemporary Deontology', in P. Singer (ed.), *A Companion to Ethics* (Oxford: Basil Blackwell, 1991), p. 205.

44 Charles Fried, *Right and Wrong* (Cambridge, MA: Harvard University Press, 1978), p. 9, cited by Davis, 'Contemporary Deontology', p. 205. For a comprehensive discussion of the ethics of deception, see Sissela Bok, *Lying: Moral Choice in Public and Private Life* (New York: Vintage Books, 1978).

45 Not all theorists would agree with the classification of Kant as a deontologist and some even claim that his philosophy is compatible with consequentialism. I will not engage with this contention here, but rather accept the widely held view of his work as an example of deontological reasoning.

46 Immanuel Kant, *The Metaphysics of Morals* [1797] trans. by Mary Gregor (Cambridge: Cambridge University Press, 1991), p. 154.

47 Ibid.

48 Kant, 'Perpetual Peace: A Philosophical Sketch' [1795], in *Kant: Political Writings*, ed. by Hans Reiss and trans. by H.B. Nisbet (Cambridge: Cambridge University Press, 1970), p. 97. For a detailed comparison of Hobbes' and Kant's different perspectives on the role of the sovereign in the external relations between states – that includes

a discussion of their respective views on intelligence – see Howard Williams, *Kant's Critique of Hobbes: Sovereignty and Cosmopolitanism* (Cardiff: University of Wales Press, 2003).

49 Whereas, for Kant, a *categorical* imperative is one that identifies an action 'as objectively necessary in itself, without reference to another end', he would associate the ethical realist and consequentialist approaches outlined above with the notion of a '*hypothetical* imperative', by which an action 'would be good merely as a means to something else'. Kant makes this distinction in *Groundwork of the Metaphysics of Morals*, in Mary J. Gregor (ed. and trans.), *Practical Philosophy* (Cambridge: Cambridge University Press, 1996), p. 67.

50 In 'Ethics and Intelligence', p. 630, Godfrey describes the 'controlled' source as 'a source that you "own lock, stock and barrel"', suggesting that such individuals are bought, blackmailed or otherwise bound to their case officers.

51 Ibid., p. 625.

52 Onora O'Neill, *Constructions of Reason: Explorations of Kant's Practical Philosophy* (Cambridge: Cambridge University Press, 1989), p. 96. O'Neill also discusses the 'moral unworthiness' of coercion in the same passage.

53 Godfrey, 'Ethics and Intelligence', p. 629. Emphasis not in the original.

54 O'Neill, 'Kantian Ethics', in Singer (ed.), *A Companion to Ethics*, pp. 178–9.

55 The judgement that this individual behaved immorally might, however, be subject to an important qualification. If the informant were engaging in deception to counter a tyrannical regime, for example – a regime that Kant would see as reducing one to existence within the 'state of nature' – then his or her action might be immune from moral condemnation. (I owe this point to Howard Williams.) Significantly, however, the informant's acts of deception could *not* be viewed as morally praiseworthy from this perspective. For the consequentialist, the goal of undermining a tyrannical regime could morally justify the means of doing so. For the deontologist, these extreme conditions might, at most, render normal categories of moral judgement inapplicable. See note 58, below. This qualification is, arguably, relevant to judging the actions of informants in states such as Saddam Hussein's Iraq.

56 Herman, 'Ethics and Intelligence', p. 184.

57 Thomas Nagel, *The View from Nowhere* (Oxford: Oxford University Press, 1986), p. 179. Emphasis not in the original. This distinction is fundamental to what is generally referred to as the 'principle of double effect'. Indeed, Nagel refers explicitly to this principle in the context of the passage cited above.

58 The phrase 'supreme emergency' was used by Winston Churchill in 1939 and is adopted by Michael Walzer, *Just and Unjust Wars* [1977] (New York: Basic Books, 2nd edn, 1992), pp. 251–5, as a conceptual category that covers grave and imminent threats to 'human values' (p. 253). (The phrase, 'shock the conscience of humankind' is also taken from Walzer, p. 107.) We are justified, Walzer maintains, in overriding moral principles of restraint in order to counter these threats. Although Walzer allows (with some hesitation) that such a justification might be invoked not only in response to threats to our common humanity, but also in response to a 'supreme emergency' in the form of a threat to a particular community, the ethical realist position that I outline above need not rely on such an appeal in order to justify means of intelligence collection. As I have argued, a 'just fear', broadly interpreted, rather than an imminent threat, is all that is needed to give legitimacy to any means of intelligence collection that serves the interest of the state if one adopts this realist perspective. As for the deontologist, even defence against a 'supreme emergency' could not *justify* intrinsically immoral actions. Some deontologists, however, acknowledge that such a state of affairs would render moral principles inapplicable, thereby removing actions in response to a 'supreme emergency' from either moral justification or condemnation. (For an example of this line of argument, see Fried, *Right and Wrong*, p. 10.)

59 Quinlan uses the phrase 'Just Espionage' in 'The Future of Covert Intelligence'; Herman, refers to the possibility of 'Just Intelligence' in 'Modern Intelligence Services' and 'Ethics and Intelligence'. Other scholars have invoked Just War principles to address covert action. See, for example, William Colby, 'Public Policy, Secret Action', *Ethics and International Affairs*, 3 (1989), pp. 61–71 and James A. Barry, 'Covert Action Can Be Just', *Orbis* (Summer 1993), pp. 375–90. For an influential articulation of contemporary Just War theory, see Walzer, *Just and Unjust Wars*.

60 A Just War position shares with an ethical realist approach the assumption that self-defence is the right of the political community. Moreover, a Just War position requires that we exercise restraint in the use of force against our 'enemies'. The principles through which this requirement is articulated rely respectively on consequentialist and deontological reasoning. For an influential articulation of contemporary Just War theory, see Walzer, *Just and Unjust Wars*.

Index